Glickman is the definition of a dedicated public servant who puts country
rvice ahead of personal benefit. This book is a great chronicle of his life
periences and gives us an insight into the values he brought to each of his
tunities—from the excitement of his first victory for Congress to his work
Clinton cabinet and to the coveted position of the head of the Motion Pic-
sociation. He celebrates his immigrant heritage and the strong religious
that were passed on from his grandparents and parents. Typical of Dan,
es his journey by poking fun at himself and reminds us of how humor
mility go a long way toward getting us through even the most challeng-
ments. Most of all, Dan reminds us of the importance of decency and the
mise that is needed to support a working democracy. There could not
re timely reminder of how important compromise and flexibility are to
ing the challenges we have as a country, and his lifelong belief of the
nce of reaching out across the aisle to get things done. The book should
st-read for our next generation to remind them that it is possible to get
one if we respect the process of give-and-take and build relationships
on respect and good will."

ery Kraus, founder and executive chairman of APCO Worldwide

Washington career, I was often asked why I enjoyed a strong sense of
My response was that the alternative was 'jumping in the Potomac.' My
an Glickman in *Laughing at Myself* makes the same point, particularly in
zy times. I have known Dan for over forty years—he was my classmate
ess, we worked together in the Clinton administration, and as the chil-
nmigrants we share the same values and beliefs. He is a good man and
tells you why."

anetta, former secretary of defense and cofounder of the Panetta
or Public Policy

Dan Glickman has long brought good humor, common sense,
, and a strong expression of his Jewish identity to Capitol Hill, the
ation, Hollywood, and now to all of us through his new book. Hailing
Jewish community in Wichita, Kansas, he conquered Washington
wood. And now he will also capture your heart and help you laugh
In these trying times, we all need more good memories, smiles, and
ere is nobody better to help us with that than Dan Glickman. King
ught in the Jewish scriptures that 'a constant joyous heart' is a good
has that, and he shares it with us here. Everyone always leaves meet-
ppier than they were before. Picking up this book and finding out
; putting it down will be much more difficult."

vi Shemtov, executive vice president of American Friends of
nd founder and president of the Capitol Jewish Forum

Laughing at Myself

Laughing at Myself

My Education in Congress,
on the Farm, and at the Movies

Dan Glickman

 University Press of Kansas

Published by the University Press of Kansas (Lawrence, Kansas 66045), which was organized by the Kansas Board of Regents and is operated and funded by Emporia State University, Fort Hays State University, Kansas State University, Pittsburg State University, the University of Kansas, and Wichita State University.

All photos courtesy of the author's collection, unless otherwise noted.

Library of Congress Cataloging-in-Publication Data

Names: Glickman, Dan, author.
Title: Laughing at myself : my education in Congress, on the farm, and at the movies / Dan Glickman.
Description: Lawrence : University Press of Kansas, 2021.
Identifiers: LCCN 2020042476
  ISBN 9780700632138 (cloth)
  ISBN 9780700632145 (epub)
Subjects: LCSH: Glickman, Dan. | United States. Congress. House—Biography. | United States. Department of Agriculture—Officials and employees—Biography. | Motion Picture Association of America—Biography. | Legislators—United States—Biography. | Cabinet officers—United States—Biography. | Kansas—Biography.
Classification: LCC E840.8.G55 A3 2021 | DDC 328.73/092 [B]—dc23
LC record available at https://lccn.loc.gov/2020042476.

British Library Cataloguing-in-Publication Data is available.

Printed in the United States of America

10 9 8 7 6 5 4 3 2 1

The paper used in this publication is acid free and meets the minimum requirements of the American National Standard for Permanence of Paper for Printed Library Materials Z39.48–1992.

This book is dedicated to my extraordinarily creative wife of nearly fifty-five years, Rhoda; my amazing kids, Amy and Jon, and my daughter-in-law, Christy; my four wonderful grandchildren, Cal, Mae, Lucy, and Leo; my brother, Norman, and sister, Sharon; and the entire extended Glickman and Yura families.

Contents

A photo gallery follows page 96.

Acknowledgments

For every step taken in one's career and throughout one's life, some-one—a friend, family member, or mentor—has probably been close by to extend a helping hand. Some people are really lucky in life, and I have had the good fortune of having my wife, Rhoda, and her wonderful family, by my side for nearly fifty-five years of marriage. Her support and political skills have helped me throughout my ca-reer, along with our two amazingly supportive children, Jonathan and Amy. The have blessed me with four grandchildren: Cal, Mae, Lucy, and Leo, who are my inspiration and keep me young. This all began with the two best and most supportive parents in the world, as well as my brother, Norman, and my sister, Sharon.

Of course my life in politics would not have been possible without individuals along the way who were willing to give me an opportunity to succeed: former president Bill Clinton, Jack Valenti, Walter Isaacson, former congressman and secretary of defense Leon Panetta, former vice president Al Gore, former senator Pat Roberts, and former senator Bob Dole.

I have also been the beneficiary of many great colleagues and staffers, without whom none of this would have been possible. I can-not list all of them because the names would fill numerous pages, but I do want to highlight Myrne Roe, who started as my high school debate coach and became one of my most trusted advisors, and Melissa Gregory, my long-time colleague, friend, and confidant, who I still rely on for political advice and to keep me grounded.

I want to thank my co-authors, Peter Weichlein and Dava Guerin, for helping me write this book; my friend and colleague

Doug Farrar for his support and editorial guidance; and Elizabeth Beller, for her editing help early on.

A special thanks to David Tabatsky, for his editing and creative input, and to my literary agent, Nancy Rosenfeld. Thank you both for your friendship.

I would like to acknowledge some other people for their help and friendship over the years, including Jason Grumet of the Bipartisan Policy Center; Terry Duffy, CEO of the Chicago Mercantile Exchange; Margery Kraus of Apco Worldwide, Rick Leach, a great friend and fellow crusader against world hunger; Catherine Bertini, who spurred my commitment to ending global and domestic hunger and fighting for better nutrition; Liz Schrayer of the US Global Leadership Coalition; Randy Russell, a great friend and thought leader of food and agricultural policy; former staff members from my congressional office; the Department of Agriculture; Walter Isaacson and Elliot Gerson of the Aspen Institute; the Motion Picture Association of America; and my colleague from Kansas, former congressman Jim Slattery, whose common sense has been incredibly welcome over the years.

Finally, thanks to the thousands of Kansas constituents who maintained their confidence in me over the years.

Let me sign off by acknowledging some advice I once received from my Jewish mother: "Folks have two ears and one mouth for a simple reason. Maybe the best advice I can give is for all of us to talk less and listen more."

Life is a succession of meeting and interacting with people. Every choice you make, opportunity you pursue, goal you achieve, and setbacks you endure involve the people who inspire you. Sometimes they remain in your life for decades, sometimes only for a couple of seconds. But every one of the people I have met has enriched my life beyond my wildest dreams and made me a better man. Thank you all.

Chapter 1

What a Country!

Where else but in America could a nice Jewish kid, born in the farm state of Kansas, grandson of Russian and Eastern European immigrants, son of unconditionally supportive and entrepreneurial parents, end up as a nine-term congressman, US secretary of agriculture and chief lobbyist for Hollywood?

One might think that my background, birth location, and ethnicity would have been a disincentive to achieve much more than a career in my father's scrap iron business. Then again, there were not a lot of Jewish farmers around to be role models, either. My story, like so many others of similar backgrounds—children of immigrants with encouraging, ambitious parents, a natural desire to strive for higher goals, and frankly a lot of luck and good timing—shows how anyone can achieve relative greatness in many different ways.

Things did not always go how I hoped. I won elections and lost them, too. College was not always easy academically. Once in a while my religion was a barrier to achieving my goals. Even though there was a lot of love in my immediate family, my parents did not have a perfect marriage, and I experienced my share of family conflicts, which sometimes involved a lot of loud fighting between my mother and father. I hated that. They were never physical, but their language could get abusive. This made for a strange and often frustrating mix of hostility and mutual love, but aside from their own issues, my mother and father were each unconditionally supportive of their kids, in good times and bad.

Growing up as the middle child in this type of environment caused to me to avoid controversy and conflict—at any cost. In my high school yearbook, a girl named Carol (who I had a crush on), wrote that I was a good guy who shouldn't try to please everyone all the time. I'm sure the conflicts I witnessed for so many years played a role in how I came to avoid any third-party conflicts and hoped everyone would like me. Eventually, once my siblings and I left home, our parents began to get along much better.

Sound familiar? I think so. Through experiencing similar struggles, most of us can understand each other better, which is essential if we are ever going to make genuine progress in this world—and God knows we need all the progress we can get.

In my case, I have always been driven by a desire to keep my reputation intact. From an early age, my father and grandfather used to pound into me the priority of a good name and being well thought of by others, above almost anything else, including money. As a result, everything I have done in my personal and professional life has been influenced by an effort to preserve my good name, even in the context of controversial issues and conflicting experiences.

As the Bible says, a good name is more precious than all the gold in the world.

This philosophy has served me well through many unpredictable and troubling times. Born at the end of World War II, I have witnessed my fair share of history, from the Vietnam War era to the Civil Rights revolution to the Trump era, with several other mind-bending twists and turns along the way. My childhood and young adulthood trained me to adapt to most of the challenges I faced by finding ways to work around problems and by being creative and imaginative when looking for solutions.

But the key to my meeting most of these challenges has been in recognizing that a credible self-deprecating sense of humor is my strong suit. It has opened doors and allowed me to learn how to get along with people, convincing them to like and trust me, and in the process get things done.

Being likable is only one step in getting people to vote for you. At the core, you have to stand for something and be principled. Otherwise, you become just another empty suit. You must share your principles with a sense of courtesy, and as I found along my way, with a tone of moderation and a willingness to keep an open mind. After all, moderation is as much about attitude as it is about ideology.

Back in the 1980s, when I laughed each night watching *The Johnny Carson Show*, I used to enjoy occasional guest Yakov Smirnoff, the Ukrainian Jewish comedian, who based his immigrant shtick on the humorous welcome to New York he received after living in a proverbial Soviet gulag for most of his younger years.

Smirnoff's sitcom *What a Country!* demonstrated the wonder he felt at the unique, crazy, and wonderful daily life he found here in America. He made fun of simple things we take for granted, like toilets flushing, a lack of lines for buying basic necessities, and less daily confrontation with police.

Smirnoff also once said something quite wise.

"Laughter is the shortest distance between two people."

This had a great influence on me. As you will discover repeatedly in this book, humor and laughter served as the glue that kept our family together and the foundation of much of the success I have been able to achieve in my life. In fact, the music of laughter was a constant soundtrack as I grew up, and I'm always happy to hear it, wherever I am.

My dad used to say that if folks think you are funny (not at their expense), and they like you, then you are much more likely to weather controversy and get things done, or at the very least, you will accomplish something even if they really don't like you. The point is, most of the time what's most important is getting things done—not scoring points for being right or funny. In many cases, in fact, "whatever works" could be the motto of the day.

Watching how my parents thwarted disaster by treating people—rich and poor—with respect and care, and always with humor, was especially instructive for me and still inspires my style. Sadly, humor is an underrated commodity, but it's something I highly recommend. If only we could have it officially prescribed throughout the hallways and meeting rooms of our Congress, public schools, and private homes.

Laughing with and laughing at, however, are two different things. Sharing your own mistakes and owning up to your own foibles in a self-deprecating way helps to break the ice in new or awkward situations. Failing to acknowledge even the simplest of mistakes turns people off. I'm not sure former president Trump ever learned that basic lesson. He never seemed to listen to anything, except thoughts that reinforced his preexisting views. Frankly, he is a bonehead when it comes to taking advice.

The art of listening is one of the great gifts God gave us. He felt so strongly about it that he gave us two ears, not one. This is a huge problem in Washington, DC. Listening often means not jumping to rash or uninformed conclusions. It also encourages independent thinking. I often think that if there were two qualities that great leaders, political or other, should possess, it's the ability to listen to and learn about alternative points of view, and when you do disagree you must not do so disagreeably. That's hard to do in this age of social media, when instantaneous and provocative responses are rewarded by the masses.

My mother used to advise me that since I had two ears and one mouth, I should speak much less than I listen. That same advice, which has been passed on countless times from parents to children, was something I often failed to follow while growing up, and I usually suffered whenever that happened. Gradually, though, I figured out that she was right, and that credo led me to lead a solutions-based public life, which is probably the reason I have rejected political extremes on all sides and have often felt more comfortable as someone operating in the middle of the road, even though this position is not necessarily relished in today's political climate.

I hear the naysayers, preaching stubborn extremism as the only way to make real change, but I beg to differ. In my mind, moderation is the only way to achieve what Daniel Webster encouraged when he said the goal of a public servant was always "to do something worthy to be remembered," which for me means substantial action to help people instead of empty words to drive them apart from each other.

By the way, moderation is not a code word for weakness but an acknowledgment that America is a diverse country, and it takes a wide policy perspective to satisfy as many people as possible. Following the principle of active listening is central to this happening.

Resiliency has been the other central attribute that has guided me to finding success in politics and life in general. It's not merely making lemonade out of lemons, although who can argue with that? Learning from genuine adversity means creating new opportunities, far beyond merely surviving a challenge. We can all agree that shit happens in life, but the trick is whether you can rise above it and create something new and positive from what once seemed so negative and hopeless. Sometimes, all it takes is a simple attitude adjustment and a willingness to solve problems in new and different ways.

"Ad astra per aspera," or "To the stars through difficulties," is the Kansas state motto, which is a good attitude to adopt when it comes to dealing with the uncertainties and vagaries of life. Essentially, we must never give up. Sometimes, that means simply keeping an open mind and heart, even when circumstances don't suggest an immediate benefit for that approach.

For example, when I faced an ethical challenge while serving in Congress, this was central on my mind. A 1992 scandal called Rubbergate (described in detail in chapter 10) infected Washington and the nation with allegations of politicians, including me, bouncing checks. This struck a dagger into what I believed was a good and honest reputation I had earned, built up over the years with a combination of intelligence and good judgment. During that time, I had accumulated a lot of good will, which helped, and my sense of humor came in handy, too.

But being funny while stupid was not enough. I needed to preserve, and at times rehabilitate, that good name and the sense of guilt that goes with worrying about it. When my honesty and trustworthiness were in question, that was always a deep blow. I also carried a fair amount of Jewish guilt, sometimes believing I had committed acts of wrongdoing that occurred ten thousand miles away from home.

Being caught up in the House banking scandal left me feeling naked and fully exposed to the world. This was due in part to the constant reach of cable television news, which made sure the world knew that I had "bounced" personal checks. Technically speaking, I didn't really bounce any checks. They were unintentional overdrafts, which were always "covered" by the Office of the Sergeant at Arms, but to the public and media they were bounced checks.

Without knowing all the facts, people who knew me no longer thought of me as nearly perfect. Being exposed like that was no fun, especially for someone who had always done his level best to avoid personal controversy and believed that his personal reputation was vitally important. It also challenged the notion in some circles that maybe I was not so likable and that my toothy smile was hiding something more insidious. Ironically, it was my natural self-deprecating sense of humor that became an enormous help in swallowing some humble pie and getting me through this and other challenges.

As a partial result of Rubbergate, I lost my reelection to Congress in 1994 after a successful eighteen-year career, and just five weeks later, as I was thinking I may have no future in public service, I was nominated by President Clinton to be the US secretary of agriculture.

This was pretty amazing, since I would have given up my House seat voluntarily to take that job. Years later, I became head of the Motion Picture Association of America, a job many thought was the best job in all of Washington, DC, in large part because I was in the right place at the right time, when the iconic leader of that organization, Jack Valenti, decided to retire.

Clinton and Valenti both liked me, so that was pretty much it when it came down to being offered those positions. Obviously, I was at least marginally qualified, but I think the real reason I got those jobs was because Clinton and Valenti thought that the people who would be working with me would be well respected, motivated, and appreciated.

The truth is, my story could only happen here in America. As the grandson of poor immigrants from eastern Europe, where my grandfather, Jacob Glickman, escaped from religious persecution in 1910 and came to America to seek refuge and freedom, I was given every opportunity to succeed—initially by my parents, who knew the value of jumping when opportunity knocked, being positive and optimistic about the future, and not taking themselves too seriously. They knew, and I hope you will too, that our country, despite reports of doom and gloom, is not going to hell in a handbasket!

Despite all the negativity and constant infusion of political discord, our country is a legitimate beacon of civility. We have a rich history of overcoming our divisions and uniting behind a common purpose: handing the next generation a better America.

Even though America has plenty to be proud of, this success is not guaranteed in perpetuity. Our institutions are strong, but a perilous failure of leadership at the top, whether it's the presidency or otherwise, can seriously damage this country's historic position here at home and around the world.

It's been said that "one man with courage makes a majority."

Conversely, one person with no shame or real character can destroy a country's reputation and purpose for a long time. I find it deeply disturbing that so many people consider this kind of behavior acceptable or are not willing to actively confront it.

I still believe in the words of Anne Frank, who wrote in her diary about her belief in the basic goodness of humankind. This may be naïve, but it is core to my beliefs.

I believe adversity can be overcome and that when faced with great obstacles, Americans will rise to the challenge. Although politics today is often more dysfunctional than productive, we can change that paradigm if we unite together and listen respectfully to our differences.

What a concept.

As Thomas Jefferson and the Founding Fathers stated so eloquently, our values will always be based on equal opportunity and the ability of everyone, no matter their background or where their grandparents came from, to thrive. The United States can continue to lead in the world if we stay true to those values, but we must be vigilant and somewhat relentless in reminding ourselves of our greater purpose and potential.

Since I left public service, I have seen the value of this unified approach through my work at the Aspen Institute and the Bipartisan Policy Center, working with numerous think tanks to make positive change. I hope to use my lifetime of experiences—good and bad—to help change the world. I don't take that responsibility lightly, although I am not opposed to lightening things up a bit in our nation's capitol!

That reminds me of a story my dad used to tell about a conversation between an American kid and a Russian kid.

"I have it so free," the American kid says, "I can go to the gates of the White House and yell at the top of my voice, 'To hell with Ronald Reagan,' and nothing will happen to me."

Not to be outdone, the Russian kid responds.

"This is no big deal," he says. "I can go to the gates of the Kremlin and yell, 'To hell with Ronald Reagan,' and nothing will happen to me."

I am not sure how that story applies to the Trump/Putin love affair, but perhaps I will run into Yakov Smirnoff again and he can explain it to me.

All I know is that his "What a country!" line always rings true for me, too.

What other country in the world would select a nice, Midwestern fella like me to assume the role of designated survivor, which I was during the State of the Union address in 1997, when I was (temporarily) placed in a secure location and directly in line to become president of the United States in the event that a national catastrophe had struck Washington, DC, and wiped out the upper echelon of America's leaders?

I have had many experiences as a survivor, but that one night was more poignant and ironic than any survivorship I had ever known, which I describe in detail in the next chapter. The rationale is that if anything disastrous should occur to those politicians, someone is ready and able to provide continuity of government.

That someone was me, and the minutes I spent "in hiding" were surreal, but they also encompassed what I learned over a lifetime of public service, that through hard work, dedication, and a bit of luck, America will give you the opportunity to succeed, allowing one to reach unimaginable heights.

Even though I was Jewish, I was still a white kid from the Midwest. Although overt discrimination against me sometimes hurt, it was pretty mild. As we have seen in events in recent years, a young Black man in America faces the calamity of racism on a daily basis, and this reality remains one of the greatest of all stains on the American experience. One of my greatest legacies, discussed later in the book, is my role in helping to eliminate the legacy of racism among Black farmers.

Notwithstanding, I have learned that moments of glory are fleeting. Being at the top can often be followed by a crashing fall to the bottom. Ultimately, it is how you react to challenges that truly matter and define who you are, as you look in the mirror and communicate with others.

During high school I thought I was hot stuff when I became the election commissioner of our Southeast High School elections. We asked students to register to vote in advance as part of maintaining election integrity. Guess who "lost" all the filled-out registration forms two days before the election? Me. Yours truly, the election commissioner. We decided to handle my screw-up by not letting the kids know all the registration materials had been lost.

Instead, before they voted we just had them certify that they had registered.

This same guy grew up and ran for Congress ten times. I guess I may have learned something from this early foible.

As for my ability to make sense of a few things for you, I have learned so many life-changing lessons from each one of my careers: as president of my sixth grade class at Fabrique Elementary School in Wichita, as a hometown lawyer, as a congressman from Kansas, as secretary of the US Department of Agriculture, as president of the Motion Picture Association of America, as director of the Institute of Politics at Harvard University's John F. Kennedy School of Government, and through my work at the Aspen Institute and Bipartisan Policy Center, trying to build bridges between Republicans and Democrats.

I know what you may be thinking: Is that even possible? Yes, I assure you it is, even though I must admit that surviving in Washington, DC, and Hollywood is not for the faint of heart. Hollywood is filled with creative, imaginative people, some of the smartest folks I have ever worked with, but some of those people are not terribly forgiving and have not learned the Golden Rule. It's a tough business, filled with enormous egos and gigantic consequences for failure.

I recall a legendary story, apocryphal and while perhaps exaggerated is likely true, that when the famous Louis B. Mayer, one of the founders of the iconic film studio, MGM, died, thousands of people attended his funeral. In fact, it was one of the largest funeral crowds in history. The story goes that the crowd was so large because so many people he treated badly wanted to make sure he was dead.

I have often said that Hollywood is Washington on steroids. On the other hand, those who do survive both worlds usually have learned that how you treat others is key to personal and economic success.

I am happy to say that through it all, I have never lost my ability or willingness to listen, admit when I was wrong (yes, I've actually done that, and still do), learn and adapt to changing trends, build lasting friendships, think big, leave something of value behind for the next generation, and maybe most valuable of all, cultivate an ability to lighten up and have a few laughs along the way.

There is an old joke I often tell about the businessman who speaks to a group of high school students and gives them this advice: "You need to remember that you have to 'jump' when opportunity knocks." One of the students says, "That's great for you as a successful businessman to say that, but the real question is, how do you know when opportunity knocks?" The businessman replied, "You don't. That's why you have to keep jumping all the time."

That has been my credo in politics and life: keep jumping and looking for opportunities, regardless of the challenge or possibility of defeat. Keep your humor, too, when things don't necessarily go your way. It helps when we remember that we are not the most important person in the world, that humility is a key factor in getting ahead, and when shit does happen, which it invariably will, what really matters is how you survive it, learn from it, and make it a building block in your life and career.

Life is short, power is a fickle thing, and you never know what's around the corner. This is a nation built on opportunity and optimism, which was true two hundred years ago and still holds true today. So if a memoir full of good things have happened for me, a Jewish kid from Wichita, Kansas, why not for you, too?

We all are designated survivors in one way or another of a complicated and tough world. Some of us fare better than others, and economic and political success are not the only determinants of survival. Outside factors, such as repressive and authoritarian regimes, can often impact our respective welfare.

This is my opportunity to share my ingredients for not just surviving life, but living it with purpose, passion, and optimism. I have learned many tricks of the trade, which will hopefully be helpful to aspiring politicians, but I recognize that my life is not totally replicable for everyone. Changing the world is not easy, no matter where you are from or going, but I am convinced that the toxicity of our current political environment might be mitigated by some of the principles that have guided my life: a strong sense of humor, respect and civility for those who have different perspectives and points of view, a belief system founded on values based mainly on the Golden Rule, looking at all times if possible to solve problems, and not creating irreconcilable conflicts.

Like the old saying goes, "If you don't have something nice to say, don't say it." If only certain people in charge today would heed this lesson, the world would be a better place. May I suggest we don't wait for this to happen by itself and that we take change into our own hands?

I have mentioned that the president of the Unites States can be an instrumental force in setting a positive tone by encouraging people to treat each other with dignity and even love. Most presidents, including those I disagree with on policy, can bring out the best in us. It wasn't just Lincoln, Roosevelt, Truman, and Eisenhower who could do this. From Kennedy through Obama, each has seen that as part of their job as president. Even Nixon demonstrated positive leadership at times. But, in my humble judgment, these qualities were dangerously missing in former president Trump, much to the detriment of us all.

By the way, Smirnoff also said, "I believe laughter is the language of God and that we can all live happily ever laughter."

What a country, indeed, and it's our obligation to fix it.

Chapter 2

The Most Powerful Man on Earth

More than any other experience in my life, the brief time I spent as the most powerful person on earth was utterly sobering. For a few hours on Monday, January 20, 1997, I was next in line to assume the office of the presidency of the United States of America, should the unthinkable have happened. That was the one and only time I was the designated survivor.

Our need to have a plan of succession in place is so compelling that the ABC television network created a series based on this theme, the aptly named *Designated Survivor*, starring Kiefer Sutherland. The soft-spoken yet fearless Tom Kirkman, fictional secretary of Housing and Urban Development, was named the designated survivor in this political action fantasy. Much to his horror, he becomes president of the United States after the US Capitol is destroyed in a major terrorist attack. I can greatly empathize with Kirkman because there's no training or real-world experience that properly prepares one to contemplate such a circumstance, let alone actually become the de facto ruler of the free world. Unfortunately, the series was cancelled after a two-year run on ABC, but it did manage a third season on Netflix. Perhaps if the hero had been the secretary of the United States Department of Agriculture (USDA) instead of the secretary of Housing and Urban Development it would still be on the air and they would be consulting me for the inside scoop.

At the time, I thought that my kids and wife would be proud of me but would still make fun of my foibles. I would go down in history as the first Jewish president—if the unthinkable happened. I hoped that the public would accept me, and we could avoid a revolution. But truthfully, I took most of it with a grain of salt. The odds

that President Clinton and all of the other constitutionally designated successors would be killed was so remote that I just viewed
it as a fun experience few others would have, and it would give me
some good stories to tell. My mother could tell her friends that her
son was the "almost" president.

Here's how it works: during political gatherings where the entire government is present, a natural-born citizen over the age of
thirty-five (usually a member of the cabinet) is selected to become
the designated survivor. That individual is given presidential security, including a military officer carrying the briefcase with the
nuclear codes, and transportation to an undisclosed, secure location.
Should the president of the United States, vice president, Speaker of
the House, and members of the cabinet all be killed, the designated
survivor assumes the role of president to ensure that a governing
authority remains in power.

We designated survivors are an elite club. Gatherings of this
type, with all of these political figures assembled in one place, are
rare and usually occur only for presidential inaugurations, State
of the Union addresses, and perhaps official State funerals. In fact,
since 1981, secretaries of agriculture have been selected to occupy
this role seven times (tied with secretaries of the interior), more than
any other cabinet member, which may suggest that we "creatures of
the land" are seen as natural replacements for such high office.

I have subsequently learned how other designated survivors
spent their ninety minutes of trepidation. Bill Daley, who was the
commerce secretary under Bill Clinton, was the designated survivor in 1998. He spent the night rather informally with family and
friends. Tommy Thompson, who was health and human services
secretary under President George W. Bush, had a tougher time since
he served in this role only eleven days after September 11, 2001. His
concerns were far more magnified and justifiably so; given the recent attack, Vice President Cheney was designated as a backup survivor that night, hidden away in a secret bunker during President
Bush's address to a joint session of Congress.

With the exception of those serving immediately following
9/11, I believe that we all shared the same odds of the entire US
government being wiped out as I had of becoming a major league
baseball player.

I was informed of my impending role a couple of weeks before the 1997 State of the Union speech. The White House chief of staff called my chief of staff at the USDA and asked if I were available, which wasn't exactly a call to vet my presidential qualifications!

I was honored to be selected, but if I am completely honest, there was the tiniest voice in the back of my head thinking something altogether unexpected.

God forbid it happens; I could be the first Jewish president of the United States!

Later that night, I shared these thoughts with my wife, Rhoda, and mentioned to her that I thought I could handle it if something terrible actually happened. I told her that the Clinton cabinet was good, that she would be a terrific First Lady, and that I would make agriculture a higher priority. Of course, I would also need a better joke writer on staff.

"Well, Danny," she said, "good luck to you with that one."

Everyone, but especially politicians, are entitled to a few delusions of grandeur.

Being the designated survivor afforded me the rare opportunity to watch the president's speech like most of my fellow citizens: on a couch, with a beverage in hand, not worried about being caught on television looking bored or drifting off for a second or two. Even on C-Span, the camera can catch you looking anything but captivated. Having every reaction frozen in posterity is not exactly a welcome thought, not then and not now.

Because I had to leave town in my role of designated survivor, I asked if I could be taken to New York City, where my daughter, Amy, had an apartment. They didn't want me to stay in DC as I assumed that they thought a nuclear attack would wipe out the entire city. Looking back, it's ironic that New York was deemed safer from terrorism than Washington.

I was whisked away in an air force jet with Secret Service agents managing my every move. All I could think about was the enormity of the moment as a three-car motorcade picked me up when we landed at LaGuardia Airport. It was a surreal experience to know that I was next in line for the presidency of the United States should the unimaginable occur.

If the worst were to happen, I wondered how I would manage my grief and the horror of the moment: How would I muster all the strength and resolve to step in and lead the nation under such dire circumstances? Even the prospect of it was terrifying.

We arrived with military precision at Amy's apartment, precisely on time. As a member of the cabinet, I was accustomed to having security from the USDA's Office of the Inspector General. But I was not used to the intensity and seriousness of the Secret Service detail I experienced that evening. I was accompanied everywhere by an imposing military officer who I believed was carrying the nuclear football. Now here's the rub: the person who would have to punch the authorization code into the nuclear football was *me*, Dan Glickman, former president of his sixth-grade class in Wichita, Kansas.

Should that horrible moment arrive, it would take mere nanoseconds for an order to go to the Pentagon's National Military Command Center. Within minutes the missiles would launch, and millions would die. Shouldering this level of responsibility, even theoretically for one evening, was intimidating and almost unreal.

I don't recall getting any specific instructions on what to do if the doomsday scenario happened. All I knew was that if necessary, I could simply turn to that large military officer accompanying me, holding that forty-five-pound bag, and trigger a nuclear strike. It was an awesome burden to put on one man's shoulders, even if it was exceedingly unlikely that the president—or in this case, *I*— would ever have to use it. I sometimes wonder if I would have had the courage to give the order to retaliate against whoever wiped out the entire Capitol and all of the people inside it, many of whom were my friends.

Amy's apartment was in downtown Manhattan, which was not a logical place for the designated survivor to hide. When we entered the building, there was a lot of nervous discussion in Spanish by the staff as to whether this was an immigration raid.

So, there we sat in her small and cozy living room, Amy and I, with Secret Service agents hovering around us, watching my every move. I listened to the speech and hoped President Clinton would talk about farming or agriculture. It occurred to me that after all those years of telling the world that agriculture was the most important part of our economy and society, perhaps he would recognize that in his speech, along with naming the secretary of agriculture as the designated survivor.

Most people who know the president realize that there is no such thing as a short Bill Clinton speech, and this one was no exception. It turned out his speech focused on the environment, crime, welfare, and his plan to balance the budget by 2002. There was hardly a word about agriculture, which clearly would have changed under a Glickman administration.

When the speech ended, and the president and Speaker of the House had safely left the House Chamber, one of the lead agents on my security detail walked over to us with a sober look on his face.

"Sir, the mission is terminated."

That was the end of me holding the fate of the world in my hands. He went on to say that I would have no more security detail at my disposal and that they would all be heading back to Washington. Easy come, easy go. I actually felt relieved because although there was a little pressure associated with the experience, I also knew it was unlikely to happen. I was also peeved at how long Clinton's speech was (typical for him) because Amy and I were starved.

"Can we give you a ride back to DC?" he said.

I laughed, thinking that only minutes ago they wouldn't let me out of their sight, and now they couldn't care less where I was going or how I was going to get there.

"Thanks, guys, you did an excellent job tonight, but I'm going to stay in New York a little longer."

Amy and I walked them to the door. My plan all along was to stay and take Amy out to dinner at a Japanese restaurant about ten blocks away. After I said goodbye to my Secret Service detail, they— along with the nuclear football—left Amy's apartment. As the door closed, my anxiety receded, and I began to think about sake and sushi.

Amy and I headed to the restaurant, and after a relaxing dinner and plenty of lively conversation, a terrible storm unexpectedly hit. New York City was pounded with unrelenting, freezing sleet. We got caught outside in the miserable weather, waving our hands and yelling at each passing taxi, but they were either taken or didn't bother to stop. This was long before Uber, Lyft, or any apps at all. Dejected and freezing, we trudged the ten blocks back to her apartment, stuck in a drenched, analog world.

"Shit, a few minutes earlier I was almost the leader of the free world, and now I can't even get a cab."

Amy laughed.

"If only your colleagues shared your sense of humor, Dad," she said. "Most of them take themselves way too seriously."

I had to agree. That type of humor seems to be in short supply in the halls of Congress. There are plenty of jokes directed at other people but too little aimed in the mirror. Though it has been difficult to find a lot to laugh about during the COVID-19 pandemic, the president's occasional verbal foibles (e.g., that he had an inherently sophisticated knowledge of medicine, or that injecting Lysol or Clorox might be a good virus disinfectant) were ridiculously funny but extraordinarily dangerous. A pandemic causing massive death doesn't lend itself to much humor, but it's tragic that President Trump was unable to be funny or empathetic.

The most important lesson I took away from my ninety minutes of designated survivorship was that life is unpredictable. No matter what—no matter who you are, or think you are—it will throw you curveballs. Life will lift you up and just as quickly tear you back down. One minute they're calling you "sir," and the next minute you're soaking wet and ignored.

If you understand this, and humbly accept it, too, you will understand a key tenet of moderate politics: one day you may be on top, but you will probably need some help the next time. Burning bridges, defying norms and conventions, being needlessly obstinate, or an absolutist jerk won't get you far in your life or career. That applies to extreme elements of both parties.

You can choose to be a moderate, both in tone and substance, with an open mind, but sometimes there is just too much shit to swallow. That applies to whether you are dealing with human rights violations overseas or with racism at home. Sometimes, the Groucho Marx prescription that "these are my principles, and if you don't like them, I have others," is just not applicable when basic principles of morality are at stake.

I have to invoke Dante when it comes to any discussion on the subject of neutrality.

"The darkest place in hell is reserved for those who in a period of moral crisis, claim neutrality."

There are certain things you just can't be neutral about.

You'll utilize this approach if you want to actually achieve something with your career. You have to, if you're serious at all about dealing with problems, passing bills, and being a conscientious lawmaker—one who makes a genuine impact and who moves the country forward by working with others toward the common good.

In other words, you can choose to be a thoughtful moderate lawmaker with an open mind.

On my way back to Washington, I had time to reflect even more on my near brush with unwanted fame and misfortune and what it really takes to work effectively in the political world.

No one gets far without a good team behind them and, above all, treating contemporaries, especially every colleague, with courtesy and respect. This is a simple rule, but as we know all too well, it's not always followed, certainly in politics and in life in general.

But it is the absolute key to success.

Being a good leader allows one to build a good team. Looking at the way in which President Trump tried to lead, it's clear that he had a lot of sycophants and yes-people telling him only what he wanted to hear, if not outright praise him like a servant praises a master. Behavior like this made his presidency less effective and forestalled true and lasting achievement, not just what he claimed to be true. In order to be a good leader, one must display respect—for one's allies and enemies—and one must earn it mutually through one's statements and actions.

We could also define it this way: bosses push, and leaders pull.

At times, I thought President George W. Bush was just not up to the job and that he delegated away too much authority to folks like Vice President Cheney. Yet he was an empathetic person, demonstrated by his immediate personal response to 9/11, and especially in the way his administration led America's transformational response to the AIDS epidemic in Africa. I thought he'd led a terrible response in our American involvement in Iraq, but he treated members of Congress from both parties with decency. Nobody is a total jerk, although Trump comes close.

Being the designated survivor back in 1997 was a big moment in my life. Being potentially the most powerful person on the planet was not an accomplishment by itself, but being chosen to occupy that role, even for a few scant hours, was the culmination of a journey that proved how success in life can be based on integrity and hard work. This was a level of acknowledgment I had never anticipated, and in its own small way it confirmed what I had been striving for all along and that I had earned the respect to even be considered for the highest office in the land. I had only dreamed of this before.

You do not have to be a self-aggrandizing chameleon to make it to the top. You can achieve incredible success by working hard, being an independent and measured voice, and not taking yourself too seriously along the way.

A sense of humor helps, and mine started to develop years ago back home in Kansas.

Chapter 3

Growing Up Glickman in Wichita, Kansas

Like many folks, I am proud of where I come from. I am a Jewish kid from Kansas, and thanks to my hometown, my religion, and my parents, I love to crack a joke.

Kansas sometimes gets a bad rap these days but much of that is not exclusive to the state I know and love. Besides Dorothy and Toto, the state is best known for farming, college basketball, and a strange fiscal policy of late, championed by ideological conservatives and voted on successfully (if you're an ideological conservative) by a decidedly non-moderate state legislature. The political winds in Kansas, though, have not always blown through the windows of Evangelical churches. In fact, the Sunflower State is the birthplace of the progressive movement, initially led by William Allen White, a native of Emporia, Kansas, who was a famous author, editor, and politician. Until his death in 1944, he was considered the face of the progressive movement and a relentless advocate for Middle America and its core values.

I am proud of the many thoughtful moderate politicians who have called Kansas home. I am proud of that legacy for our state. I am proud of the common-sense pragmatism that defines much of Middle America and remarkably produces thoughtful, progressive politicians of high integrity and character.

I grew up observing many Kansan residents who considered politics to be a noble pursuit, and they behaved accordingly throughout their careers. It was clear that they respected the process of legislating and enjoyed making a difference in people's lives.

But Kansas has changed since the era of Senators Bob Dole and Nancy Kassebaum, who exemplified the moniker of "Honorable" and made us Kansans proud. Today, Wichita is not only the largest city in Kansas, with a population approaching four hundred thousand, it is the home of one of the largest and most influential employers in the state, Koch Industries, which spends tens of millions of dollars to support ideological conservative and libertarian policies and advocacy groups.

The Koch network has helped to spawn a politics of unlimited campaign spending in the United States, which is now replicated nationally, to pursue their agenda. Much of this spending is not subject to proper disclosure rules, so the public often doesn't know who is giving what to whom. Dark money. Figures on both sides of the aisle have joined in this metastatic race for money, although it is more prevalent on the political right than the political left.

Since the Supreme Court passage of the *Citizens United* case in 2010, strong, ideologically focused groups like Koch Industries and their principals have been able to spend unlimited amounts of money to support or inhibit political candidates and various causes without any trace of their fingerprints—through dark money channels and disguises. This enables them to finance a lot of people and policies I disagree with, and I wish they would not continue giving our state such a dubious reputation. No one seems to be calling them out much in public, which I'm sure is conveniently intentional. Let me purposefully mention someone who was unfortunately singled out—former governor Mike Hayden, elected as a conservative rural force, who became an environmental and conservation champion while he served as governor and afterwards.

Kansas has a long history in moderate politics and has produced some of the country's greatest civil servants, such as Alf Landon, Dwight D. Eisenhower, Kassebaum, Dole, Kathleen Sebelius, John Carlin (former governor), and many other Democratic and Republican lawmakers. It's sad that the Kochs have become the face of Kansas to the nation, but to be honest, they reflect a changing tide in our state's electoral whims. In recent years, Kansas has moved more and more to the right and is now as close to a one-party state as you can get, producing a growing number of hardened partisans who have emerged from what used to be a fertile ground for pragmatic moderates. I've seen a hint of change lately, though, spearheaded by the election of Laura Kelly to the governorship, the first Democrat to hold that office in many years. She calls herself "the least political governor you've ever had," and seems to really want to work with both parties, which as a moderate is music to my ears. And I might add that even leaders of Koch Industries thought Donald Trump was too extreme in his tone and politics.

Kelly is emblematic of the values of a Kansas upbringing, which still hold the seeds of moderate politics. We've seen a tremendous shift to the right in Kansas over the past few election cycles, but I know that this does not fully reflect the voice of the people. While much has changed in the Kansas Statehouse in Topeka and the far-right megaphone is as loud as ever, I know that Kansans are still good people and have not sold out their values to the highest bidder.

Our state's long-standing reputation has been built from its agricultural roots. Farming and raising livestock are a big part of the Kansas legacy, and there's no doubt that it's played a major role in my own career in Congress and as secretary of agriculture. We're also not called the Wheat State for nothing. In most years, we grow more wheat than any other state in the country, which might also make us the gluten capital of the world.

But Kansas isn't just a giant farm in the breadbasket of America. A lot of industry is generated here beyond agriculture, from oil and gas to manufacturing and construction, including one sector that was important for me as a child and as a congressman: aviation.

Wichita was the aviation capital of the world for many years, the corporate home for industry giants such as Cessna, Beech, major parts of Learjet and Boeing, as well as dozens of auxiliary suppliers and subcontractors. In fact, when I was growing up, nearly half of all planes manufactured in the world, both small and large, were built in my hometown.

My parents took advantage of Wichita's aviation innovation by taking us to many of the city's air shows, which is where I fell in love with planes. For people of my generation, the idea that you could get on a plane and fly somewhere was astounding, especially as a child growing up watching people on horseback in real life and on TV, in shows like *Gunsmoke*, *Bonanza*, and *The Lone Ranger*. The prospect of flying was more exciting than anything else I could imagine.

We'd visit the Wichita airport just to see the planes take off and land, especially the TWA constellations, those iconic triple-tail airplanes used for their transcontinental routes. Once we had our fill of those awe-inspiring visual treats, we'd cap off our family excursion with a visit to the local A &W Root Beer stand, one of the first restaurants to be franchised in the United States, or the first White Castle hamburger joint, which was built in Wichita.

I don't know if my excitement about planes came from seeing them as a path to get out of town in the future, or if it was the thrill of seeing people moving all over the world. It sure seemed like most people were traveling with a smile on their face, excited for the experience and their next destination. Going to an airport was a totally different experience then, too. In those days, we could walk around the terminal free and clear, without having to pass through any security. Planes went to places like Chicago or Los Angeles or New York, and before long they were connecting people to cities we'd never heard of or imagined visiting. Air travel today can feel as crammed as being on a bus in rush hour. It's not exactly what I'd call glamorous, either, though I still get a kick out of going to Dulles Airport in Virginia and hopping on a plane.

As a child, flying on a plane seemed inconceivable and maybe the coolest thing ever for a young person to think about doing someday.

My elementary school in Wichita was situated right under the flight path of McConnell Air Force Base, so as a kid I got to see B-52s and B-47s flying over us all the time. While some people were bothered by airplane noise, I always thought it sounded like a symphony to go along with the visual magic show it never failed to provide.

Witnessing so many strides in aviation was one of many fond memories of my life growing up in Kansas. The Glickmans were a gregarious group and our roots run deep. I am a third-generation Kansan, and proud of my hometown, which is known as "The Air Capital of the World." Wichita is also known as "Doo-Dah," a nickname it picked up in the 1950s, supposedly to counter the hype surrounding its better, more traditional nickname. Some claim that Doo-Dah is meant to reflect the laid-back nature of Wichita's culture and its people's attitudes. For me, it represents the Doo-Dah Diner, a favorite locale for homemade biscuits and gravy.

Wichita was well-known as a big oil and gas town, filled with dozens of independent oil and gas operators, including my dad, back in the 1950s. The city also produced dozens of entrepreneurs, millionaires, and successful businesses, such as Pizza Hut, Koch Industries, and the Coleman Company, among many others. I mention this because although Kansas is universally considered small-town America, cities like Wichita were the rural equivalent of an entrepreneurial incubator, producing great companies, innovative leaders, big agriculture, and much more.

Growing up in Wichita, home of the conservative movement in America and a city of entrepreneurs with a tiny Jewish population, literally made me who I am today. How ironic that a Jewish kid from Doo-Dah got elected to the US Congress—as a Democrat, no less, in a highly unusual way (see chapter 6)—and then became the leading spokesman for our nation's farming and agriculture communities.

Only in America. Only in Wichita! Only in Doo-Dah!

I am who I am today because of Kansas, because of the values instilled in me as a child growing up in the Midwest, and because of the opportunities Kansas afforded to the entire Glickman family. It's like a three-legged stool. I truly believe that I am who I am today because of my heartland values, my supportive family, and a basic optimistic belief that I could accomplish almost anything I set my sights on. I also believe that my religion turned out to be a big plus for me throughout my career, and I am sure I felt, even thought, that in some sense I am no Moses, but I have been a modern-day secular ambassador for the Jewish people.

My grandparents arrived in Kansas at the beginning of the twentieth century. My grandfather left Belarus (then part of Russia, also known as White Russia) at the age of seventeen, entirely on his own. Like many immigrants of his era, he arrived in the United States with nothing of value and few options to make a living. He found work in the salvage and scrap metals business. Back then, this was an exclusively Jewish industry and didn't require any level of formal education. My grandfather would collect scrap metals, like iron, copper, and aluminum, disassemble them, and sell them by their weight and purity. At the time, few people were even in the junk or trash business. It was the ideal vocation for my grandfather because he could use his body for hard labor while also employing his brain and can-do attitude to grow a business. It also gave him a chance to learn English while earning a living.

Being Jewish in Kansas means you stick out. That was still true when I was growing up, but it must have been especially so for my grandparents. Yet my grandfather was proud of his heritage and was an early founder of one of only two Jewish congregations in Wichita, and he served as president of the synagogue for ten years. He was not devout in the ultra-Orthodox sense, but for him his religion represented the strength of his people to make their own way through one adversity after another. He was not the most observant Jew and did not partake in many of the daily Jewish rituals, but he insisted that I receive Jewish training as a young boy and celebrate a full bar mitzvah ceremony when I reached the age of thirteen, which I happily did.

My grandparent's religious leanings were not exactly traditional. We picked what we felt was relevant to our lives as Jews in a decidedly non-Jewish world, and we didn't lose any sleep by keeping score of every ritual we observed or skipped. My family wanted me to be proud of who I was, even if in a place like Kansas, this made me different.

My grandfather met my grandmother in Wichita. They were both Jewish immigrants living in a small town with almost no other Jews. She came from what was the Austro-Hungarian empire, somewhere on the border with Poland. They decided to get married pretty quickly, because after all, if you wanted a Jewish wife or husband in Wichita at that time, pickings were slim! There was no resident yenta nor were there any religious matchmakers. That industry would have to wait for a bigger pool of candidates and the internet.

My father was born nine months and one day after my grandparents got married, so clearly, they were both interested in expanding their family, not to mention Wichita gets quite chilly in the winter and it's natural to want to keep warm.

My father, Milton, certainly inherited the humor gene. He was a popular and exceptionally funny man. No joke was too corny or too long, and he coveted jokes as others might collect rare coins or stamps.

His one-liners were priceless.

"You know, I proposed to my wife in a garage, and then I couldn't back out."

"Your mother and I have sex almost every night—almost on Monday, almost on Tuesday, and almost on Wednesday."

"The other night I swallowed a muffler; the next morning I woke up exhausted."

"The other night I wondered what happens to the sun when it goes down at night, and when I woke up the next morning, it dawned on me."

He was a machine when it came to one-liners.

"Danny," my mother once told me, "I had to listen to your father's jokes and stories for sixty-three very long years."

My poor mother. I guess after all those years, even the funniest of jokes can get a bit stale. For my father, his muse and passion was humor, and it was a daily joy for him. He grew up during tough times, and having a fun and easygoing attitude was not necessarily what one would expect, given his early experiences. He was born on December 22, 1916, and raised during the Great Depression. He quit college at the University of Oklahoma after my grandparents literally ran out of money. That was one of the main reasons he and my uncle decided to go into the family scrap iron business.

The Glickmans were hardworking, dedicated, and determined people. Nothing ever stopped them from coming up with novel ideas, and they were not afraid of taking risks or experiencing failures. My father never appeared outwardly depressed. But at times he could be moody and downcast, and his mood swings could come out of the blue. This was especially evident after the death of his parents and his brother, Bill. Though he always tried to reflect positivity and put a good face on things, especially when he was experiencing a business challenge or setback, I could always see when he was worried, which was often. I'm convinced that being alive during the Great Depression and growing up with those clouds over his head made him the real survivor.

As my grandfather's business expanded, my dad and uncle went into business with him once they became young adults. Over the years, like many entrepreneurs at the time, they had their ups and downs. We never really talked about how tough their business was, particularly their struggles during the Depression, because my grandfather, father, and uncle never complained. I believe people back then were much more self-reliant and resilient than they appear to be today.

"Danny, what good would complaining do anyway?" my dad used to say.

I suppose that attitude also saved him a fortune on therapy. While I have never gone through any serious psychotherapy myself, even if I needed it at times, I do think that similar qualities in my father's self-reliance and perseverance became important ingredients in how I handled adversity in my life.

My father's joking style even extended to his business, where he was quite successful, like his father. Plenty of people, especially in politics, have absolutely no sense of humor. Some even think it's a weakness or a flaw. But my father showed me that you can be funny and even a bit silly in business and still do extremely well.

Possessing a strong sense of humor is such an important part of who I am and how I have always thought about my career. Make people laugh, make people comfortable, and try to build consensus around basic points of agreement. A sense of humor and a little humility can go a long way toward accomplishing agreement in every aspect of life, including politics. In that arena, if people like you, you are closer to gathering support and finding success. It all starts with being liked.

Likability is certainly one of the most important parts of my own political success. You can be likable for a lot of reasons: humor, empathy, honesty, kindness. The one thing that gets in the way of being liked, no matter what, is ego. If you think so highly of yourself that you have contempt for others, then people will see through that. It is amazing how many politicians have such inflated egos and then wonder why they lose elections or have trouble running for higher offices. For me, being funny was a central and organic way to be liked, and we know how much politicians value that type of thing.

Luckily, my own father was a great role model for the benefits of being an affable fellow with a gentle, humorous soul.

I loved my dad's stories. Here is one of my favorites:

"Danny, there are two songs to sing every morning when you get up. It's your choice. The first is, 'Oh no, I hate to wake up in the morning,' and the second is, 'Oh what a beautiful morning.' If you sing that last song, you'll have a productive and positive day."

This sounds incredibly corny, but we are talking here about Kansas in the 1950s ("Hello Toto") and the Glickman family, who understood the comic absurdity of living as Jews in the heart and soul of Christian Middle America.

My dad was a perpetual optimist, especially in dealing with his business.

Even when business was not good, he would always say,

"Business is terrific," because, as he shared, "The Depression taught me that people would much rather do business with successful people than unsuccessful ones, with optimists rather than pessimists." Fake it till you make it? Maybe.

Both of my parents taught me and my siblings to treat everyone with respect, "and that goes especially for business customers," they often said. That was a good lesson for me to learn when I first got into politics—thinking of my constituents as my customers, except for the fact that if they wanted to return the merchandise (me) they would have to wait two years for the next election.

Milton and Gladys Glickman were well matched in many respects. Her sense of humor was also pivotal to her life and an integral part of her character. Compared to my dad, her funny bone was more subtle, natural, and understated. They were a good team, a handsome couple with splendid personalities, who were friendly to everyone, affable, and extremely easygoing. My parents were both popular in Wichita and beyond, and people admired their congeniality and how well they got along, but that doesn't mean they had a perfect marriage. In fact, I witnessed a fair amount of internal bickering at home. Nevertheless, they were committed to their union and stayed married for sixty-three years, which is no joke.

My mother used to tell us this joke about their marriage:

"I never once thought of divorcing your father," she said. "Murdering him, yes."

My dad told a similar joke.

"When your mother turns forty, I'm going to trade her in for two twenties."

Move over George and Gracie.

To be fair, our household did not exactly operate like a stand-up comedy club. Just like Don Corleone, my father ran a tight ship, and he believed that it was his responsibility to take care of all aspects of family life, so what he said became the rule of law. My mother, on the other hand, was less confrontational and didn't have as many rules for running the household or their lives together. They enjoyed a good and productive partnership, and as time went on, especially during their last twenty years, they appeared to be the best of friends. As the middle child, my role was the family peacemaker. As I look back, I realize more and more how that played a significant role in my commitment to bipartisanship when I began my political career. For all I managed as a middle sibling, I could have been nick-named "Moderate Dan."

I ultimately became closer to my mother because she was less judgmental and volatile than my father, and like most Jewish moth-ers, she believed I could do no wrong. Well, at least most of the time. She wasn't so happy with me at all during an unfortunate incident with my Aunt Shirley and Uncle Bill that involved a pad of butter. My parents were arguing quite a bit with my aunt and uncle at the time, and one night when we were all having dinner at a Wichita restaurant I decided to act and take things into my own little hands. I didn't have a lot of options, but ever the loyal family member, I concluded that the best way to support my parents and let my aunt and uncle know that I meant business was to take a pad of butter and spread it all over Aunt Shirley's beaver coat. Don't ask me how a pad of butter had anything to do with a family feud. I thought at the time that a nasty deed like that would make my mother happy. Big mistake. She scowled like I'd never seen her do before. Clearly, she was annoyed at me for behaving badly, but she never punished me. I suspect she might have been secretly happy that I took the initiative and defended the Glickman honor. I still smile whenever I see a pad of butter.

Both of my parents were my biggest cheerleaders. They sup-ported me throughout my entire life, as well as my siblings, es-pecially when it came to our intellectual pursuits in the academic world and our professional projects. Their support was shown with a hug, a homemade dinner, and of course, a joke. You could wake my parents up in the middle of the night, and without objection they would take me to a small-town parade and drive a convertible with the top down and a metallic placard on it saying, "We're Dan's parents." They were Twitter before computers were invented.

As they grew older, my parents' love of baseball became almost an obsession. They remained focused on their business but devoted more and more time and energy to their favorite sport. My father was the ultimate baseball fan and loved everything about the game, from the thrill of a ninth inning grand slam to the smell of hot dogs and popcorn. Incidentally, he loved movie popcorn even more, and he loved to drive me and my brother and sister to the local theatre, where we would go in and buy popcorn for him. The theatre owners all knew the entire Glickman clan and our affinity for popcorn. I'm sure that's also where my love of movies originated, and maybe my agriculture career as well. After all, there's no pop without the corn.

My parents' interests were laser-focused around the ownership of their beloved AAA baseball team, which they managed from 1969 to 1984. I sat in the stands many times, hoping the Aeros would strike out the opposing team, score more home runs, and of course, win more games than they lost. Still, regardless of their record, it was fun to spend a lazy summer afternoon as the proud son of the owner of the Wichita Aeros.

Despite outward appearances, the team was not particularly successful in an economic sense, mainly due to poor attendance. We were affiliated with the Chicago Cubs most of the time, and until they won the World Series in 2016, the Cubs were one of the worst teams in the history of professional baseball. However, win or lose, my parents were always positive, and reveled in the overall baseball experience.

As owners of the team, you would think they would have had an air about them that was off-putting or even snobbish. On the contrary. My parents would talk to anybody about anything. It didn't matter if someone was rich or poor, powerful or run-of-the-mill. My parents could connect with anyone and make them feel as if they were the most important person in the room. They loved America and loved their family, but there was no doubt that baseball, and all the people associated with it, was chief among their passions.

One time, the great Ernie Banks came to visit my dad in Wichita. Ernie, "Mr. Cub" Banks, was a shortstop for the Chicago Cubs from 1953 until 1971 and was a good friend of my dad's. He was also a local hero in Wichita, and of course, Chicago, even more so when he was inducted into the Baseball Hall of Fame in 1977. After he retired from playing professional baseball, he was the Cub's PR guy and came to Wichita to meet with my dad. Unfortunately, after he arrived, he realized that he had forgotten to bring his suitcase.

"Ernie, don't you worry," my dad said. "Go down to Henry's and buy what you need and put it on my tab."

Ernie was more than happy to oblige. A few weeks later, when my dad received the bill from Henry's, he almost busted a gasket. He told me that Ernie spent nearly $2,000, and that was in 1972, when $2,000 would have been a fortune to spend on what essentially was Ernie's weekend wardrobe. Ever the diplomat and a man of good cheer, my dad let it go. To him, losing a few thousand dollars was a small price to pay for not embarrassing a good friend, not to mention a baseball legend.

I think part of this approachable and self-effacing quality was the result of my dad being a Depression-era kid when he learned that being kind and likable was the foundation for everything good, with friends and in business. Regardless of the reason, both of my parents were genuinely friendly to pretty much everyone.

"You don't make lasting friendships by being demeaning or critical of others," they always said, "and the way you treat people is part of your character. Word gets around and people talk, so don't give them a reason to speak badly about you."

This was my parents' golden rule and it stuck with me through thick and thin.

My dad's sense of human dignity and his enormous collection of jokes made him a Wichita fixture and local legend. He was among Wichita's favorite sons—a successful business owner and entrepreneur, the owner of a AAA baseball team, and an involved and passionate community advocate with a sterling reputation.

He also became good friends with many professional sports figures across the country. That made his joke playlist even more compelling. Here are two of his favorite baseball jokes that we heard all the time.

"Did you know that baseball was invented in the Bible? In the *big inning*?"

"Why does it take longer to get from first base to second base than it does to get from second base to third base? Because there is a *short-stop* between the bases."

To be honest, sometimes after hearing Dad's jokes over and over, they lost a bit of their luster. But his animated delivery and funny facial expressions, in true Glickman style, always kept me and my mother, brother, and sister in stitches.

There was no question that my parents' popularity was helpful to me in my many political races. This is ironic since neither of them was terribly political. They didn't consider themselves Republican or Democrat. Kansas was full of people who embraced conservative values but were politically moderate and pushed what today would be considered as progressive policies, for example, being an early adopter of civil rights policy. That is the political environment in which my parents shaped their views and ideology, and when they did get politically active, it was usually to support moderate Republican points of view. My running as a Democrat was by no means a break with family tradition, especially since a moderate Democrat in Kansas was not all that different from a moderate Republican, and moderate Democrats were not an extinct species in Kansas politics at that time.

My parents were great. They gave us everything we needed to do what we wanted, and they raised me with strong values and ethics. My parents both lived until their early eighties and died within two weeks of each other. Like most people from happy and stable homes, I feel as if I owe them everything.

My mom and dad were careful to not use humor or satire in a hurtful way, or to make fun of vulnerable people. Their humor was silly and funny, and I think they both loved Johnny Carson for that reason. While my dad loved the one-liners, I preferred the self-deprecating humor. I often wonder if my parents were alive today what they would think of the mean-spirited humor that permeates late night television and the internet. My father would probably feast on puns.com and drive my mother crazy with his endless reporting on what he found.

When I took my mother to the White House for a congressional picnic during the George H. W. Bush administration, she displayed her dry wit in spades. Of course she was excited to be there, as would anyone standing outside the south lawn of the White House for the first time in the company of the leader of the free world.

When I introduced my mother to the president, he said to her, "Oh, Mrs. Glickman, we just love your son, but we wish he would convert."

He obviously meant that I should convert to a Republican from a Democrat. With a straight face and a deadpan delivery she replied in her own subtle fashion.

"Oh, Mr. President, we can't do that, we love being Jewish."

President Bush raised one eyebrow ever so slightly, and with a smile, he put his hand on her shoulder.

"Mrs. Glickman, don't worry, I got the message; I won't try to convert your son again."

It was a crushing blow when my mother died from a stroke and my father died from lung cancer so shortly after. We do not believe that she ever knew my dad had been diagnosed. He wasn't feeling well, but back then there was no thought of him having a life-threatening condition.

December 1999 was the toughest month I have ever experienced. For me and my siblings, the emotional pain was almost unbearable. Losing both parents so close to one another was horrible. It took us a long time to get over not hearing our dad's jokes or our mom's effusive praise for her three children. It was a loss like no other I have ever experienced. But somewhere amidst all the pain there remains another uncanny moment.

My mother and my sister never full trusted my dad in one respect. Let's just say he had a gregarious nature. When we were all gathered at the funeral home, with hundreds of Wichita's finest in attendance, we noticed something rather unusual. Several young women were there, obviously overcome by emotion at the loss of my father. We clearly didn't recognize any of them. Suffice to say, my father's gregariousness was more pronounced than we ever imagined.

After he died, we found several dozen legal pads laying in inconspicuous places in his office—all filled with jokes, lots and lots of them. I sat down behind his desk and started reading them. To my amazement, they were all handwritten, literally thousands of them. It was like he was a professional writer for Johnny Carson or *Laugh In*. I smiled, as poring through those legal pads brought back his voice and mannerisms, as if he were standing right next to me delivering his one-liners and puns. Clearly, my father took this humor thing seriously! Many times, people from across the country who had heard my dad's propensity for instantaneous humor would call him for jokes. Former Speaker of the House Jim Wright used to request his material on a regular basis. I introduced them to each other in the late 1970s and they shared the same birthday. They became fast friends. I'm not sure if Jim became any funnier but at least he tried.

That's really what I carry with me from my parents. Humor helps you stay grounded and build relationships.

President Dwight D. Eisenhower, one of Kansas's favorite sons, expressed this best.

"A sense of humor is part of leadership," he said, "of getting along with people; of getting things done."

This came from a soldier, the guy who led the Allied assault on Europe!

Being a Glickman and growing up with such colorful, kind, and loving parents and grandparents made all the difference. They gave me courage, determination, guiding principles, persistence, humility, and most of all, the appreciation and importance of a good joke.

We loved humor so much that after my parents died, my brother, sister, and I donated $100,000 to Wichita State University to create a seminar program in political humor in their honor. As you can imagine, this became quite popular with the students. Over the years, we hosted several well-known speakers, including the comedian Mo Rocca, the political scientist Norm Ornstein (he is actually really funny), the Capitol Steps, and more serious speakers, such as David Broder and David Gergen.

We attracted large crowds—fifteen hundred people—and the seminar leaders always talked about my parents during their introductions. Al Franken once told a politically incorrect joke while I was in the audience with my family, along with the senior leadership of the university and thousands of students. This was before he became a senator, when he and Norm Ornstein performed at one of these lecture series as a team. Al and Norm were (and are) close friends and grew up as Minneapolis neighbors.

At one point in the joke, Franken specifically referred to the male sex organ coming out of the forehead of a person. Our family gasped. I was worried that they were going to cancel the seminar and keep the money. There was total silence for a moment, but thankfully the wife of the president of the university began to laugh hysterically, and then the crowd joined in.

I always want to be funny, but the lesson here is to know your audience, which is exactly what any successful stand-up comedian needs to do.

We all carry within us the spirit of those who came before. I am keenly aware of how my grandparents and my parents guided me to become the person I am today. They set me off on a trajectory that has given me an incredibly satisfying and exciting life, personally and professionally. I am indebted to them, and I hope I can give the same to my children and grandchildren.

If I can pass on a few things to my kids and grandchildren, it would be the following: Don't take yourself too seriously. Get enough sleep. Laugh as much as possible, and use your imagination, which is more important than all the smarts you will ever possess.

And by the way, the Wichita baseball team for a while became known as the Wingnuts. Go figure.

Chapter 4

A Cafeteria Jew on the Prairie

Growing up in Kansas gave me a typical American upbringing, and being Jewish helped me develop an appreciation for what it means to be different as well as a desire to understand and engage with people whose alternative points of view are based on their life experiences.

Curiosity and a willingness to connect are fundamental for being a political moderate and, I would argue, a good person. In Congress and in life we constantly encounter people who think differently than we do, for a variety of reasons, but unless you can appreciate that and let it guide your interactions, you can never genuinely connect with others.

I always tried to put myself in the shoes of the person I was dealing with, which usually proved to be a disarming technique. It was especially effective with the farmers I dealt with over the years. I think they knew my knowledge of agriculture was pretty limited, but I showed genuine concern and care about their problems.

As a child, I had an intuitive understanding of this, which I attribute in part to my Jewish culture. As I matured and became a congressman and secretary of agriculture, I felt a deep responsibility to the Jewish community—to be an unofficial ambassador of my Jewish heritage.

Kansas in the 1940s had only a handful of synagogues, including the one founded by my grandfather and a few others. Out of three hundred thousand residents, there were only about three hundred Jewish families in Wichita. Throughout my elementary, junior high, and high school years, there were only about a dozen Jewish students in my school. I knew most of them through synagogue or wherever else we met for various holidays, but I was always was comfortable befriending everyone, as I did not want to limit myself. Both of my parents were comfortable being part of the entire Wichita community, and that tradition carried on with me and my school activities. I was pretty popular, active in debating clubs and school politics.

During Christmas celebrations, I felt a little self-conscious because we were different; however, I didn't let that prevent me from being part of my class or my community. I was active in student government, the debate team, and I sang in the kid's choir during Friday night services at our local synagogue.

Throughout my young life, especially in high school and college, I always found being Jewish as largely positive and helpful to me in many ways. It meant having involved and caring mentors and family members, a wide range of cultural experiences, a strong set of values, and lots and lots of books. I embraced my heritage, and my friends and peers largely did too.

Even though my parents owned the Wichita Aeros minor league baseball team, and I was exposed to sports during most of my life, I always preferred to let an enjoyable book transport me to faraway places. No one in my family was that surprised when they realized that I was not going to be the football team's quarterback or a record-setting hitter on the baseball team.

Early on, it became evident that I would much rather read a book or complete a Cub Scout project than hit a baseball or make a tackle. The only exception was my skill as a golfer, which earned me a letter for playing on the Southeast High School golf team.

Much to my parent's chagrin, I constantly carried a pitching wedge or a nine iron around the neighborhood so I could practice my shots. I would try to hit a golf ball across the street or over the roof of my neighbor's house, thinking that was equivalent to hitting it over a natural hazard at a golf course. When I inevitably broke our neighbor's front window and hit the back of a bus on Douglas Avenue, I was convinced to stop putting Wichita at risk.

Nevertheless, I felt no pressure to become a jock. The only expectation hovering over me was that I put all my effort and positive energy into succeeding at whatever I chose to pursue. That was the Glickman mantra, and my parents could not care less whether I applied it to Shakespeare rather than Babe Ruth, or to debating instead of hitting home runs. While I eventually took another rather nonath-letic path in life, I learned the art of jumping in when opportunity knocked. Vigorous work and the importance of education were the hallmarks of my early experience as a young Jew growing up in the Midwest.

Our family was what I refer to as "Cafeteria Jews."

Take for example our consumption of pork. We did not keep a kosher house, but we never ate pork or bacon at home. That all went down the drain, though, when our family went out to eat. Bacon was definitely on the table. When it came to food, we chose what to observe, where to eat what, and when it was appropriate to put that into practice.

For the most part, I never found my religion to be an imped-iment during my school years, even though I am sure there was occasional suspicion about what a Jew was really like. I was not oblivious to this, but I can't recall any time it came up. My parents were both well integrated in the community. My dad was on a local bank board and popular in the Wichita area, and both of my parents were close with local and state politicians.

One thing that was never off the table was me having a bar mitzvah. There were not many of those celebrations in Wichita, so mine was destined to be quite a production.

Jews celebrate bar and bat mitzvahs when boys and girls turn thirteen and theoretically become "adults." I remember mine as a big event. We invited everyone in town that we knew, Jews and non-Jews, as long as they could show up. I performed the entire Satur-day morning service, which was not the usual procedure, but my brother had set the bar pretty high four years earlier, so naturally I had to keep up. I must admit I nailed it. I was thrilled, too, because most of the Jewish community was there to see me, as were many of our non-Jewish friends.

Clearly, this was the kickoff of a long career that involved pub-lic speaking, having the spotlight squarely on me, and connecting with people from all over the community. There are no Republicans or Democrats at bar mitzvahs. There are only people hungry for a good meal.

After the service, my parents hosted a large party at a local hotel—mostly for their friends. I think only one of my friends was there. When I walked into the ballroom, I couldn't help noticing an enormous ice sculpture that was impossible to miss from a mile away. Had we had men in space at the time, they would have said, "Yeah, it was so cool being up in space. We could see the Great Wall of China and Dan Glickman's ice sculpture."

"Danny" was carved into the ice, which was pretty embarrassing for a thirteen-year-old. As the evening went on, and the band kept playing popular songs that adults liked, I began petering out. I sat down at the head table, grabbed a bite of filet mignon, and started falling asleep. My parents called a cab and sent me home while they kept on dancing with their friends. As they partied, I slept, and I think they hardly noticed I was gone.

I have always felt that being a Jew in America's heartland is a huge asset. It served me well from my early years through adulthood. I only met a few people who made an issue out of my religion, either overtly or behind my back. While campaigning for office, I found it interesting that some people were curious because they had never met a Jew. This was especially true in parts of farm country.

During one of the Middle Eastern wars in the 1950s or 1960s, I heard the mother of one of my closest friends make a strange but typically naïve comment.

"Dan, I don't understand why Jews and the Arabs can't get along like good Christians."

I didn't know whether to laugh or cry. I think that witnessing this type of naïveté, as well as growing up in a small community instead of a big city, gave me a purpose. Over the years, I felt a stronger sense of purpose, based on my Jewish heritage. I considered it my responsibility to act as an ambassador of the Jewish community. Looking back, I knew that because I was one of the few Jews that people in Kansas had ever met, I did not want to give anyone the opportunity to judge me or my work as inferior based solely on my heritage. I wanted to represent "my people" by putting forth my absolute best as a means of demonstrating that we were fundamentally no different. Once people got to know me, any apprehension they may have felt just faded away.

"That Dan Glickman; he's Jewish, but he seems regular enough."

"Yeah, I wasn't sure what to think, but he seems okay."

"I might even go to one of those Batman Mitz things if they have good food."

Being Jewish was never a material factor in my political career, either in the lead up to being elected to Congress or during any of my tenure in Washington, DC. This was partially due to good campaigning as well as the respect that the Glickman family had amassed over many years serving the Wichita community. After all, in 1976 I defeated an eight-term incumbent Republican congressman named Garner Shriver. Ironically, his chief of staff was also Jewish and had strong ties to the Wichita community.

My Jewish heritage was certainly on my mind when I was appointed to serve as the secretary of agriculture during President Bill Clinton's administration. Not only was I the first Jew to occupy that position but I was also keenly aware that I was breaking a stereotype, since few Jews went into farming, though many worked in the food industry. One might argue that there was one influential Jewish farm administrator before me: Joseph in the Book of Genesis, but who's counting?

I used to get a kick out of the way President Clinton introduced me at events.

"Ladies and gentlemen," he'd say, "please welcome the first Jewish Secretary of Agriculture, Dan Glickman."

I could see that he enjoyed introducing me that way and it didn't come off as weird or awkward at all. Clinton was both serious and amused about his first Jewish USDA secretary, fully understanding the anomaly of Jewish people involved in American agriculture.

There were plenty of Jewish people in President Clinton's cabinet, in my law school, and in many other places I have lived. But there are definitely not a ton of Jews in the agricultural production industry. I never felt this was a problem for me, but I was a curiosity to some folks in the communities I visited while serving as secretary of agriculture.

Being Jewish meant I had a little convincing to do to let America's farmers know that I was on their side, since many of them had never met a Jew in their life. Once again, humor was my most successful weapon. To break the ice with the farmers I represented, I used my arsenal of self-deprecating jokes, such as, "You might be wondering what my chief qualification is for getting my job here at USDA. It was my Jewish mother's constant admonition to 'eat, eat, eat.'"

Once at the Iowa State Fair when I was the guest of the Iowa

Pork Producers Association, they hosted a special lunch for me. Assuming that I did not eat pork, they were respectful and served me a large steak. But the waiter kept pulling the steak from my plate and putting a huge pork chop in its place, thinking that someone in the kitchen had made a mistake. I had never seen a pork chop that huge, although I must admit I did not have a lot of experience with that type of meat.

A reporter covering my visit witnessed my predicament.

"Secretary Glickman, don't you eat pork?"

I was actually stunned by the reporter's question. I thought he was pretty ignorant, actually, but I did not respond. Quite honestly, his question did make me a little nervous, as I didn't know him or what he would write. He actually mentioned it in a short piece in the paper the following day, but only to the extent that I ate a big steak at the pork producers' lunch. This subsequently made me quite popular with the Iowa Cattleman's Association.

Ultimately, I didn't eat the pork served to me at the Iowa State Fair. I must admit that when the reporter asked me why I didn't eat pork, not only did I think he was stupid but I actually had a moment of Jewish anxiety, as I was not sure if I would be carrying on the tradition of a thousand years of being "different." This was early on in my USDA experience and that fleeting moment of fear dissipated when they quickly put a steak on my plate. Because I was hungry, the anxiety quickly passed. No one, including me, asked if the steak was kosher.

After that day at the state fair I became a huge advocate for the pork industry, helping with exports as well as fighting low prices, among many other issues they faced. How else but with a sense of humor, or at least a sense of irony, can you be a Jewish secretary of agriculture advocating for the pork industry and all the people who depend on it being successful?

Shortly after I was appointed as agriculture secretary, I visited several farms and a cattle auction in West Texas to inspect the serious drought conditions and do what I could to help. When we were walking around the auction site, I made an offhand comment to the people giving the tour.

"I think I smell rain in the air."

I had seen the weather report on television that morning. That night, they got more than two inches of rain. The next day when I returned, the woman I met with the day before came up to me, smiling, obviously quite pleased about something.

"Secretary Glickman, I had my doubts about you, but what they say about your people being the chosen ones is absolutely true."

My rabbi would have been impressed.

West Texas soon became one of my favorite places to visit.

I grew up with typical Kansas values, but being Jewish was atypical in that predominantly Christian environment. While those facts are unique to my own experience, they tell a story that is central to the heart of the American experience. This "same, but different" component is a central part of American society, and it often defines a critical reason for our national success. Diversity of thought and culture are the cornerstone of America's greatness. We are a great country because so many people, including Jews from all over the world, were given a chance to succeed, regardless of their origins or backgrounds.

In politics these days, it seems that the extreme views held by so many elected officials is partially a result of an inability to even see the other side's perspective as valid. As someone who grew up integrated into a Kansas community but also with a separate (but equal) Jewish identity, that was never a problem for me.

I am so proud of my Jewish ancestry. Three main reasons for that include being part of a continuum of history of a great people, learning and respecting the value of traditions, and getting to understand the beauty of Jewish humor and comedy.

I am living proof that contributing a different experience and heritage to the melting pot of our great nation is an asset, not a shortcoming. It seems to be forgotten by some Americans that almost all of us, except Native Americans, came to this country from somewhere else.

Most came to this country to escape economic calamity, religious or other persecution, or simply to seek a better life in the land of boundless opportunity. It saddens me that as our recent president, Trump, whose ancestors came here from Germany to seek their fortunes, looked at immigration as a weakness in this country, not a strength. This should bother anyone, as most of our ancestors came here from somewhere else, and for many, it was not terribly long ago.

Recent immigrants are often the most patriotic and successful of all classes of Americans. We need to fix our immigration system, but we should do so while acknowledging that immigration makes this country great and defines the soul of who nearly all of us are, here in the land of the free and the brave. This is why immigrants are so embedded in American democracy and history. This is why we should cherish them.

And when it comes to pork . . .

Chapter 5

Finding Myself in the Midst of Turbulence

As I headed off to the University of Michigan in 1962, America was becoming a deeply divided country, full of protests, strife, and upheaval. Race relations and civil rights were certainly driving the divide, but as I arrived in Ann Arbor and entered campus life, I found much of the unrest there was focused on the Vietnam War; the protests against it began in earnest soon after I settled in, still wet behind the ears and looking to figure out my future. Having grown up in Wichita, I arrived on campus with scant awareness of the war and concepts of world peace and global affairs. Support for Israel had always been part of our Jewish tradition; otherwise, I had a lot to learn.

This was the era of Tom Hayden, the former husband of actress and activist, Jane Fonda, who was a Michigan student when the school became a center of the anti-war effort. Hayden was a key member of the Students for a Democratic Society (also called the SDS), who gathered together in 1962 just ninety minutes away from campus to write the infamous Port Huron Statement, which became the manifesto for the "New Left" and the Vietnam political generation. A small portion of the Introduction is included here:

> We are people of this generation, bred in at least modest comfort, housed now in universities, looking uncomfortably to the world we inherit.
>
> When we were kids the United States was the wealthiest and strongest country in the world; the only one with the atom bomb, the least scarred by modern war, an initiator of the United Nations that we thought would distribute Western

influence throughout the world. Freedom and equality for each individual, government of, by, and for the people–these American values we found good, principles by which we could live as men. Many of us began maturing in complacency.

I suppose I was one of those kids, "maturing in complacency," but I already knew when I entered college as a teenager that I wanted to contribute significant, positive change to the world. I just needed to figure out which specific direction I should head in so that I could eventually achieve that purpose. My inclination in that direction came from a general curiosity and a love of reading history. Discovering Winston Churchill was particularly interesting and inspiring. I also met Harry Truman when I was younger when he spoke at a dinner in Wichita. My dad and I picked him up in Kansas City sometime in the mid-1950s to drive him to a speech in Wichita, and we spent four hours with him in the car, where he regaled us with a great amount of history. Dwight D. Eisenhower was in his first term as president, and when my dad asked Truman what he thought about Ike's performance, all he said was, "he was a great general." I don't think there was much love there. The other thing I remember was Truman's specific dislike of a politician named Richard Nixon. He said not to trust him. I will never forget that.

My brother Norman had attended Michigan years earlier and stayed for one year before transferring to the University of Colorado. I guess I wanted to prove that I could make it there in Ann Arbor, which was known for its rigorous academic life.

I didn't know Tom Hayden well, but I met him on several occasions on the Diag, what we called the primary gathering place on campus, named for the many diagonal sidewalks leading toward and through a large, open outdoor space.

At the time, I thought the Port Huron Statement was extreme. My general attitude, coming from my moderate roots in Kansas, had me skeptical of radical positions. Looking back, though, I believe that what Tom and his cohorts put together played a pivotal role during such a big moment in one of America's most tumultuous period in politics. Sometimes, radical ideas need to be out there, debated in public so that the country can confront divisive and difficult issues and find common ground to solve them.

Up until then, the university community was progressive but

not exactly known to be radical in any shape or form. Two years earlier, John F. Kennedy (JFK), who once referred to Harvard as "the Michigan of the East," had chosen the steps of the Michigan Union on our campus to deliver his famous 1960 campaign speech where he laid out his plans for establishing the Peace Corps. Later on, I thought briefly about joining the Peace Corps, but marriage and law school got in the way.

Dr. Martin Luther King Jr. spoke to a sold-out crowd in Hill Auditorium two years later, proclaiming that "the American dream is as yet unfulfilled," and in 1964, Lyndon B. Johnson (LBJ), by then the president, outlined his Great Society reforms during a commencement speech.

The appearances on campus by these three iconic figures provided just some of the backdrop for my early years at Michigan. The school has a long history of advanced, pioneering research, which has attracted investments from government agencies as well as private corporations, and this has not always sat well with the student body. This all came to a head during the 1960s when I was a fresh-faced Jewish farm boy looking to expand my horizons.

One doesn't often realize in the moment the true weight of the historical importance of an event or a place in time until years later. As a newbie at Michigan still figuring out everything from my politics to my personal interests to who I really was, I didn't have the judgment to recognize the gravity of the moment for American history. But I do remember that nearly everything we did or thought was overwhelmed by the war, and our daily life on campus was impacted by the news, especially reports of casualties and protests on other campuses, in urban centers, and even within yards of where we might have been studying in the library or gathering for a meal. Vietnam was literally thousands of miles away, but at the University of Michigan it was always on our minds and the effects of the war surrounded all of us.

In a sense, the war became the center of student life as soon as we were all eligible to be drafted. By the end of 1965, President Johnson had already ordered approximately eighty-two thousand troops to Vietnam, and his inner circle of military advisors were hungry to send more. That meant an increase in the drafting of young men into service and an end to automatic student deferments.

All of us, young men and women alike, knew someone who had

been drafted or was about to be sent off to war. The imminent fear of being pulled out of your classroom, handed a rifle, and shipped off to a foreign country to shoot at other human beings, and possibly to be maimed or killed, really brought it home to all of us. No one could pretend that this wasn't really happening, and it should come as no surprise that many of us on campus did not take kindly to this horrible and seemingly futile situation. Like most of my friends, I worried about being drafted, but my student deferments kept me out of the draft until the war was winding down. My parents were very anti-war. They constantly believed that it was a terrible mistake, and in my own time, propelled by the energy on campus, I came to agree.

My fellow students at Michigan didn't just accept their fate. They protested, and the actions they took were everywhere on campus. One could see signs all over the central campus, and protest booths seemed to spring up everywhere, with students providing instructions on how to move to Canada or put together a case as a conscientious objector. The protests themselves, and the larger news about the war, impacted all of our daily decisions and filled our lives with a bizarre and incomparable pressure. Being drafted in the midst of a college experience was anxiety producing to say the least and challenged any trust we had in our government.

In October 1962, we had our first awakening to the idea that US foreign policy could have such an impact on our personal lives. I remember eating at my fraternity house, Sigma Alpha Mu, and listening to President Kennedy's message about the Cuban Missile Crisis when he announced the embargo of Cuba. We were all eighteen to twenty years old (except me, I was still only seventeen for another month) and up until that point had been thinking about classes, grades, and girls.

Suddenly we were being forced to face the fact that we might all be drafted and have to go to war over Cuba. As it turned out, the Russians backed down and the United States reached an agreement over the placement of missiles. But sitting there with my fraternity brothers at Michigan, as we heard about an exotic, far-off island in the Caribbean—full of Communists, too—I had the first taste of what it might be like to have our personal lives impacted by our nation's leaders. We were all eligible to be drafted and none of us wanted to end up in combat instead of in the classroom.

By the way, our fraternity was known as an animal house, long before the John Landis movie came out and became such a hit. It was a pretty wild place, even in those days, and was known as the Jewish "jock" house. I wasn't particularly wild or a jock, but otherwise I'd say I fit in pretty well. One thing I am not proud of was that our fraternity was one of the few on campus to hold its pledge formal on November 23, 1963, just a day after the assassination of our president. I'm still not sure why we did that. Maybe it was just youthful stupidity, which just goes to show how questionable it is to send such young people off to war. I was no John Belushi, that's for sure, but I liked the guys and loved the fraternity.

The assassination was a shock. Kennedy was the first president I felt a kinship with, due to my age and his enormous charisma.

The Cuban scare was relatively brief, and it was nothing compared to what came next, thanks to the escalating war in Vietnam. Over the next several years, the University of Michigan, along with the University of California-Berkeley, became the primary centers of war resistance among America's institutions of higher learning. Between daily protests by students and faculty, speeches galore, and draft dodger meetings, there was almost no other topic being discussed on campus. We couldn't escape this even when talking to our families, who continued to ask us about what was happening on campus every time we spoke.

I was more of an observer than a protester. I'm not sure why, except most of my friends were not actively engaged in the anti-war movement and I guess I was under the illusion at the time that I would not be impacted by it. I still believe I am more of an observer than an activist working to aggressively change the world. That doesn't mean I don't care deeply about alleviating global and domestic hunger, or making Congress work better, or keeping our food safe, or fighting racism. It just means my style is less confrontational. That is genuinely me.

Among the guys especially, there was a serious question whether or not the Selective Service System would keep the deferment in place for currently enrolled students, and that freaked people out. We all felt we were ripe for the picking. Did it keep us up at night? Sure did. The Selective Service created a qualification exam, which was supposed to be a prerequisite to keeping your student

deferment and was first given in 1966. I took it that year one morning at Wichita State University during a break in my senior year.

The test was colloquially referred to as the Vietnam or LBJ Test.
It seemed similar to the college aptitude test I had taken four years
earlier, but it was heavily based in math. As I recall, you had to score
a seventy to keep your undergraduate deferment and an eighty to
keep your graduate deferment. Because I was a senior at Michigan
by then and had already been accepted to law school at George
Washington University, it was pretty nerve wracking to discover
that I scored an eighty, right on the nose, barely enough to keep
my deferment. I guess my basic math skills miraculously got me
through. Nonetheless, the test was later struck down by the federal
courts, but the damage had been done for a lot of us, at least in the
short run. We were convinced that the war was for real, and the re-
alization that it could impact me personally was made much clearer,
which took a toll on both my psyche and physical health.

The entire episode was not good for my blood pressure or my
sleep during those weeks and months. Imagine the pressure of
taking and scoring highly on the SAT to get accepted into an elite
school. Now compare that to getting tested to see if you might end
up in Vietnam—in combat, getting shot at, where hundreds if not
thousands of people were dying every week. It was an anxious time
to be a young American, and the draft did not discriminate between
Republicans, Democrats, or Independents. If you had a pulse, you
were eligible.

In the middle of the main area of the University of Michigan,
the Diag was the heart of central campus, where from morning until night students assembled around tables of anti-war materials,
staged demonstrations against the war, and hosted speakers galore
who talked nonstop about the war and how to avoid getting drafted.
The intensity of the activity increased each year and seemed to reach
a peak as we headed toward graduation in 1966. By that time, I was
engaged, but the deferment for married couples was limited to only
those with children. My father encouraged me to have a child out
of wedlock simply to avoid being shipped off to Vietnam; although
I appreciated the idea, I wasn't ready to become a father any more
than I was prepared to get blown up by a land mine.

None of my friends got drafted while we were in school

together, but once we graduated, many lost their deferment status. Some were drafted and had no choice but to join the Army and hope for the best.

While I was more anti-war from a personal perspective because I didn't want to go to war, my parents were opposed for philosophical reasons. Hayden and the other organizers were not a direct part of my school experience. At the time, fairly early in the war, I was mostly focused on more traditional activities. In law school, this all became more timely and real. The professors and students understood better than most policy makers in Washington, DC, that we were in the wrong war and couldn't win it. At Michigan, though, as a young man enamored with my life on campus, I was just afraid of being killed in a country I knew barely anything about.

Many of the faculty were actively involved in the anti-war movement. I especially remember an economics professor, named Dr. Kenneth Boulding, who organized the first anti-war teach-in, where professors explained their views on why the war was wrong or ill-fated. I took a class with him and will never forget his dedication to the anti-war movement and the fervor of his belief, unmatched by all but the most committed students. His wife, Dr. Elise Boulding, was seminal in developing the intellectual framework around peace building, and I worked with her years later to establish the United States Institute of Peace.

Notwithstanding the constant protests and the steady uproar over the Vietnam War, I was able to carry on a somewhat normal existence at school. I participated in fraternity events, I was part of a theater production of Leonard Bernstein's *Wonderful Town*, and I attended my classes as usual.

Historians argue about the Vietnam War in terms of our national interest, our military advantages or disadvantages, and other high-level analyses. But for a boy becoming a young man during a time of war, the fear of being drafted and sent to fight and possibly die in the jungles of a distant land made the politics of the day quite real. This was true for millions of Americans on campuses all over the country and even more so for the guys who were not enrolled full-time in school and especially vulnerable to the draft.

For me, nothing can sharpen the mind toward understanding the impact of public policy like the threat of being sent to war in a campaign known for its high rate of casualties. When it becomes personal like that, all bets are off when it comes to viewing the greater good.

I ultimately received a 1-Y deferment as my blood pressure was high when I took the draft physical. It still is. At that time, I felt I was lucky to escape the draft. That said, military service is one of the most honorable and notable ways in which Americans can serve their country. All veterans, including those who served in wars that were later deemed mistakes, should be applauded for their service. But what makes Vietnam so important to me and people of my era is the failure of our political leaders to honor the sacrifices made by our military in committing them to a war that was unwinnable, and frankly, pointless. It's easy to say that in retrospect, but it was such an important lesson for my generation, and one I took to heart as I embarked on my career in public service.

Being drafted into the army to go to Vietnam could feel like a death sentence. But at times, for example, in the Second World War, the draft was an important force for breaking down barriers between different groups of Americans. Shared service in that type of situation can demonstrate what binds us together, not what keeps us apart. It allows Americans an opportunity to interact with their fellow citizens, regardless of race, class, or hometown, and it does so in the context of commitment to the country. These benefits are why more and more people support some form of national service.

In that era of great political strife, which defined nearly all of my university years, national elections became pivotal moments for me and my fellow students. I spent much of my time on campus organizing my fellow undergraduates on behalf of candidates and working on various local, state, and federal elections. While I was driven to political participation, understanding early on that each of us has a stake in the process, I was not particularly motivated by the cause of the day. I just found politics captivating, especially given my interest in history, and I was enamored with all the multiple layers of communication and interactions with people. Honestly, I was not driven at this time by any particular cause other than the satisfaction I felt from bringing people together.

College was more of a social experience for me, but I did begin my entry into politics in 1964 as part of the University of Michigan's Students for Romney and Johnson. I liked George Romney, a moderate Republican, and LBJ was certainly preferable to Barry

Goldwater when it came to who would be our next president. At the time, splitting a ticket between parties was much more common. As opposed to today's politics, serious consideration was given to individual character and policy ideas over pure party identification. Can you imagine that?

Governor George Romney was appealing to me because he said our leaders in the Vietnam War were brainwashing us, and he did so at his own political peril. I respected him for that. It was a brave thing to do as he went against his party, and his honesty about the war earned my support. He was a political giant in those days, a cagey politician who had been highly successful as an automobile industry executive in Michigan. It helped that he was an excellent governor of that state and had developed broad appeal among folks on both sides of the aisle.

I will never forget the excitement I felt when I went to the Detroit Airport in 1964 for an LBJ presidential campaign appearance. A group of us from school attended the event, and we held up signs that read, "Michigan Students for Romney and Johnson." Our group was standing nearby when LBJ made his exit. I saw him read my sign before he caught my eye and looked right at me.

"You're half right," he said.

I told that story to George Romney's son, Mitt Romney, who later became governor of Massachusetts, ran for president, and is now a senator from Utah. He appreciated the reminder of how his father's powerful message had united many different people with diverging political ideologies, especially during those turbulent times.

Mitt took a great political risk when he chose to become the only Republican senator to vote to convict President Trump during the impeachment hearings in early 2020. Courage and independence certainly run in the Romney family and Mitt has done well to uphold his father's legacy. If only more senators would follow his example.

I learned another crucial lesson about politics during my days as a college student: leadership can make big things happen. Great politicians possess intangible qualities that make for great leaders. One of those is charisma and another is authenticity. Good character is critical, too, of course, but perhaps the most important one is an ability to inspire people.

I recognized political giants, such as John Kennedy and George Romney, as leaders who could inspire me and others of my generation. President Kennedy was a hero to me and to most people I knew. He was young, dynamic, and brought to the nation a message of inclusiveness and motivation. I was in my second year at Michigan when those shots rang out in Dallas on November 22, 1963, and President Kennedy was assassinated. The gut-wrenching feeling I experienced that day as I heard the news and watched a traumatized nation try to process the loss will never leave me. Sometimes, I still can't believe it really happened. Each year on the anniversary, I'm brought back to my days at Ann Arbor and the promise we felt back then for a bright and magnetic future with JFK; like everyone else, I still mourn for Kennedy, but I also feel a smile come over me just before a wave of sadness and melancholy because I know damn well that our country has yet to fulfill the same potential that we all felt possible while JFK was our president.

Good leaders at all levels of politics and public life are critical, especially in Congress and the White House. I hate to say it, but Donald Trump lacked almost all the key leadership skills required for his position. *Almost* all? Who's kidding who here? Which leadership skill *did* he have? He was missing good character, good judgment, and the ability to inspire. To be blunt, Donald Trump lacked any (or all) of the leadership skills required. I really think he has no redeeming qualities. None. Zero. Period. Fortunately, Joe Biden is a man of character and hopefully is one who can provide the good leadership the country so desperately needs.

Having great people in Congress can theoretically overcome bad leadership and flawed decision-making from the White House, but as we have seen in 2020, this is not always the case, not as it was "back in the day."

Exemplary congressional leaders over the years include Bob Dole, Nancy Kassebaum, Everett Dirksen, Mike Mansfield, Tip O'Neill, Dick Lugar, Sam Nunn, Jim Clyburn, Steny Hoyer, and Nancy Pelosi, just to name a few. More recently, the late Senator John McCain showed everyone that doing what you believe is right, even if it goes against your party, can get you reelected, not to mention genuine respect. And no leader inspired more Americans than the late Congressman John Lewis.

Voters understand the power of being an independent person

with good judgment. People like the aforementioned have been keeping our political and constitutional system in good shape. As these great men and women pass from the world, we must encourage a new generation of exceptional leaders, and to do so we need to create space for them to lead us against the great challenges of the present and the future. We must encourage independent and thoughtful people, and not simply fill the Congress and the White House with rigid, mindless ideologues, indebted to their financiers at nearly all cost.

Thankfully, I didn't spend my entire college years on a soapbox. I didn't spend my time only working for candidates and the student government. It was college, after all and I did my fair share of enjoying myself. I wouldn't call it "debauchery," but I enjoyed myself. I liked being with crazy people I guess, but I was pretty normal during those times. Funny, but quite normal. The fraternity was filled with jocks (not me) but high academics, too (not totally me). It was a carefree place.

Best of all, it was in the state of Michigan that I met my future wife, Rhoda Joyce Yura, an incredibly smart and funny woman from the city of Detroit, whose relatives for the most part attended the same university. Even our son Jonathan became a U of M grad.

To this day Rhoda and I share a deep passion for politics, a love of movies, and an ability to crack each other up. We took musical theater together and both appeared in several productions, including *Wonderful Town*, which was when we met, singing and dancing in the chorus of that show.

During our senior year, she came down with a case of hepatitis and was hospitalized for several weeks. I tried to visit her every day, and during the ninety-minute round trips from Ann Arbor to her hospital bed in Detroit, it became crystal clear to me that I either loved the drive across this swath of Michigan or I could not live without her.

I proposed to Rhoda in her hospital room, and we were married on August 21, 1966, just a couple months after we both graduated from the University of Michigan. We are still married after fifty-four years, which only goes to show you that spending all that gas money on Interstate 94 was a good investment.

The University of Michigan gave me the tools I needed, and I graduated as a young man with a much better understanding of who I was, where my skills could take me, and how I might succeed in my quest. I was active in campus politics and student government, and eventually became president of my senior class in the college of liberal arts. This election was mostly a ceremonial position, as national politics took center stage on campus, but even at that young age, I was fairly ambitious.

By the time I graduated, I had made three decisions that would determine every aspect of the rest of my life: to marry Rhoda, enroll in law school at George Washington University, and move with my new wife to Washington, DC, to be close to the action.

I knew that going to law school was the next logical step if I wanted to be in politics. By then, that was my aim, since becoming a commercial airline pilot, a professional baseball player, or an acclaimed Broadway star all seemed a bit out of reach. Law school came kind of by default, a natural progression for me and a lot of friends. Plus, the prospect of being drafted after college led a lot of us to stay in school. There's nothing like being motivated to live.

Ever since I can remember, I've always wanted to do something that mattered. Public service, and certainly politics, were more of an avocation at that time than a vocation, but contributing something to make the world a better place was attractive to me because of this drive to make a difference. I didn't always think of it in those terms, but I guess I could feel that my efforts and talent were being put to good use. On the other hand, I guess I have always relished putting my natural leadership skills on display, whether it was in grade school, high school, college, law school, or wherever I was heading next.

Local and national government, especially under the umbrella of an elected office, is a place where you can serve your country and improve people's lives at the same time. I first learned this at the University of Michigan, and I will always be thankful for spending those four years with the maize and blue of the Wolverines.

As the university motto says, "Artes, Scientia, Veritas," or "Arts, Knowledge, Truth," three inarguable ingredients any successful politician should emulate.

Chapter 6

Right Place at the Right Time

Soon after Rhoda and I arrived in Washington and settled into a tiny apartment in the DC suburbs, I trekked up to Capitol Hill and started walking the halls of the Senate, hoping someone would find me employable. Law school was going to keep me plenty busy, but Rhoda and I couldn't live off love and good humor. We needed food, and money for rent.

In today's security-conscious environment, especially in the nation's capital, a kid from Kansas loitering in the Russell Senate Office Building would surely attract attention and would probably be escorted promptly out the door. Back then, congressional offices were quite a bit more accessible, and I knocked on one door after another, determined to find a lead. My best qualifications were tenacity and perseverance. I really wanted to work on Capitol Hill, and even back then I dreamed of becoming a congressman.

Incidentally, if you're a young job seeker reading this book and hoping for insights on how to get into politics, let me recommend strongly against my job search strategy. I hear that handcuffs can leave bruises, to both your wrists and your reputation, so considering how times have changed, may I suggest that you instead email your resume to potential employers.

In my case, I got lucky. My persistence eventually paid off and somebody heard from somebody else that a senator ("I think from Colorado, but I'm not sure . . . ") was looking for a staffer, "but I hear it is only part-time and a low-level position, probably not worth your time."

Truth be told, I was not as enthusiastic a law student as many of my colleagues at the George Washington University Law School.

I did well enough, excelled in moot court, an activity where we simulated real court or arbitration proceedings, and was even invited to write for the school's prestigious law review. Instead, I took a part-time job in the Senate, working for Senator Peter Dominick (R-CO). I was not, however, the legal scholar who dissected every minuscule phrase of a Supreme Court decision to ascertain the higher philosophical meaning behind the justices' thinking. That was not my sweet spot. I was certainly determined to do well and remain competitive with my fellow students, but whereas many of them had visions of becoming the next Atticus Finch, my goal was always to work in Congress.

The rumor turned out to be true. Senator Dominick was looking for a part-time staff member and the job was going to be as lowly as one could imagine—working the autopen, a device that automatically reproduced the senator's signature at the bottom of every letter that left his Senate office. I sat in his office for hours, slipping in the unsigned letter to constituents, carefully watching the pen automatically signing the letter, and pulling the letter out quickly. I could do up to one hundred per hour, and the signature looked personal and authentic. It helped that I was paid about five dollars an hour, which was a hefty sum in those days, allowing Rhoda and me to even enjoy a few of Washington's great restaurants.

While the autopen may have fallen out of fashion, the long tradition of junior positions on Capitol Hill hasn't changed much at all. I didn't hesitate for a second when they offered me the job. If you want to begin a life in politics, you have to start somewhere. Operating the autopen was my ticket to the big time, and I didn't hesitate. It helped that my part-time schedule working for Senator Dominick fit perfectly into my law student life. I went to his office and took care of the mail in between attending classes and lectures. Somehow I also managed to keep up with all of the required reading and casework. The work ethic I had involuntarily picked up in Wichita came in handy in Washington.

The task of opening a congressman's mail continued as well when I served in Congress. I often came into my congressional office on Saturdays when no other staff was around, and I proceeded to open all the mail by hand. This drove my staff crazy, and I'm sorry about that, but reading what were mostly handwritten, personal letters gave me an immediate and current understanding of what folks at home were thinking and feeling. The problem was, I wasn't always known for neatness and I often threw away the envelopes without considering the fact that I was also getting rid of the return addresses. That meant our front office sometimes looked as if it had been burglarized. This was before texts and emails, and what a great way reading the mail was to keep my ear to the ground and connect with my constituents.

I have always had a thing about mail. I think it originated when I worked in my dad's office during high school. I used to watch him anxiously wait for the checks to arrive in the mail and then see how he happily opened each one of them.

I learned a valuable political lesson from my "low-end" job in Congress. Those letters I answered and always personally signed, unlike the mass emails and social media posts of today, connected me directly with the folks who took the time to write them. They gave me a bird's eye view of the issues in Colorado, both good and bad, from the perspective of real voters who took the time to gather a paper and pen, write down their thoughts and concerns by hand, fold up their pleadings or manifesto, put them in an envelope, add a stamp and a return address, and bring them to a mailbox. Each step in that process is another action that personalizes the effort and only adds to the commitment and thought behind it. To me, writing and sending a handwritten letter takes more care and intention than simply dashing off an email or posting a Tweet. I think I paid close attention to those letters because of the people and concerns they reflected. Thank goodness for the US Postal Service and their letter carriers.

At times, Hollywood and television have glamorized the life of elected officials and those who work for them. *House of Cards, Madame Secretary*, and *West Wing* made it seem like the business of politics is a high-powered and glitzy profession. But those letters, the ones I spent countless hours opening, reading, and responding to, represent the true nature of what's involved in elected office. Every district in every state is populated by thousands of constituents trying to live their lives, working and raising families. From time to time, they encounter problems with federal policy, such as tax issues, business permits, or a community looking to rebuild a public park. Some constituents write letters to their member of Congress or their senator, seeking help and a better understanding of how the political sausage is made. This kind of casework is what real politics is all about and I was fortunate to learn it early on from a ground floor position.

My time in Senator Dominick's office was formative for me and occurred during a pivotal time for the country. No doubt I was in the right place at the right time. My first few years in Washington in the late 1960s and early 1970s were during a volatile time that shaped the country and our collective conscience like few other periods in the nation's history. The Vietnam War continued to dominate the headlines, and day after day, reports from Southeast Asia disclosed deeper truths of what the United States was doing, stuck in a quagmire that was producing body bags by the hour. As President Lyndon Johnson expanded the theater of war, the number of young American men who were drafted, guys from my generation, including many friends of mine, rose into the hundreds of thousands.

This was the first televised war, too, and watching the nightly news with our friends and neighbors, as bombs exploded and killed so many innocent people, was deeply disturbing and created more and more polarization in multiple sectors of our society.

The country was deeply divided between those despairing over the madness they were witnessing, and those supporting the president and our troops. The older generation had fought and won the Second World War, and to say they saved the world was no hyperbole. Those veterans believed deeply in service, and they saw America as a uniform force for good. These are important traits of a brave generation of Americans, and they must be acknowledged and respected, but the lessons they imparted to my generation made it hard for many Americans to rightfully question those in leadership positions who were leading us deeper and deeper into an untenable situation. I think even the most patriotic vet had to wonder if the war in Vietnam was even remotely winnable, and if it was, what would the winner really win?

Not all Americans of the "greatest generation" supported the war. My dad was particularly anti-war. Remember his suggestion that while Rhoda and I were dating that I get married quickly and have a baby to obtain deferment from service? "Just have the baby," he said, "and you can get the marriage part done later." Having children out of wedlock was a huge social no-no in the 1960s and didn't exactly ring any romance bells for me, either.

My father's suggestion showed how scared he was that I would be drafted and possibly killed. He wasn't alone; many of my friends were afraid of the same thing and for some of us, even the supposed protection of being in graduate school was not totally comforting.

The daily body counts were horrifying and depressing. I didn't want to fight and die in a war I wasn't sure was the right thing for our country. Vietnam presented a much different prospect than World War II, where the threat of Nazi and Imperial Japanese world domination made the cause just and noble and clearly in the national interest.

While fighting a hot war in Vietnam, we were also embroiled in a Cold War with Russia that could have gone nuclear any second. The Soviets, clearly taking advantage of the turmoil occupying our attention at home, brutally suppressed any hint of democratic uprisings behind the Iron Curtain, most notably and terrifyingly in Prague in 1968. Keep in mind, too, that just a year earlier, the Middle East had exploded during the Six-Day War, when Israel took no prisoners simultaneously fighting its neighboring states of Egypt, Jordan, and Syria. Whatever side of these conflicts you may have been on, everyone could agree that the world seemed to be teetering on the brink of chaos and all kids of destruction.

Domestically, the predominant challenge in our society was race relations. In 1967, in the state of Virginia, just across the Potomac River from where I was going to law school, interracial marriage was still against the law. That same year, a case called *Loving v. Virginia*, which came before the Supreme Court, empowered men and women of different races to marry. This was a watershed moment, which led to more positive change. Later that same year, Thurgood Marshall became our nation's first African American Supreme Court justice. These were tremendous accomplishments for the nation as it grappled with the legacy of racism, seeking to tear down unjust laws and lift African Americans up and over the divide of Jim Crow America. But such accomplishments came with backlash too, from violent bullying on public school playgrounds to secretive Ku Klux Klan rallies deep in America's woods. While progressive events in the courts were as beneficial to racial equality as the desegregation of public schools, we also faced the horror of the assassinations of Dr. Martin Luther King Jr. and Bobby Kennedy.

When Dr. King was killed on April 4, 1968, it had an immediate and significant impact on Washington, DC, and I will never forget living there during that terrible time. Washington, DC, which at its heart is a Southern city with a majority African American population, experienced terrible race riots following Dr. King's death. I was in Senator Dominick's Capitol Hill suite when news of Dr. King's assassination slowly spread from office to office. As we learned of this tragedy, we were unaware of the reaction that was growing across cities all over the United States, including its capital.

Distraught citizens, mostly African Americans but many whites as well, took to the streets to vent their pain, anger, and frustration. Soon this grief turned into rioting, with looting of stores and cars set on fire. None of this was immediately apparent to those of us laboring away in the senator's office while all of this chaos was happening in another part of the city.

That changed soon enough for me when I was told to take the senator's car and get it gassed up. As a lowly legislative assistant, I didn't think twice and headed down into the parking garage, where I carefully backed the senator's Cadillac out of his parking space. Everything seemed pretty swell. There I was, taking this gorgeous car for a little joy ride—until I pulled out of the underground garage and basically entered a war zone. I could smell smoke immediately, hear the screaming and chanting of thousands of enraged protesters, and was surrounded by emergency vehicles trying to make their way to the epicenter of the riots. I was scared, but being young always tempers fear. I wouldn't do today what I did on that day, that's for sure.

The only nearby gas station was several blocks away, and undeterred, I pointed the Cadillac in that direction. What should have been a five-minute, four-block ride turned into complete gridlock for at least forty minutes as I watched the gas gauge getting lower and lower. After traveling exactly one block in slightly less than an hour, I admitted defeat, turned off the main street, and backtracked for another half hour to return to the garage.

Today, doing something like this would set my anxiety to emergency levels. But back then, it was an adventure, and one I never forgot. I came back with no gas, and the only thing I had to show for my efforts was a perturbed chief of staff who had to explain to the senator why he most likely would run out of gas on his way home.

That was not the end of my exposure to DC's tumult following

Dr. King's death. My commute was usually an easy half-hour drive up 16th Street to my apartment in Silver Spring, Maryland. But as I sent the senator off with an empty gas tank, getting myself home took several hours, and along the way I ran headfirst into clashing protesters and police. There were endless streams of smoke in the air, and the US Army placed tanks around major federal buildings. This was the closest thing to a war zone I could have imagined and I wondered what real military vets must have felt seeing all of this unfold in their neighborhoods. One reason I think legislators in Washington can allow themselves to vote for sending our young men and women to war is that most of them have never personally witnessed a war up close and firsthand, even as a civilian. Perhaps if they had, their decisions would be different.

Finally home, I received word from the law school that all students were asked to support the city in handling the enormous number of arraignments hitting DC's court system. There simply weren't enough lawyers to ensure a due process of the law, and law students filled in the gaps. My brother, by then an attorney himself, couldn't help himself when he commented that he sure hoped George Washington University Law School had taken out extra legal malpractice insurance on our behalf.

Attending law school in the nation's capital, it was impossible not to realize the significance and gravity of each of these events. While political activism was more widespread during my undergraduate years than among my peers in graduate or law school, we still were aware of the political climate and apprehensive about the world and our roles in it. Every other day it seemed there was some sort of protest taking place in front of the White House or the Capitol, a large percentage of which were against the war in Vietnam.

I was working in the office of a Republican senator who served on the Armed Services Committee. It was certainly a moment that gave me pause, as I am sure it did for many of my colleagues at the time. Were we doing the right thing?

There was so much strife and anxiety in America about our foreign policy, the way we treat our fellow citizens, and the fundamental question about whether this was and still is a great nation. Yet even in these spaces, lawmakers found room to work together to solve huge and challenging problems in other areas. Though it often goes unheralded, many of the most significant parts of landmark civil rights legislation arose from a collaboration between Republicans and Democrats. We still haven't addressed systemic racism in American society, but it was a start back then, and the struggle that we are having as a society today must never be conveniently swept aside.

Collaboration on civil rights between Republicans and Democrats was key to getting things done. Despite all of LBJ's foibles concerning the war in Vietnam, he eventually took the country in the proper direction when it came to civil rights. His persuasive leadership on the issue made the difference in getting meaningful legislation passed. This was influenced by his history of being born into poverty in Texas and his commitment to the poor, his grasp of the historic significance of civil rights as a national imperative, his understanding of Dr. Martin Luther King Jr.'s power and moral influence, and his personal relationships with members of both parties on Capitol Hill. All of these factors came together as seminal reasons for why historical civil rights and voting rights legislation came to pass in the 1960s.

That brand of moral and courageous leadership is still needed today, but it must be driven by leaders who are willing to risk their political careers to follow in the footsteps of people like Lyndon Baines Johnson.

The relationship between President Johnson and Senator Everett Dirksen proved pivotal in passing the Civil Rights Act of 1964. The records show that when a cloture petition was filed to get the bill to the Senate floor, LBJ insisted that then majority leader Mike Mansfield put Republican senator Dirksen as the first name on that petition. He did this to show the Senate and the world that this effort was bipartisan. Can you imagine that happening today?

I don't think Congress has become blatantly racist. In fact, the current numbers of women and minority members in the House (not the Senate) belie this, and nonwhite men and women are growing in numbers. It's more that Congress has become insensitive to the problems of race in America, witnessed by my experience seeing the racial discrimination of farmers while I was a House member and the failure of Congress to address those issues until fairly recently.

While I served in Congress, I felt that I was part of something really big and important. I recall a Daniel Webster quote about "doing something worthy to be remembered" that is etched behind the Speaker's chair in the House, which I looked at every day I served.

Throughout this time, both the Senate and the House met regularly, passed budgets and appropriations bills, and did the people's business. Of course, there was some partisanship. After all, this was politics, not a game of backyard beanbag. But everyone shared a commitment to producing results for voters, and you can only do that through legislation and a willingness to work together. I know this sounds almost alien, but it really happened. I was there!

The trick is to engage in constructive partisanship. There will always be disagreements, as long as there are two people still living on Earth. Sometimes, I think too much is made out of the idea of ending partisanship. We will never end this type of conflict, so we must view it from a larger perspective, which includes popular concepts such as getting things done, or getting, as author Roger Fisher says, to "yes."

Despite the tumultuous times for the country, my own career proceeded swiftly. My time as the letter-signing guy was relatively brief and I enjoyed several promotions after starting that first position working for Senator Dominick. Throughout law school, I kept my part-time schedule and gradually earned more and more substantive assignments. I became a legislative correspondent, communicating directly with the senator's constituents back in Colorado while also focusing on specific issues assigned to me by his senior staff. Persistence and determination paid off, and by not dismissing an opportunity as too menial, I became an official senate staffer, contributing to Senator Dominick's public service and handling tasks of increasing responsibility. This was my first true taste of working on Capitol Hill. As I came to understand how I fit in and what impact I could make via the legislative process, I was hooked.

While working with Senator Dominick, I came to realize that the press secretary is one of the most important staffers for any congressional office. Senator Dominick had an outstanding journalistic mind working for him: Brian Lamb. He and I hit it off from the start. This may have been because we were close in age—he is only four years older than me—or because we both loved music, or as a result of his alma mater, Purdue University, regularly playing (and losing) to my alma mater, the University of Michigan, in Big Ten football.

Whatever the reason, working for and with Brian was one of those experiences that stuck with me for the rest of my career.

Press staff on the Hill are still critically important today. Though the medium may have changed from local newspapers to social media platforms, carrying the message of your work to your constituents largely through the press operations in your office is one of the most important parts of electoral politics. You can pass the most important bills or secure the biggest federal contributions to your district, but if none of your voters know about it, then you won't be getting sent back to office!

Brian and I are still friends today. In 1977, he told me about this crazy idea to create a cable television channel that would broadcast all the live proceedings from the House and Senate floor and its committee rooms to members' offices throughout Capitol Hill. At that time, I was a member of Congress who could help him obtain permission to place his cameras in the House chamber for the first time in history. He called his brainchild the Cable Satellite Public Affairs Network, and the acronym would become a household name: C-Span. I remain a huge advocate of C-Span and its role in bringing government into the homes of millions of Americans in an unfiltered way. I helped Brian convince a skeptical Congress that their proceedings were a good thing to put on television. C-Span has brought Congress to the American people, warts and all. Not everyone likes the transparency, and some of the political theater created for C-Span encourages public cynicism. But I think now more than ever it's vital to provide Americans with the chance to see their government in action.

Transparency is a great "disinfectant" for politics.

I loved my time working for Senator Dominick, but I eventually graduated from law school in 1969, which meant it was time for me to figure out what was next. I decided to at least try to put my law degree to work in a more traditional legal setting rather than Capitol Hill. As a young man with bills to pay, a wife, and a new family, the decision seemed right at the time. It also meant moving on from Senator Dominick's staff. I wonder what might have happened, what direction my life may have taken, professionally and privately, if I had stayed with that office. I may have worked for him until his defeat in 1974 to Gary Hart, but that would have meant missing out on my chance to reestablish my Kansas roots, which led to my own election victory in 1976. The irony is that Gary Hart was a Kansan by birth, but then again, that didn't help him years later when he got on the wrong yacht.

Instead, after passing the bar, I landed a coveted trial attorney position with the Securities and Exchange Commission (SEC) in Washington. For me, still a kid from Kansas at heart, I was thrilled and looked forward to the new challenge.

The SEC was gaining exponential importance as the American economy embraced the securities industry as a key component to growth. Proving yet again how everything in life is intertwined and one experience builds upon another, working for the SEC as a trial lawyer in the late 1960s left me, about ten years later, as the only member of Congress on the Agriculture Committee with experience in securities regulations. This background was invaluable in understanding the implementation of the Commodity Exchange Act, the law that regulates agriculture and other futures and derivatives. That hugely important act fell directly into the jurisdiction of the House Agriculture Committee, and therefore provided me with a unique opportunity to combine my SEC experience with my service to America's farmers.

Thanks to that one year working for the SEC, I eventually became *the* congressional expert on legislation impacting futures markets, which have now become a huge business. Taking this thought one step further, it is interesting to note that to this day, I serve on the board of directors of the Chicago Mercantile Exchange, the world's largest futures exchange. This, too, can be traced back directly to my SEC post in the late 1960s.

The work was interesting, if not sometimes fascinating and I got much out of it, especially later in my career. But I wasn't truly happy in that job. After about a year with the SEC, I was at a crossroads. Rhoda and I needed to decide what we were looking for in life. By now, there were three of us: our son, Jonathan, was born in May 1969, and life's responsibilities had taken on a much bigger meaning.

Rhoda and I loved living and working in Washington—Rhoda as a teacher for seventh and eighth grade English and science in a nearby public school in Prince George's County and I as an attorney. We knew how lucky we were to be living in one of the most interesting and vibrant cities in the world.

On the other hand, it felt like something was missing for us, and eventually, especially after Jonathan was born, it became obvious what that something was: family. We missed the feeling of being "home." Washington, DC, was interesting, but it wasn't where my family and roots resided. Deep in my mind, the desire for a political career was lurking and with my Kansas roots, I wasn't going to move to Alaska.

Though we had friends, colleagues, and acquaintances in Washington, we were missing our family and the comfort that comes with establishing roots. After having been away from the Midwest for quite a while, and for me, Wichita since 1962, we decided it was finally time to come home. This meant giving up—at least for the time being—my exciting work in Washington. However, it also meant returning to family and the comfort that comes with being back home, and frankly as I saw it, closer to a possible career in politics.

For Rhoda, things were a bit trickier. She loved her teaching position, and there was no telling if there would be viable opportunities in Wichita. While heading back to Kansas represented a homecoming for me, it was different for her. She would be moving in with the in-laws, giving up her freedom and autonomy, and placing herself in the hands of the Glickman family. All joking aside, this could not have been an easy transition for her, and to this day I am incredibly appreciative of her agreeing to give it a shot.

In 1971, Rhoda, Jonathan, and I moved from Washington, DC, to Kansas. Just a few months later, in June of 1972, our daughter, Amy, was born. We were content to be back with family and establishing our own Glickman headquarters.

But it didn't take long before we grew bored. So bored, in fact, that upon hearing that a certain senator from Kansas was looking for a staff attorney, I flew from Wichita to DC for a job interview. Bob Dole was a first-term Republican senator looking to staff up, and one of the lawyers I was working with in Kansas arranged a meeting for me with the senator.

When I met him, he had just made a big leap in his political career. Even though we represented differing political points of view, both of us embraced pragmatic and moderate philosophies that enabled us to do a lot of good for the people of Kansas.

Bob Dole is an extremely perceptive listener with an astute political mind. Hearing me describe my aspirations and reasons for wanting to work for him in the Senate, he advised me to stay put in Kansas and establish myself back home. He understood that my real goal was to return to Washington as a lawmaker, not as a staffer (though he probably envisioned me as a Republican colleague, rather than a pesky Democrat). His counsel, to spend some more time in Kansas getting to know the people, the issues, and the challenges there, turned out to be some of the best advice I have ever received.

Seeking advice from people on the other side of the aisle may seem ridiculous to partisans in today's political climate. But for me, Senator Dole always helped me as a fellow Kansan and as a friend. We shared a common instinct in that our first inclination was always to lean toward cooperation. Although our viewpoints often differed on the specific issues, we were able to maintain our healthy relationship, regardless of party or the campaign season.

If I could bottle Senator Dole for today's Republicans, I would do it in a heartbeat. Dole's greatest strength, for Republicans and Democrats alike, was his desire to get things done, and the only way to do that was to work across the aisle. Collaboration was the key to success, much more than ideology. Both sides of the aisle, but especially Republicans, need to follow that lead right now. But Dole and I were not friends in the classic sense. The Doles and the Glickmans did not socialize. We were competitors but we had common interests in our love of Kansas and country. Neither one of us were naïve enough to believe that politics was anything more than an intense and competitive business.

Senator Bob Dole is a legendary political figure and a true testament to Kansas values. For the rest of my career, I would spend a lot of time working with him one way or another. Our relationship started with that 1971 job interview and built from there. But as things often do in politics, we next found ourselves on the other side of political divides.

As I began my effort to get to Congress, I actively campaigned against him in 1974, and he returned the favor by bringing out the Republican vote during my 1976 congressional run. When Senator Dole joined Gerald Ford as his vice president and running mate, it inspired a lot of Republican voters to come out in Kansas.

I have often been asked, "Since you were close to Dole, and at times considered him a mentor, how and why could you want to run against him?"

Perhaps my ambition and love of politics were greater than my love for Dole. Just because I respected him did not mean I was part of his political team.

Every time Bob Dole came up for reelection, mostly because I was one of the only prominent Democrats in the state, I took a hard look at running against him. This included forming an exploratory committee and raising funds for a 1986 Senate run. Every time I ended up deciding against it because Bob Dole was such an institution, and polling, as well as my gut instinct, told me he was pretty much impossible to unseat in that state. Bob knew that I wanted to run against him and become a senator from Kansas. He also knew that I probably couldn't beat him. But he never let our indirect or direct competition on issues and in elections get in the way of our professional relationship.

My connection with Bob Dole symbolizes everything that is right about politics and career politicians. Though from opposite parties, we were never enemies. Political adversaries, yes, personal enemies no! We campaigned against each other and supported whoever was running against the other. Bob Dole, as a loyal Republican, probably helped unseat me by campaigning and fundraising for Todd Tiahrt in 1994, but on issues that supported Kansas and our constituents, especially agriculture and aviation, we were partners and worked extremely well together. We worked together as colleagues, which in the true sense of the word, means respecting each other and seeking out each other's opinions. Dole and I both understood that politics was important, but the needs of our country and our state were paramount.

When it came to politics, Bob Dole was no wimp. He didn't treat me with kid gloves just because we had a good professional relationship. He realized I was ambitious and certainly had my eye on his Senate seat, so he ensured through political means that I wasn't going to get in his way. He made specific decisions and used situations to protect himself from a challenge by me.

For example, during my 1994 race, he actively helped my opponent and made robocalls that tens of thousands of voters in my district heard in the run-up to that election. He also encouraged some donors to help my opponent financially. I was pissed at Dole but understood it through a political lens. It reminded me of the famous line in *The Godfather II* when the mobster Hyman Roth tells Michael

Corleone, "Michael, this is the business we have chosen." Although politics isn't the mob (do I need an asterisk here?), there are some interesting parallels.

Dole's moves were completely rational for him, and I didn't begrudge him for it, though I do wish he had been less effective. On the other hand, he supported me years later when he played an instrumental role in delivering Republican votes for my unanimous confirmation as secretary of agriculture. When I was subsequently vetted for the position of CEO of the Motion Picture Association of America, I even listed Dole as a character reference.

This kind of cooperation and respectful mutual support is key for current and aspiring politicians to understand, and it begins with one's tone and a willingness to embrace moderation. It's also about understanding how our system of government actually works and how to make it function on behalf of our nation and its citizens.

My motto: Don't let the political become the personal.

Politics is a serious business; it's competitive, and it's important. But politics is not war, and your opponent is not your enemy.

Bob Dole exemplified the importance of building bridges, not burning them. For us, our differences rarely, if ever, became personal. Another thing Dole demonstrated, both to me and the world, was that despite any consideration of partisanship or political dogma, he made his empathy for the disabled, minorities, and the poor a focal point of his work.

That's a good lesson for us all, and he was particularly effective in these issues because of his own personal experience with poverty, war, and suffering from disabilities as a result of fighting fascism as a soldier in the Second World War.

Any discussion about Bob Dole has to include his sense of humor, which was often acerbic but equally self-deprecating. As a war veteran with lingering disabilities, he had plenty to be grumpy about but he was almost always genuinely funny. He served briefly as the chair of the Republican National Committee during the Nixon years, but proved far too independent for Nixon to keep him on.

When describing the team of H. R. Haldeman, John Ehrlichman, and Richard Nixon, he said they should have been known as "Hear no evil, See no evil, and Evil." Not too endearing to the Nixon team, I'd say. And who can forget the 1998 television commercial Bob Dole did for Viagra, their first ever, which was probably their best, too, when he said in what appeared to be a campaign spot, "You know, it's a little embarrassing to talk about ED but it's so important to millions of men and their partners that I decided to talk about it publicly."

I'm pretty sure that went a long way to improving marriages, at least in Republican households, and it said a lot about Dole's ability to not take himself too seriously. He knew that humor was the glue in building bridges, and I learned a lot from him about that process.

Life experiences make a big difference. My own ups and downs certainly shaped me, and I didn't let the sport of politics stop me from doing what I felt was right. Frank Sinatra sang, "I gotta be me," which is hard to argue with, and Shakespeare, in a play you may have heard of called *Hamlet,* put it more eloquently when he said, "To thine own self be true." Of course it was Polonius who said that in act 1, scene 3, and he was somewhat of a dubious character, but the sentiment is certainly worth emulating.

Being authentic in the eyes of voters and in your own life can only be achieved by being true to yourself. It may not always lead you to be what the crowd wants or to say what they want to hear. But it is so essential to living a good life and can make you successful in politics when people can feel you are being genuine. When it comes to a quality in politicians, authenticity does not get the credit it deserves.

My big concern about the failure of congressional leadership today is the failure of so many politicians from both parties, but especially Republicans, who hide behind their party's labels and support their party and their president unconditionally with no room for independent thinking. I think the Founding Fathers would turn over in their graves if they knew that members of the Article 1 branch of government would effectively give up their power and independence to the head of the Article 2 branch of government. Hiding behind the mask of one's party is never what the Founding Fathers intended.

The relationship Bob Dole and I enjoyed was reflective of my entire political career, in that I never was such an entrenched Democrat that I could not find things in common with a Republican. I think the world of Bob Dole and remain in awe of the service he rendered to our country, starting on the battlefields of World War II and culminating in his run for the presidency in 1996.

We would be a better country if we had more Bob Doles. I admire lawmakers Chris Coons of Delaware, Dick Durbin of Illinois, Mitt Romney of Utah, Nancy Pelosi of California, Jim Clyburn of South Carolina, Sherrod Brown of Ohio, Tom Cole of Oklahoma, and many others. They all respect their colleagues and work across the aisle. Newer and younger members of the House are especially impressive; many other members are veterans and really appreciate service.

I still thank Bob Dole for turning me around the first time we met on that job interview I had with him in 1971, in his Senate office in Washington, which set me on the path toward my first run for office. It was clear that I was ambitious, and I went back to Kansas and started looking for a way to enter the world of politics.

An opportunity presented itself in 1973 when a seat opened on the Wichita Public School Board. The Wichita public schools had caught my attention, even though my kids were not yet of school age (Jonathan was only four, Amy barely one). The school system, which included almost one hundred schools, was the largest in the state, with more than fifty thousand students and about five thousand teachers, and it had a large budget. But its sheer size was not what piqued my interest. Instead, I was concerned over its fiscal management, specifically a dubious real estate deal that was receiving quite a bit of media attention.

One of the largest banks at the time in the state of Kansas was the Fourth National Bank, which is now part of Bank of America. This bank was making a real push to sell its headquarters in Wichita to the school district, to be used as its new administrative headquarters. Many of the issues about the proposed deal just didn't add up. As I followed the story, I became convinced that the bank was unloading a decrepit piece of property that would saddle the schools with an oversized headquarters at an unconscionably inflated asking price. It seemed to me that the taxpayers were going to be left footing the bill to bail out the bank instead of investing that money more intelligently for programs that would benefit the kids of Wichita.

Right then and there, it all lined up in my mind for the first time: my Kansas roots, my desire to become involved in politics, the benefit my legal skills could offer, the community involvement, the public service I was seeking, and an issue I could argue with true passion.

I decided to run for a vacancy on the Wichita Public Schools Board.

My first campaign focused on an issue all taxpayers could appreciate, and it was decidedly nonpartisan. My campaign slogan was "Our Kids Come First." Obviously, this was a play on the importance of kids and education over a bank unloading a crappy building on the school district. It was not a particularly difficult campaign, and my task consisted mainly of getting my name out and introducing myself to the voters. Name recognition and hammering away at the bank/school building deal were the bread and butter of our efforts.

Three board members were being elected at-large, which made it a little easier to campaign. Going after this bank and other community leaders while standing up for the little guy was my first experience becoming popular with voters by doing what is right. It was my first test of speaking truth to power, even though in this case, power was the Wichita business and political establishment. But I had the public on my side. People could see this was a raw deal and thanked me for standing against it. Because speaking truth to power involves a lot of risk, it is not always successful. But as the old expression goes, "no guts, no glory," and this risk was a necessary ingredient to make changes in this Kansas school district.

On Election Day, my passion and confidence were rewarded with a seat on the board.

Since then, so much about campaigns has changed. But at the end of the day, I believe the voters still want the same thing from their candidates: people who realistically fight for them, identify problems, and try to solve them. It's pretty basic. They want to shake your hand and see what you're really about, even if you shake up the establishment in the process.

I had successes and failures in trying to take on the establishment. But ultimately, just being seen as someone who would try to go against the powers that be showed my identity and character to the public as someone independent who could get things done. This absolutely laid the foundation for my future in politics.

Serving on the school board is one of those public service

opportunities where you can have a direct and positive impact. Being an elected official can be a real ordeal, so seeing results from your efforts is special. I enjoyed the hard work with my fellow board members and was extremely impressed with the talented superintendent of schools, Dr. Alvin Morris, who did an outstanding job.

Just two years later, in 1975, I was elected president of the board, which gave me the opportunity to help lead an effort to pass a massive school bond issue, calling for the construction of many schools, and to bring much-needed financial resources to the district. My position also put me in the public eye on an almost daily basis, which certainly helped me in future races.

Though I ran for the school board because I felt strongly about the good I could do for Wichita's public school kids, it was not lost on me that the position presented a broader opportunity. The public school system encompasses about 70 percent of the Fourth Congressional District of Kansas and nearly 100 percent of the district's media market. School board meetings, visits to schools, football games, and even home visits were an excellent way to meet many of the people living in the district.

I made a point of traveling throughout the school district and eating lunch with the kids as often as I could. That was my favorite part, eating with the kids, especially at high schools, where I listened to them complain about the quality of the food. Little did I realize that twenty-five years later I would be heading up the federal agency largely responsible for the food served in the school lunch program. Hopefully, the menu has improved over the years.

All in all, I got to know the people, hear their concerns, help them with school issues, and connect with them while getting a read on their concerns beyond the educational arena. I built a reputation that served me well during my first run for Congress. People knew I was accessible, hardworking, conscientious, and willing to partner with others for the greater good. I also earned a reputation as an independent thinker, who had no problems crossing party lines if common sense and common ground solution were required. No elementary, junior high, or high school was too small a place for me to visit. I learned the importance of reaching out and interacting with constituents no matter who they were or where they lived. I met so many terrific people!

You could say I became the living embodiment of the importance and value of "showing up." This cannot be underestimated.

Unfortunately in today's politics, that independence is punished rather than encouraged by a process that empowers extremists. Much of the debate about the problems with our political system centers on the lawmakers themselves. I don't absolve legislators of the responsibility to lead by any means, but voters need to provide positive encouragement, donations, and ultimately ballot box support for those lawmakers who try to work across the aisle to get things done. Town hall meetings, where you look your constituents in the eye, are sorely missing from today's politics, where most voter interaction is conducted via social media.

If I hadn't focused on agriculture, then education would have been a great place for me to put my energy once I reached Congress. Clearly, serving on the school board for four years gave me invaluable insight into how public policy choices affect every single child in every single public school classroom for many years to come.

For example, desegregation and busing were decisions that preceded my service on the Wichita Public School Board by several years. The effects of those decisions were still being felt throughout the district. Busing had been implemented for a good and understandable motive: to offer the same level of education to all kids, as you need to diversify the school population by mixing groups of students outside their school cluster. But pulling kids out of their communities and parachuting them into "foreign" environments that were often openly hostile to them was not ideal, to say the least.

Busing had a significant impact, particularly on African American communities, which saw precious resources allocated toward busing instead of fixing neighborhood schools. Their kids also became disenchanted with their public school experience due to issues far outside the realm of classroom instruction.

In Wichita, the concept of busing was based on fighting traditionally segregated public schools, and it resulted from a federal lawsuit filed against the school district by the US Department of Health, Education, and Welfare, the predecessor of today's Department of Education and Department of Health and Human Services. Incidentally, one of the senior officials involved in this lawsuit was a young Leon Panetta. Without either one of us realizing it, our paths had already crossed years before we worked together in Washington, first in Congress and then for President Clinton.

Panetta helped to integrate the Wichita public schools in the early 1970s and was elected to Congress from California in 1976 as part of my freshman class. We became good friends. In 1994, as White House chief of staff, Panetta had a great deal to do with President Clinton choosing me to be secretary of the USDA.

I came to see that politicians who rose to higher office via school boards or who had worked in a city hall tended to have a better understanding of pragmatic lawmaking than those who arrived from the outside or with limited public service experience. Once you are in the community trenches, fighting for concrete issues on behalf of taxpayers, and you actually know these people on a first-name basis, you understand that getting things done *is* the highest calling in politics. And that relies on developing deep personal relations on Capitol Hill, a crucial skill when it comes to having any impact on passing an agenda.

Whether I realized it at the time or not, my years on the Wichita Public School Board were an essential foundation for my later success as a congressional candidate and as a representative of the people.

Looking back, I'm so glad Rhoda and I left Washington, DC, and returned to Kansas, as it was the right place at the right time and afforded me an education, which served me well into the future, both at home and once again in Washington.

Chapter 7

Crossing Party Lines to Sing
My Way to Congress

By the mid-1970s, I came to a crossroads in my political life. While I never fully identified with the Republican Party, I instinctively thought of myself as a Republican during high school, college, and law school. I based my leanings on the slightly right-of-center thinking of my parents, influential public personas—such as George Romney and Bob Dole—and of course, working for a Republican senator. It took some deeper analysis and reflection to understand that I was a Republican more because of circumstance than any deep conviction.

At the early stage of my political career, I could have been a Republican or a Democrat. But three things ultimately put me on the Democratic path in the mid-1970s. First was my respect for the Docking family, and especially Democratic governor Bob Docking, who was a conservative in fiscal policy but more progressive and inclusive on social policy and ran the state well. The Dockings were to most Kansans like the Kennedys were to folks in Massachusetts. The Docking family was close to my family, too. Second, the Kennedy and Johnson administrations were much more progressive on social issues, especially impacting the poor, and emphasized job creation and education reform. Third, the Democratic Party was by and large much more dedicated to racial inclusion and diversity, issues I cared about deeply. Gradually, over a few years, my thinking became more aligned with the Democratic Party values of John Kennedy and leading Democrats who had been elected in Kansas.

Though these individuals certainly made my case for switching easier, the seminal policy issue for me was the Vietnam War. The way the Nixon administration handled Vietnam pushed me toward the Democrats and gave me a strong reason to change my affiliation. Politically, Vietnam was dividing us as a nation, and as I saw first-hand in Ann Arbor, Washington, DC, and Wichita, America felt like it was coming apart at the seams. Protests were happening daily, and when I returned home at night to watch the news, Walter Cronkite brought the destruction of the battlefields right into our living room. At war's end, nearly sixty thousand Americans had died, and more than three hundred thousand were wounded. Many of them were people around my age, and I personally knew too many. Folks were returning to Kansas and the rest of the country with tales of savage destruction and senseless death. Most of my generation could never accept why this war was necessary or how we had gotten embroiled in such horrific butchery half a world away.

Even though the Nixon White House promised a de-escalation of the war in Vietnam, Cambodia and Laos became new battlefields. The Pentagon Papers, published in 1971 by the *Washington Post*, re-vealed a troubling history of the Nixon administration deceiving the American public. At a certain point, I came to feel that Nixon was exploiting my generation, as was the Republican Party at the time. Of course, I didn't blame Republican voters, but it did cause me to question whether the Republican Party was right for me. As all of this unfolded, and more and more information became clear, an increasing number of my peers opposing the war found a home with the Democratic Party.

Clearly, the Vietnam War was a mixed bag for Dems on these issues because Lyndon Johnson suffered politically as a result of the war, but the Democratic Party had more leaders (Hubert Humphrey, Robert Kennedy, Jimmy Carter, and others), who were dedicated to the end of the Vietnam conflict.

The question of race relations was an equally important issue for me and many of my generation, and this overlapped completely with the anti-war movement. Even though the GOP was the party of Abraham Lincoln, I felt that Democrats were more in line with my generation's attitude toward race relations. I was strongly com-mitted to the civil rights movement and greatly admired Dr. Martin Luther King Jr.

It became particularly clear to me during my time in Washing-ton that race and civil rights issues were among the most important things that government needed to take on and solve. Millions of

American citizens had suffered persecution, oppression, and violence for hundreds of years, trying to pursue the American Dream like anyone else, despite what they had faced.

It wasn't just unfair; it was unpatriotic.

Racism defied the essential idea of equality enshrined in our national character by our founding fathers. Of course, many of those men were slave owners, but their ideas of freedom and equality needed to extend to all of America's citizens. I felt back then, in the midst of the movement, and still feel strongly today that social and racial justice is one of the most critical challenges facing the US government and Congress, in particular. Of course, the 1954 case of *Brown v. Board of Education of Topeka, Kansas* had placed my home state in a central role in the struggle for civil rights, but ten and twenty years later, progress was still painfully slow.

As I contemplated my future political affiliation, I felt that Kennedy and Johnson had been much more supportive of the African American citizen's push for true equality than the Nixon White House. In the background, of course, one of the biggest scandals in American history was uncovered: Watergate. Compared to Vietnam and civil rights, Watergate had less of an impact on my decision to become a Democrat. Still, corruption and scandal in government didn't exactly make me want to stay a Republican.

My fairly loose affiliation with the Republican Party wasn't only an awkward talking point at parties, it was a question of my core identity.

By 1974, I could no longer identify with the Republican Party of that era. The Nixon scandal triggered that, along with rumors of anti-Semitism among higher-ups in the White House. My values were different and the changes in DC had become increasingly troubling.

It's important to remember that parties evolve and change just as society does. I am struck by how today's Republican Party is changing (again) in ways that leave many of its traditional supporters behind. I have met countless former members of Congress who were rock-ribbed conservative Republicans, but now they no longer feel like the values espoused by today's party reflect their beliefs. Fiscal responsibility, balancing the budget, and what are today considered liberal views on immigration and human rights used to be heavily supported by Republicans. The party of Lincoln was the party of equal opportunity for all. Historically, the Democratic Party had been dominated by some racist voices in the South. This has all been flipped on its head, to say the least.

For me, what it ultimately came down to was simple. I agreed more with Democratic politics than Republican politics. This was a rewiring of how I grew up in Kansas, where as a young man I placed yard signs for a Republican candidate for governor, became one of the leaders for Michigan Students for Romney and Johnson, and volunteered at the 1964 Republican Convention that nominated Barry Goldwater for president. My work for Senator Dominick helped me get a job interview with Senator Dole, a Republican giant of his time.

I never felt as if I identified solely with one party and always considered myself a political centrist with moderate views. I was constantly evaluating the political positions of both parties to determine what I thought was right. In politics today, this kind of free thinking is seen as a betrayal of party loyalty, but I have always considered myself more loyal to functional, just, and representative government than to any one party.

There have been many high-profile party switches in national politics. Nearly all of them appear to be taken out of political opportunism. My switch was not high profile, nor was it "necessarily" cynical or opportunistic.

To be honest, I was driven in part by the real possibility in 1974 and 1975 that the incumbent congressman was weak, and I had more of a chance to win the race as a Democrat than running against him in a primary as a Republican. In all fairness, my motives were probably a bit mixed.

I have learned that one of the first principles in political life is flexibility, inspired by an old line from Senator Everett Dirksen when he was accused of changing his position on a key spending issue.

"I am a man of principle, and my first principle is flexibility."

An open mind—imagine that!

All joking aside, where is the flexibility in Washington today?

In Kansas especially, no one could credibly accuse me of switching parties for political benefit. This breadbasket state was and remains one of the most Republican states in the Union. Because Kansas was a conservative state, my political network up until that point was with the Republican Party. By declaring myself a Democrat, I was giving up the support of many people who knew I had political ambitions and the connections and finances they represented.

However, at the state level, Kansas had a long history of electing conservative Democrats to statewide office, such as former Kansas governors George Docking and Bob Docking. We had precedent for some pragmatic Democrats making it through an otherwise Republican gauntlet.

At that time, Kansas's Fourth Congressional District was not gerrymandered into a one-party district. We elected Republicans to Congress but voted primarily for Democrats for governor and state legislatures. Kansas wasn't quite as uniformly Republican as it is today, but it was no cakewalk. Still, I felt my change in party affiliation was the right decision.

I had one enormous advantage when it came to the political space to be a moderate in Kansas. The Democratic Party was not as left leaning as it was some other states. This was also a time when my views as a moderate Democrat could just as easily have been seen as those of a Republican.

Having been on the other side of the aisle politically gave me the ability to understand the viewpoints of Republicans and respect their ideas, even when I disagreed with them. Throughout my career, this contributed to my ability to work well with my Republican colleagues.

I have always felt a need to search for common ground. What drove me as a lawmaker was passing bills, amending laws, and getting things done. In our system, bipartisanship is simply the most, and often the only, productive way to do that. One aspect of today's hyper-partisanship is that unless you win 100 percent of what you want, you will not work with the other side. Getting "only" 90 percent is seen as a loss and giving the other side 10 percent is considered a win for them, which is sadly viewed as a no-no. With that type of mindset, it is nearly impossible to work toward compromise and embrace any type of bipartisanship.

Today, extreme partisanship means that whatever views the other side takes on an issue are automatically wrong and even immoral or unethical in the eyes of your own team. Much has been written about the problems of partisanship, not least of all by me. But from a purely political perspective, such black and white party structures have taken any true competition out of our political process. Both Republicans and Democrats have built ideological monopolies and a system that ensures their electoral success, while leaving no room for free thought.

I must remind you that partisanship is not inherently evil in politics, just as long as it is mainly constructive and trends toward substantive accomplishments for the people. It sounds trite, but the fact is, we *are* all in this together.

My generation's shift toward the Democrats, plus the reaction to the scandal-plagued Nixon administration, set the Democratic Party up for a big election in 1974. The Democratic post-Watergate landslide did materialize and brought a new class of young and well-educated lawmakers into power who shared a drive to infuse the party's traditional platform with their modern and fresh ideas.

While 1974 was too early for me to consider running for Congress (although I did think seriously about it), seeing the impact of these new members leading a peaceful revolt against the congressional old guard really got me thinking about the 1976 campaign. This next step in my political career could be the time for me to jump at the opportunity to go higher in elected politics. Being ambitious, it looked to me that the timing might be right for a big step up from the school board to running for Congress, skipping the more conventional step of campaigning for a seat in the state legislature.

I had been involved on the periphery of the 1974 election, volunteering for the campaign of former congressman Bill Roy, who ran against Bob Dole for a US Senate seat from Kansas. Roy had been quite an effective congressman in the Topeka area of the state. He was an obstetrician who had delivered thousands of babies, which meant he had also performed a few medically necessary abortions. Dole beat him, but only by a single percentage point, in part because he raised the abortion issue quite aggressively—and successfully, which also shows how closely divided even a traditionally Republican-friendly state like Kansas had become in the post-Watergate era. In fact, the Dole-Roy race was one of the first senatorial races in the country where abortion became a major issue. It's interesting how abortion has become a seminal and divisive political issue, in Kansas and elsewhere, which affected me directly in my losing battle for reelection in 1994.

By the way, it took Bob Dole a long time to forgive me for volunteering for his opponent.

I also took note that in his 1974 reelection campaign, Garner Shriver, one of several incumbent Republicans on the state and federal level who was reelected by a small margin, defended his seat with only 49 percent of the vote in a three-way race that included a relatively obscure Democratic challenger. Such a close race from an unknown Democratic challenger certainly led an ambitious young lawyer from Wichita to believe that a race for Congress as a Democrat was not impossible.

There wasn't one specific moment that I can point to as my epiphany to run in 1976, but these factors taken together—the success of the 1974 class in Congress, Nixon resigning, which wounded many Republicans, lots of positive attention for my work on the Wichita Public School Board, and incumbent Republicans in Kansas keeping their seats by tiny margins—all fed my determination to make a run for Congress in 1976.

The school district I had been serving was nearly two-thirds the size of the congressional district, with the same media market I had worked heavily during my tenure. The power of local television, which I had used aggressively to promote my various activities, was not lost on me as I thought about a run for higher office.

This was my chance.

Many folks at home actually discouraged me from running. But one virtue of being thirty-one years of age is that political "realities" of running against a long-tenured incumbent congressman are not a match for youthful exuberance and perseverance. That is why I am encouraged that many younger Americans want to run for office lately, even if the establishment keeps telling them to go slow. If I had listened to those leaders who urged me to wait, I would probably still be in Kansas, practicing law and gaining weight at White Castle.

Power is never given; it's taken.

My friends and family initially got me off the ground and helped me believe I could pull it off. Rhoda staffed the campaign office, and my parents jumped into campaigning with their usual gusto and humor, making themselves available for parades, meetings, or simply babysitting on an oft-needed, twenty-four-hour basis. Thanks to them, I already enjoyed some positive name recognition in the community.

Our kids, though young, contributed as well, often going with me door-to-door and looking extraordinarily adorable in campaign ads and news stories. My school system experience was essential to my profile and gave me instant credibility in the district because these constituents had seen me in action and could vouch for my candidacy and credentials.

This campaign was a family and grassroots effort, with very little money spent on pollsters or professional campaigners. It seems quaint by today's super PAC, data-driven, top-down campaign strategies, but anyone who has ever run for office can tell you that no amount of money or expensive consultants can win you a race. You must go out into your community, hear what constituents have to say, and show them that you are on their side.

Democrat or Republican, it takes wearing out your shoes and showing up at barbecues.

When you put yourself out there in a campaign, you end up finding out how much your friends and family really love you. My mother, for example, came down to my campaign headquarters and worked the phones, calling potential voters throughout the district. She was so passionate that at times my campaign staff had to gently restrain her, especially one time when they overheard her talking to a potential donor.

"What do you mean you're not voting for my son? I can't believe you, that's crazy! He's the best candidate, and if you don't see that, well, there's something really wrong with you."

I'm not sure if my mother's passion cost me any votes, but it didn't win me any either.

My opponent, Garner Shriver, was an exceptionally decent man and a moderate Republican. He was pro-choice, which would not be tolerated in today's Republican Party. I didn't want to run a negative campaign that tried to tear him down. But I had to be realistic and point out our differences.

Frankly, I don't think going to the dark side would have worked, even if I had wanted to go in that direction. I believe that in almost every situation, being positive is a better campaign strategy than being negative. I don't mean that you should hold off criticizing your opponent's record. This is politics, after all. To that end, I focused my campaign on the theme of fresh ideas and new energy. Shriver, on the other hand, had been in Congress for sixteen years, and I'm pretty sure he didn't take me too seriously.

I realize writing this book how often I say a version of, "things were different back in my day," but nowhere is that more evident than my first campaign. My best estimate is that the entire race cost about $100,000 for each candidate, including my opponent, the incumbent congressman. Incomprehensible in today's politics! A budget of that size is hardly enough to fund one week's worth of campaigning. It's staggering how much money is spent and wasted in modern political campaigns.

Of course, I needed money to get my message out, but we really didn't run any ads until close to the August primary date, and then again close to Election Day. My most powerful ad attacked Shriver's record but not him personally.

"Garner Shriver has been in Congress for 16 years," it began. "The following is a list of his major legislative accomplishments."

The screen went black for fifteen whole seconds, with a drum beating increasingly in the background. Garner responded with a similar-looking ad, pointing out his work on the Appropriations Committee, which was supposed to point out my lack of congressional experience. Every time he ran that ad, I think I picked up support because voters were reminded of my television spot against him and of our age difference. The ad I ran surely created some controversy here and there.

"Why are you saying those things about that nice man, Shriver?"

I don't think I would have won the race had I not created an edge between us, which was so laughably mild compared to what we see today.

The heart of my 1976 campaign was giving the people of Kansas a chance to get to know me personally. I must have knocked on more than thirty thousand doors, literally walking the entirety of the district. There was no such thing as a cell phone to permit fundraising calls while I was walking door to door. Sometimes I was by myself; sometimes Rhoda and the kids were with me, and sometimes Rhoda and my parents covered one side of the street while I took care of the other. We walked dozens of precincts and met tens of thousands of people in the process.

I was able to pursue this strategy because I did not spend all my time fundraising. This grassroots effort gave me the chance to talk with Republican constituents too, who discovered that I thought like them on many issues. The process enabled me to showcase my independence.

Today, walking to thousands of homes would be viewed by political consultants as at best, a waste of time and at worst, malpractice (of course, in the era of COVID it would be next to impossible). Now candidates spend most of their time on the phone, raising money. But you can't be a good representative if you don't spend any time with your constituents or if you only spend time with the rich ones.

Besides the many tough conversations in-person canvassing can trigger, I shouldn't ignore the many ego boosts that come with meeting my constituents. Once, Rhoda and I were in the small town of Hillsboro, a Mennonite community approximately sixty miles north of Wichita. Driving down the street, we couldn't miss the big welcoming sign.

"WELCOME DAN GLICKMAN"

It turned out that Hillsboro was national headquarters for a church called "Bible Light," and because of their huge support for Israel, they were also big supporters of me. Rhoda and I thoroughly enjoyed campaigning in Hillsboro, and it was no surprise that the Glickman campaign did well there on election night.

The necessity of focusing on fundraising above all other activities deprives our elected officials of the opportunity to connect and demonstrate to constituents that most of our public servants are men and women of good character, regardless of party label. Today's candidate is forced to act like an ATM machine, fundraising like crazy to raise money, which they turn around and dispense at an inconceivable rate to keep the campaign machinery churning.

This is a major contributing factor to our hyper-partisanship. So much of the money spent in today's politics is raised for the sole purpose of barraging the person you are running against with ad hominem attack ads. The act of campaigning has become the job, not the act of governing once elected, and all other activities are in service of the next campaign. This leaves almost no room to legislate and no spirit of cooperation.

It's not that every person running for office wants to win at all costs, but the frenetic rush to raise and spend large sums of money encourages campaigns, which are not aligned with the pressing problems facing the country. People respond to bigger donors even though they claim not to. It defies the laws of nature to kick someone in the ass who is a major campaign contributor. That is why the emphasis on smaller donors is so important. And candidly, the public responds to the negative more than the positive in the ads this money buys. But I am somewhat heartened by newly elected members in the recent elections, especially younger Democrats, who seem to be able to raise and spend money but also campaign on a higher level of issues and values.

Jesse M. Unruh, the legendary former assembly Speaker in California, once said: "If you can't take their money, drink their booze, eat their food, screw their women and vote against them, you don't belong here."

Politicians like Willie Brown and others have repeated this sentiment in more civilized terms, but the essence of it remains and Unruh wasn't wrong with another of his famous quotes:

"Money is the mother's milk of politics."

There is a certain science required to be a lawmaker, along with developing the art of communication, a technique that has been forgotten or lost by many of our current elected officials. Politics is a people-driven business. By that I mean that no politician will ever be successful without connecting with people on a personal basis. To do that, you have to be willing to reach out to people and have a desire to connect with them, no matter who they are. You actually have to care about what happens in their lives and see how you can help them. If you're not interested in shaking hands and chatting with whomever opens the door, then you have no business running for any office, including Congress.

During my many years in public service, I learned that a friendly, positive, noncombative attitude was helpful in making friends with folks who were not natural ideological allies. If they liked you, then they were more prone to hold you in higher personal regard and were less persuadable by ad hominem personal attacks. As a progressive Democrat from a conservative Republican state, this was my way to get elected and be politically successful. Plus, it's just my natural personality. Yes, I'll say it. I'm a nice guy. I am! It's not only natural. I choose to be this way! It's a commitment to embody our better angels.

For many people, social media has become their primary way

of connecting with voters. It's certainly efficient. One tweet can instantly reach millions of people. But is it actually connecting with them? Although Facebook or Twitter allow high-profile politicians to speak to the media, and the most committed supporters, parties, or issue-specific activists to broadcast their message with relative ease, I still think nothing beats face-to-face conversations with voters.

No one personifies this gap more than Donald Trump. He, like no other candidate in the primaries or the general election, communicated specifically with his base on a daily, almost hourly basis via social media and he made them feel heard. That's one lesson we can learn from the 2016 Trump campaign. One, because in my judgment, that's about it. But that said, if we ignore the power of social media—in anyone's little hands—to influence a political campaign, then we do so at our own peril.

The flip side of this strategy, however, is that Trump and others made absolutely no effort to meet people who don't support them. In fact, he actively insulted them. Despite his initial success, this is not a tenable political strategy. While burning bridges with those who don't agree with him is a core part of his personality, I have to wonder if it will eventually catch up to him in ways he hasn't foreseen. At a certain point, he can't claim to be America's president and he will have no right to ask for America's votes. It turns out that his strategy was unsuccessful, and his loss to Joe Biden was driven largely because he burned so many bridges, particularly among women, minorities, and suburban voters. And frankly, he was a man of deficient moral character.

Here lies one of the main differences between politics today and politics forty years ago. Because of the media landscape, voters are receiving unhealthy doses of outrage and party propaganda each day through a variety of platforms. Voters may think they are connected to a candidate or elected official by social media and cable news, but they are being fed nonstop propaganda and trash talk by dedicated professionals hell-bent on destroying their favored candidate's opposition. We're not meeting the real candidates anymore; we're meeting the version that some focus group told a campaign professional they'd like to see in the next ad.

Most campaigns in my era were people driven, and when I was an active politician, I was successful in that way. I feel sorry for today's candidates who are deprived by the current system of the enriching experience I had when running for Congress. Yet they enable it! There was shared intimacy between voter and representative that went to the heart of public service. Until fairly recently, most members of Congress and the Senate held numerous town hall meetings and other direct ways of meeting constituents face to face. During congressional recesses, when representatives supposedly go home to meet with their constituents, we see elected officials hiding from the people, as if they are afraid to meet with them and face the consequences of their votes. I wish we could legislate obligatory town hall meetings because in a free system it is important that elected officials meet their constituents eye to eye. These telephone town hall meetings with pre-staged questions are a joke.

Seeing the "whites of their eyes" and engaging directly with voters is a fundamental pillar of good politics. Personal contact is being lost, and the political cost to the country created by this vacuum is severe. Look at tribalism in the Bible. How did that work out?

I am not sure, for example, if a campaign manager in today's political climate would allow their candidate to literally sing and dance—basically making a fool out of themselves—in front of thousands of constituents. But that's exactly what I did during the annual Gridiron show, one of Wichita's oldest and most well-known stage shows that raises money for scholarships.

There I was in 1976, singing, "I'm Danny Boy, I want to be your Congressman," to the tune of "Danny Boy," in the best Jewish-Irish tenor I could muster. My opponent came onstage for his own song right after mine, singing a parody of "Old Man River." At the time, he was sixty-two, and I was thirty-one. The contrast the two of us presented, perhaps highlighted by the two different songs we sang, was not lost on the audience. Ironically, singing a version of "Danny Boy" at this Gridiron show, and then singing "Hey Big Spender" at the one in 1992, were key factors, first in my political success, and then later in my political survival.

Those Gridiron evenings were pivotal in connecting with voters, showing my lighter side as a candidate, and taking the sting out of campaigning against someone I respected as a person. I bet if that video were on YouTube today, social media trolls would be spreading snarky comments across Wichita and the world. Social media tends to make anything into an object of mockery. Then again, I might receive thousands of delightful sympathy cards.

I spent a lot of time in my district's rural areas, the location of some of the largest wheat-producing counties in the country. This was not at the expense of the city folks in Wichita, but it was a strategic decision my campaign made. Forty percent of the district was in the rural part of central Kansas. We just figured that with my background, I needed to make a concerted effort to connect with the many farmers who made up such a vast percentage of the district.

I was once quoted as saying I had never pushed a tractor before. Then a farmer I met explained to me that you *ride* a tractor, you don't push it. I can still recall the bemused look on the man's weather-beaten face as he slowly told me, "You ride them." Lesson learned.

I needed to get to know the constituents living and working in our rural areas and smaller communities. It helped that my father's scrap iron company had done a lot of business with the farmers around Wichita and had always treated them with respect and fairness. As a result, I enjoyed some name recognition, but I needed to translate how a Wichita-based lawyer like me would advocate on behalf of Kansas farmers.

I had some good mentors on agriculture issues who liked me and felt that Shriver had ignored them during his eight terms in Congress. One huge ally in this mission was a local wheat farmer named John Adrian of Harvey County. He gregariously took me under his wing and campaigned with me constantly outside Wichita. This afforded me credibility with his peers so I at least had a chance to state my case. Showing up at the door with a farmer beside me was a hell of a lot better than showing up alone!

My daily travels took me all over the countryside, including Reno County, home of Hutchinson, the second largest city in the district, as well as a big wheat-producing hub. It also sits on top of one of the largest salt mines in the world, where in addition to mining salt, it provided the perfect climate to become a repository for Hollywood movies to be saved and protected for posterity. This became yet another link to my future at the Motion Pictures Association of America.

I won that county with more than 60 percent of the vote and essentially tied in Wichita and Sedgwick County. I did not neglect Wichita in the process, however, especially the working-class base, which included aircraft manufacturers and their unions.

Whereas my success was based on farmers and rural voters

coming out in droves to support me, Democrats today have pretty much abandoned any hope of winning in the rural sectors of their districts and focus their resources instead almost exclusively on urban areas.

Nonetheless, there is some evidence that the Republican stronghold in rural America is weakening. The farm economy is shrinking; poverty and income inequality is extraordinarily serious in small towns and rural America, and Trump's trade policy has made a joke of farmers having solid access for their products to reach the rest of the world. Dems used to do well in rural America; gun and abortion issues have benefitted Republicans in some of these areas, but the current economic issues of small towns and farms may be turning the tide. Dems just have to focus more attention on heartland and rural voters and be more than a bicoastal party.

It has become so difficult for candidates to appeal to anyone outside of their base. Most strategies now rely on turning out as many core supporters as possible rather than trying to convince people you're the right candidate for the district, regardless of your background.

I am not naïve. I would probably never convince the folks in my district influenced by Koch Industries to support me, along with naturally targeted supporters in labor unions and minority populations. But I did not ignore any group or demographic. I needed as many votes as I could get in a majority Republican district.

I must have done something right if I got elected nine times!

This is a good political lesson and serves us well in life, too. You might find a few votes and make a few allies by being open to all different kinds of people, rather than focusing on a narrow number and a particular base voter bloc.

Some of the issues that usually play against Democrats did not affect my political life at that time. They would later, especially in 1994, but that initial 1976 run for Congress did not include any serious discussions about abortion or gun control, as far as I can recall.

Instead, we talked about jobs, the energy crisis, and how Congress could support America's farmers. The main thing that separated me from the incumbent was my message of dynamism and the fact that my energy level was incredibly high and his was not. I looked and talked the part, like I was already a member of Congress ready to go to bat for my voters and to work tirelessly, day and night, to produce for Kansas. While I was skinny, fit, and had lots of black hair, all that could be said about my opponent was how tired he looked. Maybe that's what happens when you take things for granted and don't fully respect your opponent.

Campaigns are a marathon, but we finally reached the end. On Election Day, November 2, 1976, I campaigned all day, doing more door-to-door canvassing, standing outside polling places, squeezing in one more interview, and running one last radio ad. I wasn't going to let a lack of determination or persistence come between me and my goal. After months and months of campaigning I was ready to get some rest, but what kept me going that last day was knowing that we were just a couple of hours away from either making history—a Democrat ousting an eight-term Republican incumbent in Kansas—or having to accept a stinging defeat.

We gathered in the party's campaign headquarters, a run-down office building in a less than glamorous part of Wichita, and watched the results slowly trickle in. I thought I had been picking up steam and felt that winning was a real possibility, but I wasn't what you might call overly confident about the outcome. The fastest votes came in from Wichita, and Congressman Shriver was beginning to pull ahead. Then the rural counties started coming in, and you could see the tide turning in my favor with each new batch of votes announced. The farmers and rural voters were delivering for me, and all the time I had spent getting to know them, hearing their concerns and learning their issues, was now paying off. The irony was that a relatively unknown, moderate, and Jewish candidate was winning in a rural, conservative, and decidedly non-Jewish area of the district.

We began to realize that we were witnessing a victory, an incredible political upset, unfolding right before our Kansan eyes. The room was packed with Democratic Party officials and operatives, as well as many Republicans who had helped me during the race.

Rhoda and the kids were there, as were my parents. My mom brought many of her friends—little old Jewish ladies—who did the hora (a traditional Israeli circular dance) all around the office. The next day's paper referred to the Glickman victory party as a veritable political kibbutz, with singing and dancing throughout the night.

I won the election!

I became the first Jewish congressman in Kansas history.

What a country!

It cannot be overstated how impossible that 1976 campaign would be today. First and foremost, the death grip political parties have on drawing congressional districts makes the primary the determinative election, with the general election mostly becoming a foregone conclusion. My district was winnable because it was drawn by people who were not committed to gerrymandering, although it did have a Republican edge. At that time, all Kansan districts leaned Republican, although a majority of voters held loose party affiliations and were proud of their independent views. In today's gerrymandered district maps, incumbents are protected from a candidate from the other party and only worry about candidates from their own party, since each district is overwhelmingly faithful to one party or the other. The primary opponents are usually the ones steering Republicans more to the right and Democrats more to the left. That is why we are witnessing a much larger number of extremists winning elected office while moderate voices, like mine, are being drowned out.

On top of that conundrum, I did not have to spend inordinate amounts of time fundraising, which meant I could devote my energy to meeting the voters—in person. This is a luxury that modern candidates no longer enjoy. The $100,000 I spent on that first campaign was—to me at least—a large amount of money in 1976, but that figure is laughably low by today's standards. Freedom from constant fundraising made me a much better candidate, and in return, a much better representative. I could focus on getting to know my constituents and learning about their issues, rather than begging some huge donor (the majority of whom have zero connection to the district) to write me a check.

Most members of Congress are decent human beings of good character, interested in serving their communities.

Individually, most members are decent people, but the tribal nature of our politics puts allegiance to party over principles and this has affected a fair number of them in a bad way. That is a sad truth. There are some cases where members come together on major stuff, such as natural disasters, National Institutes of Health funding, or cancer research, but the big issues of American leadership in the world—income inequality, true tax reform, commitment to science and technology, fighting racism, and rebuilding America's infrastructure—get left behind while the rest of the world moves ahead of us. I don't think it's a matter of no backbone or morals among members, but there are too few independent thinkers in Congress, and too many Republicans were afraid to confront former president Trump on anything, from his policies to his behavior.

During my time as the director of the Aspen Institute's Congressional Program, I got to meet with dozens of members of Congress from both parties. Many of them are as talented, patriotic, and well intentioned as the folks elected in the 1970s.

The difference is that I first ran under a system that empowered me to truly represent my constituencies, be independent-minded, and work with other members on crafting solutions for our nation. I worked with Republicans when I thought they were right. I won because I was a moderate, and I succeeded as a representative because of my moderate approach.

Today's members often get punished for working with colleagues from the other side of the aisle, and their willingness to compromise makes them a target in highly contested and expensive primaries. The media, especially social media, will go after candidates who don't seem conservative or liberal enough. Tearing people down is the name of the political game, and this is turning off and pushing away the next generation of political leaders.

It is worth noting that no major, enduring piece of legislation has become law without bipartisan support. Not Medicare, Social Security, the Clean Air Act, the Civil Rights Act—nothing.

Walking the streets of Wichita or the fields outside of Hutchinson gave me an invaluable education and insight. I spent so much time with the farmers of my district when I was campaigning that when I arrived in Washington on January 3, 1977, to be sworn in as part of the 95th Congress, I always had the House Agriculture Committee in the back of my mind. This was not the most obvious committee assignment for a Jewish lawyer from Kansas's largest city, but it made all the sense in the world to me.

The opportunity to serve America's farmers was paramount in my mind, as they were obviously a hugely important part of my Kansas constituency. It turns out that the Agriculture Committee assignment was profoundly instrumental in my long-term political career. It led to my subsequent appointment as secretary of agriculture. In addition, I worked on issues such as commodity futures regulation, and I was active in food and nutrition programs, such as food stamps, which ignited my passion for tackling domestic and global hunger issues.

Meeting those farmers in that first campaign and agreeing to fight for them in Washington, DC, set the trajectory for the rest of my life.

Arriving in Congress and being assigned to the House Agriculture Committee was the culmination of everything I had worked for thus far. Earning my law degree, working for Senator Dominick, gaining invaluable experience as a trial attorney, running for and winning the Wichita School Board seat, and convincing the voters of the Fourth Congressional District of Kansas to place their trust in me all led to this point. It just felt right. I was home.

When I got to freshman orientation in DC, we were seated alphabetically, with all the brand new members of Congress lined up by name. The guy on my right was a freshman from Missouri, by the name of Dick Gephardt. The guy on my left was Al Gore, a freshman from Tennessee. Not a bad year to have a last name starting with the letter "G." Many years later, after both had tried and failed to win the presidency, I told them I was glad that at least one of us had amounted to something in life.

I am forever grateful to the people of Wichita and its farming communities for giving me the opportunity to serve as their voice in Washington. My Wichita small-town roots have always been at the core of who I am as a person and they have given me an appreciation for the diversity that is America.

Too often in the past, Democrats have been guilty of forgetting or ignoring what heartland America is all about. The values and integrity that form the foundation of this part of the country—Middle America, for God's sake—have shaped me as a human being, regardless of having lived and worked most of my life in the bubble of the coastal elite.

Wichita is a special place with special people. Even though my birthplace is home to a big part of the conservative movement in America, it nonetheless listened to this Democrat upstart and was open-minded enough to elect him to Congress on nine separate occasions.

With those years on the Agriculture Committee leading to my appointment as secretary of agriculture, I attribute every success I have had in life directly to the people of Wichita and its farming communities.

Long live Doo-Dah!

*Author at age five circa 1950—
lots of hair!*

*Family picture with me in
front of my mother; my sister,
Sharon; my brother, Norman;
and my father on vacation at
Glenwood Springs, Colorado,
1954.*

My son, Jon; my wife, Rhoda; me; and my daughter, Amy, in 1981.

My children, Jon and Amy, circa 1987.

Glickman family at seventy-fifth birthday party for Milton (my dad) in 1991.

Rhoda and I meet Jimmy Carter during his pre-presidential campaign appearance in Wichita in the summer of 1975.

Standing with Wichita school board member Evelyn Whitcomb on the US Capitol steps where we met former congressman Garner Shriver (right, who I defeated in November 1976). Whitcomb and I were both members of the Wichita Board of Education when we went to visit Shriver as our local representative. This is from either summer of 1974 or 1975 (probably later). Note the clothes.

Rhoda and I celebrate at a congressional campaign victory party on the night of the election in 1976.

Preparing for Congress right after Election Day November 1976.

Outside my congressional office—1507 Longworth Building.

An early congressional fundraiser in Kansas with Rhoda in 1977.

Yours truly on the phone with a constituent while working in my congressional office.

Former Agriculture Committee chairman and later Speaker of the House Tom Foley and me discussing Kansas wheat prices in 1979 or 1980.

Former congressman Jim Leach (Iowa, left), me, and Mike Synar (Oklahoma, right), testifying in House committee in the 1980s on campaign finance reform legislation.

Riding in a convertible in a traditional Kansas Fourth of July parade in 1984.

Reading through materials in my office in preparation for a House committee meeting circa 1992. Note Kansas stained glass by window.

President Clinton signing the landmark General Aviation Reform Act in August 1994 with me, Senator Nancy Kassebaum, to the left, and representatives from various areas of the aviation industry.

Standing with Senator Bob Dole and reviewing the tally sheet that reflected I was confirmed 94–0 as USDA Secretary on March 30, 1995. Photo courtesy of Dole Institute of Politics.

At my USDA swearing-in ceremony in March 1995. Al Gore holds up photos of us from when we were both first elected to Congress in 1976.

Representing the United States as USDA secretary in November 1995 at a United Nations meeting on food security. Behind me is former senator and then ambassador George McGovern and Undersecretary of Agriculture Jim Schroeder.

Working on a USDA conservation and water project with actress Bette Midler outside New York City in 1996 or 1997.

Visiting a corn farm during a drought in upstate New York with Senator Chuck Schumer (far right), former congressman Tom Reynolds, and an unidentified New York state farmer in 1997.

Doing an agriculture radio show from the Oval Office with President Bill Clinton in 1997.

Visiting Wichita with President Clinton in 1999 to visit a job-training facility started by Cessna Aircraft Company.

Having an animated conversation with three other members of the Clinton cabinet (Bill Daley, Donna Shalala, and Bruce Babbit).

Annual pardoning of the Thanksgiving turkey at the White House with President Clinton; my wife, Rhoda; me; and our daughter, Amy. In the right corner you can see Hillary Clinton.

Speaking at the National Nutrition Summit in late 1990s, where an anti-meat activist threw a tofu cream pie at me.

Nelson Mandela and I at his home during a USDA visit to Africa in 2000. We spent four hours talking about his life.

Photo of actor Will Smith, me, and Congressman Charlie Rangel during a Motion Picture Association symposium in 2003. Will Smith spoke of the impact of the movies on American culture.

Chapter 8

How I Fertilized the Agriculture Committee

Before running for Congress, my key qualification for agricultural issues was that I liked to eat. On paper, I would not have been mistaken for an agriculture expert or a farming advocate, but I was committed to finding solutions on behalf of my Wichita constituents and America's farmers, especially after those good people had supported me so strongly in my first election. That's why I joined the Agriculture Committee. Although I did not personally plant any crops or raise any farm animals, I worked hard to understand and serve those who do.

I had not been expected to win the 1976 election, and since few of the national political groups had targeted the race, I had not built any deep relationships with national Democratic leaders or House leadership as some of the other contenders of that year had done. As a result, I had not pushed particularly hard for any prime committee assignments.

In all candor, a seat on the Agriculture Committee was not my first choice. Like most of the freshmen who entered Congress with me, I wanted a seat on the powerful Ways and Means or Appropriations Committee. But my new chief of staff, Myrne Roe, my high school debate coach, was an astute political observer. She knew that agriculture was a fundamental and crucial part of Kansas politics, which meant that much of my budding career would be based in agriculture and farm policy. Her instincts were right, and my career flourished as a result.

Congressional leadership determines committee assignments. They do this with a mix of considerations over political consequences and background experience. If you have important constituents as I did but little experience in that committee's topic of jurisdiction as I also did, then you still had a shot to get on that committee out of pure political consideration.

That's why we probably never had a member from downtown Los Angeles serving on the Agriculture Committee, although we did have one from Brooklyn. Fred Richmond was a Democratic representative and used his service on the Agriculture Committee to work on inner-city issues such as urban gardens and food stamps. On those issues, he and I worked closely together.

In my case, the Agriculture Committee was central to the concerns of my constituents, that is, rural farmers and urban consumers. My election victory was a result of the farmers around Wichita getting to know me, buying into my message and vision, and placing their trust in my abilities. The notion that they believed in me gave me confidence, a key ingredient for anyone running for office.

I certainly was not one of them, but those farmers supported me anyway. Growing up in the city's Jewish community with a father who split his time between his business and his obsession with baseball did not translate easily to the experience of a third-generation Kansas farmer whose daily life was consumed by worries about wheat prices, droughts, and tornadoes. Sensing a need to connect—and genuinely wanting to—led me to talking a lot about agriculture and the importance of the family farmer to American security and strength. Whenever I could, through direct contact and media interviews, I reinforced that message.

Most of my public messaging was devoted to two subjects: protecting farmers and farm income, and protecting jobs in Wichita's aircraft industry. Of course I did a lot of other stuff, but I made personal friends with lots of Kansas farmers and helped them manage the bureaucracy of the USDA, which I later ran. I connected frequently with Kansas agricultural media. One farm broadcaster in particular, Larry Steckline, in Wichita, became a close personal friend and served as my unofficial eyes and ears on Kansas farm issues.

Despite coming from different walks of life, those farmers and I came together over a shared understanding that at the end of the day, the job is to raise crops, and when nature changes the circumstances in which those crops are raised, you have to be flexible and innovative.

I took the practicality and smarts of Kansas's farmers with me to Congress. In some important ways, the flexibility those farmers employed in the face of Mother Nature and her unpredictable effects is the same kind of mentality moderate lawmakers could use to their benefit. Set a goal. Make a plan. When a situation changes, change the plan to achieve the goal.

I quickly found a crucial commonality through humor. I connected with these rural constituents because I didn't take myself too seriously and could ham it up with the best of them—pun fully intended, thank you very much.

There is a good reason Kansas is known as the Wheat State. It continues to be one of several national leaders in agricultural exports, such as wheat, cattle, and to a lesser extent, corn, soybeans, and pork. Millions of acres of Kansan soil are devoted to pasture and crops, and the combined value of Kansan farms reaches into the billions of dollars, more than most nations on the planet.

Kansan farmers feed the state, the nation, and the world.

Not only that but the agricultural industry in Kansas provides jobs for thousands of people, not just on farms but in related industries, including supplies, transportation, and food processing. In 1976, the year I entered Congress, there were almost eighty thousand farms in Kansas, and many of them were in my congressional district.

As with many industries across the country, America's farming system has gone through a metamorphosis. These changes had significant implications for me as a lawmaker and for federal agriculture policy in general.

For the past few decades, more and more small family farms have been gobbled up by larger, more financially stable farms. Smaller farms—and this was especially true for my Kansas constituents—had a tough time dealing with the market volatility and the frequent low prices that come with depending on only one or two crops. In the high plains of central and western Kansas, farm policy (and the weather) did not facilitate much diversification in agriculture, and farmers were often forced to produce only one or two crops, year after year.

When I initially ran for Congress, I was astonished by the constant threat of economic catastrophe that small family run farms were facing. Due in large part to low income and the capital costs associated with farming, the number of small farms had decreased dramatically.

For example, a sophisticated tractor could cost as much as $250,000. Small-time farmers need to have state-of-the-art equipment to stay competitive and often require loans to pay for such expensive items, which means they are forced to mortgage their future on the uncertainty of crop production levels and commodity prices.

With these steep financial hills to climb, many individual farms have been bought up by larger, better capitalized farms that can absorb the ups and downs of modern agriculture. Farmers continually struggling to survive looked to Washington, DC, and their local representatives for assistance—and they still do.

I was just beginning to grasp these challenges during my first campaign. I heard from many of my farming constituents about the threat to their family's existence because of crop prices, government overregulation, and an inability to compete with large corporate or individual farms. The next generation saw no future in taking over the family farm, which was the saddest part to me.

There is no question that agriculture policies have favored larger farmers, and family farm size has increased dramatically over the years. For example, a two-hundred-acre wheat farm with some cattle on it might have been profitable in 1950, but the capital costs in agriculture and technological improvements in farm machinery, among other things, have squeezed out smaller farmers. Also, farm policy in previous farm bills has encouraged consolidation in almost all parts of agriculture, from row crops, to fruits and vegetables, to dairy, and to meat and poultry. Larger farmers get bigger government payments, even with payment caps approved by Congress. This consolidation has led to concentration in certain parts of agriculture, especially in meat and poultry, where three or four companies control nearly 80 percent of meat processing.

While at the USDA, I worked to help smaller producers promote organic agriculture. I also promoted farmers markets and direct marketing of farmers' goods from producer to consumer, where smaller farmers could get a bigger share of the economic pie. Even so, the overall food system (and congressional action) still favored larger producers. The bigger you were, the higher the subsidies, mostly due to congressional actions in farm bill after farm bill, which I also participated in and often supported while in Congress, along with most other farm state legislators.

I did work with others inside Congress and at the USDA to cap farm payments to larger farmers. Certainly, politics and campaign contributions played a role here, like they do in most industries. The major food and farm organizations had their political action committees (PACs), whose money went primarily to Agriculture Committee members who tended to support these policies, but I don't ever recall seeing or receiving a contribution from a small farmers' PAC.

Nonetheless, recent problems with the food supply chain, especially evidenced during the COVID-19 crisis, has demonstrated that food supply chains need to be more decentralized and less dependent on larger operations often staffed by low wage and immigrant labor. Much more attention should be focused on the health and economic welfare of workers in meat, poultry, and produce processing facilities.

Ironically, two of the major "hot spots" during the COVID-19 crisis were nursing homes and meat packing plants. Farm policy is complex, and for the most part, decisions have been left to agricultural interests alone.

Napoleon once said, "War is too important to be left to the generals."

Frankly, farm and food policy are too important to be left exclusively to agricultural interests. Everyone eats, and everyone has a stake in insuring economically viable agriculture for our nation's farmers and ranchers. That means safe and affordable food for consumers, and workers being treated fairly. Sounds simple, but it's still a major struggle.

From the late 1970s until the early to mid-1980s, we experienced the worst farm crisis since the Great Depression. This was especially true for grain farmers in the Midwest, the plains states, and large parts of the south. Bankruptcies were declared in epidemic numbers, due to low commodity prices, high interest rates, high debt, and falling land values. The most striking example was the continued loss of family sized farm operations, which had already begun but accelerated during the late 1970s and early 1980s.

I promised my constituents I would do everything I could to help. As I dove into my new role as a legislator and member of the Agriculture Committee, I quickly realized that the committee was the most bipartisan of any on the Hill. That suited me just fine.

I also realized that the committee had jurisdiction of two primary areas: agriculture policy, which mostly includes regulating production, and nutrition, which oversees how what is produced affects the consumer. In a sense, these two issues—production and nutrition—give the committee jurisdiction over decisions that affect every American, whether it's a Kansas farmer producing corn or a city dweller who purchases food. During my era, these issues were ripe for finding compromise across the aisle. My colleagues understood that policy choices that helped only farmers or only consumers would never get enacted. Combining support for these large and politically diverse constituencies was the key to the bipartisan nature of our committee.

My first committee chair was Tom Foley of Washington state, before Foley became Speaker of the House. One could quickly discern his serious approach to the issues, balanced by an even-handed approach based on inclusion and collegiality. Foley and I became close friends, and for my first couple of years on the Agriculture Committee, he took me under his wing. Based on our districts, we found a lot in common, as many of the issues important to his Spokane constituents also mattered a great deal to my Wichita voters.

Foley became majority whip in 1981, which meant he stepped down as chair of the Agriculture Committee. He then served as majority leader and eventually Speaker of the House until 1994, when he lost his seat in an astonishing upset, the first Speaker to lose a reelection bid since 1862.

That was the same year I lost my seat. Having a leader with a large agriculture constituency was extremely helpful to me as I pushed through countless pro-farming bills while serving on the Agriculture Committee. It certainly didn't hurt that Foley and I were close friends and we had shared interests in the issues.

Today the leadership in Congress, especially on the Democratic side, is decidedly urban, with few urban members serving farm or agriculture constituencies. I believe there is a growing recognition among young Democrats in Congress that they can no longer ignore rural issues. In many cases, rural and urban voters share the same interests: competent governance, fiscal responsibility, good health care, and a strong America on the global stage—all common-sense issues.

When Tom Foley left the committee as he rose in the party's leadership structure, Kika de la Garza of Texas became our new chairman. He and I eventually worked well together, but we had a rough start. De la Garza had a reputation for being a bit rough with junior members of the committee, a character trait I had seen in action. Moving from the cordial Tom Foley to the abrasive Kika de la Garza had me worried. I even voiced that concern to one of my colleagues.

"The Ag Committee is really going to suffer from this change in leadership," I said.

Unbeknownst to me, I was overheard, and to my great horror I was quoted in some of the farm trade press the next day.

Knowing that I had to face my new chairman for the first time after having slammed him in print, I was nervous. Initially, all seemed well, and he and I chatted amicably as the other members gathered for a hearing. Just as I thought I had dodged a bullet, he turned to me and pulled the article out of his suit pocket, waved it in front of me, and gave me a dressing down that did not bode well for my future on the committee. I apologized; he seemed to accept it, and we moved on, or so I thought.

Over the next few weeks, de la Garza carried that article around with him and never hesitated to wave it in my face when he felt the occasion called for it. To his credit, he managed to move beyond my initial slight, and we ended up becoming close, particularly when I became chair of the Agriculture Subcommittee on Wheat, Soybeans, and Feed Grain. Succeeding Tom Foley was a tough act to pull off, but Kika de la Garza became a good chairman of the overall committee.

I learned a good lesson from my faux pas: watch what you say in public, as there is no such thing as an off-the-record conversation, and sometimes swallowing a little humble pie doesn't hurt. Thank God there was no Twitter back then. At least this way, de la Garza and I actually communicated with each other instead of through our phones.

The Agriculture Committee is an essential committee with a wide jurisdiction. It isn't necessarily one of the most high profile committees that gets big headlines, like foreign policy, but occasionally it has its moments of high national attention.

One such moment arose during one of the most difficult issues our committee faced while I was serving my second term in office. After the Russians invaded Afghanistan, the United States led an effort by the Western allies to isolate the Soviet Union and punish Leonid Brezhnev for this blatant act of aggression. Conditions for America's farmers were already dire, and many of my constituents were struggling to hold on to their family farms. When President Carter enacted a grain embargo against the Soviet Union, preventing US grain from being exported to Russia, the situation for many Kansan farmers went from bad to near catastrophic.

While the effect on Russia was minimal—they simply increased their grain imports from Ukraine and then later Brazil and Argentina—for America's farmers, the grain embargo was hugely detrimental. First and foremost, the price dropped tremendously, cutting directly into a farmer's ability to make a living. This resulted in grain ports across the country shutting their doors, and even after the embargo was lifted, those facilities never reopened.

Despite President Reagan's restoring of grain exports to the Soviet Union, it was too late. The Russians had discovered—thanks to the embargo—that they could meet their grain demands via other, often cheaper, sources. To avoid the danger of a future embargo, the grain trade between Russia and the United States never recovered. I believe that Jimmy Carter's loss to Reagan was a direct result of the embargo.

As a Georgia peanut farmer, Carter had counted on America's rural communities to deliver him a second term. But once Reagan issued his campaign promise to end the embargo, many farmers flocked to the Republicans and some never returned to the Democratic Party.

As a Democrat representing farmers, the political risk to me was significant given that President Carter made a decision that directly hit the bottom lines of thousands of my constituents. Even though many pundits believed that Carter's actions on the grain embargo were politically risky, they also felt it was a solid effort to confront Soviet oppression.

They all seemed to miss a fundamental fact: while politicians in DC fretted about Russia, people in the heartland needed to eat and make a living. The real issue was the incredible importance of agriculture exports to maintain the strength of the farm economy. At the time, the Carter grain embargo was perceived as a dagger in the heart of that business model.

As a student of American politics, it pained me to see this enormous shift occur. For the most part, since that time until very recently, the national Democratic Party has politically neglected rural America and has paid a price for their negligence. Multiple factors shifted the party in this direction. Carter's grain embargo was an early catalyst in this long-term, transformational political change, turning farmers and many rural Americans in grain-producing areas into lifelong Republicans. The politics of guns and abortion tended to favor the Republicans as well, especially in rural areas.

It has now become popular to focus primarily on turning out your own base and trying to win elections by exciting the most partisan among us. This strategy has been effective at times, for Republicans in particular. But politics should really be an effort to convince as many voters as possible to support you, regardless of where they live or their political affiliation. By simply picking up and leaving rural America, Democrats are actively hurting their ability to win, from county-level seats all the way to the White House. When you factor in partisan tribalism, a candidate in rural America has a steep hill to climb if running as a Democrat.

In today's Congress, few Democrats represent the rural heartland. Although following the 2016 election some thoughtful Democrats are beginning to recognize the problems resulting from being an urban elitist, coastal party, they must deal with other factors as well, especially the perception in rural America that Democratic policies on issues like guns and abortion are too far to the left of center. Whether it's true or not is almost immaterial because in our current climate of social media propaganda, perception *is* reality.

I vehemently opposed the grain embargo, not only on behalf of my constituents but also spurred by my political intuition, and I was not shy about saying so in public. President Carter, though a good man and a great former president, was not an exceptionally good politician when it came to how the sausage is made in Congress. Sometimes, moderates need to take votes that go against the broad views of their party, their president, or popular opinion. But rarely can politicians find a good reason to vote directly against the interests of their own constituents. When local interests align, it's not as hard to go against the grain.

My opposition to my own party on this issue earned me a reputation as an independent who put his people above his party, which reinforced for my farmer constituents that I was my own man, not some party hack. I was joined in my opposition by many members of Congress from both sides of the aisle, all of us from areas where the direct effect of using food as a weapon was most intimately felt. Opposing the grain embargo provided the first time Bob Dole and I worked hand-in-glove on behalf of our Kansas constituents. It was the first time, but certainly not the last.

During the farm crisis of the late 1970s and early 1980s, a small fringe group, generally referred to as "posse comitatus," decided to hijack the farmer's protests for their own anti-government purposes. Many of the participants and activists in the farm protest movement were great and decent people, but unfortunately a few of them subscribed to this group's message of hate. Posse comitatus became the forerunner of today's militia and far-right movement: anti-government, anti-Semitic, and driven by all sorts of conspiracy theories. They made the farmers' protests part of their message. Somehow I, being a vocal supporter of the farmers, found myself associated with some very extreme groups. This was clearly as uncomfortable for them as it was for me. A local television station interviewed one of the militia members and when the journalist pointed out to him that Dan Glickman was a Jew, he paused for a long time, clearly struggling with this astonishing piece of information. Eventually, he replied.

"Yes, but he's not a Zionist!"

All was well in his little world again, but even though they say that politics can make for strange bedfellows, I'd much rather choose my own partners.

The Agriculture Committee was a perfect place for me to develop bipartisan relationships with my own delegation. During those first years on the Agriculture Committee I got to know and appreciate Pat Roberts, who represented Kansas as a Republican senator in Congress for twenty-four years. I first met Pat when he worked for Kansas representative Keith Sebelius, father-in-law of

Kathleen Sebelius, the forty-forth governor of Kansas. Congressman Sebelius was one of the most influential members on the Agriculture Committee, and because of his seniority and importance, I wanted to know and get along with his chief of staff. Senior congressional staff often run for a seat when their boss retires; there have even been a couple of instances where a former staffer has run against a former boss for the seat. That is how Pat Roberts came to represent the First Congressional District of Kansas in 1980, serving in the US House until 1996.

Pat Roberts and I, along with Bob Dole, became known as "the best Ag team in Congress," because even though Roberts and Dole were Republicans, we were allied on the agriculture issues affecting Kansas, especially those impacting wheat and cattle. Much later, both men were extremely helpful with my nomination for secretary of agriculture and Pat Roberts even testified before the Senate on my behalf. He and I have similar senses of humor, and working with him was always a lot of fun. Over the years, Roberts got to know my father and even made a point of coming to Wichita to attend an event in his honor. He roasted my father thoroughly, telling some hilarious—and even wildly inappropriate—jokes.

On another occasion, Roberts elevated my dad to "expert witness" before the Agriculture Committee. This was during the Reagan administration, when the plight of America's farmers had gotten worse, not better. To highlight how Reagan cared more about supporting defense contractors than the agricultural sector (at least in our opinion), Democrats held a "rump hearing," an unofficial gathering of committee members from one party only.

I chaired the event, and we had the actresses Jessica Lange, Jane Fonda, and Sissy Spacek as our witnesses because all three had just played distressed farm wives in major Hollywood productions. My dad happened to be in town, and since this was not an official hearing of the Agriculture Committee, I invited him to sit up on the dais, the section of chairs usually reserved for members of Congress, their staff, and issue experts.

Pat Roberts stopped by, not to show bipartisan support but rather his opinion of the event as a mere stunt. When he saw my dad, he was pleasantly surprised.

"Milton," he said, "I am so glad to see at least one true expert at this hearing today."

I don't think this bought Roberts much goodwill from Jessica, Jane, or Sissy, but my dad sure got a kick out of it.

One highlight of our professional relationship was the annual Dan and Pat show, which he called "The Pat and Dan Show." This was a panel as part of the annual meeting hosted by the Kansas secretary of agriculture and was moderated by Barry Flinchbaugh, Kansas State University Professor of Agricultural Policy. We did this event at least ten times, and each one was as hysterical as it was substantive. It didn't help that Flinchbaugh, a leading national voice on agricultural policy, was also incredibly funny. The three of us spent as much time cracking each other up as we did delivering thoughtful analysis.

Barry Flinchbaugh made fun of our receding hairlines. Pat Roberts made fun of Barry's and my expanding waistlines, and I teased Pat about some of the more questionable Republican policies he and his conservative colleagues were espousing.

Back then, one could still do that: have a sense of humor while disagreeing.

Not only was it funny, we benefited politically from these meetings and jokes. The gatherings received significant publicity in Kansas, in the farm press, too, and it was humorous and bipartisan in nature. Several hundred farmers from across the state attended, and the event allowed me to continuously reestablish my credibility on agriculture issues. It also showcased a Republican and a Democrat working together. Incidentally, the state secretary of agriculture during that time was Sam Brownback, who became a Kansas senator and then governor.

Does this type of bipartisan collegiality and willingness to work together still exist today? Of course, it does, but you don't hear about it often. A group of bipartisan lawmakers yucking it up about how much they agree on farm policies is not going to be covered by partisan media. But back then, we had media coverage for every one of those panels, plus press coverage when we came together to announce policy on behalf of our farming constituents.

Dare I say politics was fun for all the right reasons?

If such an event was covered now, one side would probably claim it to be outrageous that their representative would spend time with someone from the other party let alone have a good time with them and those in attendance.

"How could you be on stage with that inhuman monster?!"

I can just picture how the headline might read in a partisan publication.

The problem with today's politics is not the type of public servants we have—at least not for the most part—but rather the environment we have created for them and the incentive structure that motivates their actions. This includes constant fundraising, absurdly drawn gerrymandered districts where primaries supersede general elections in importance, the growth of partisan media, and the breakdown in the congressional legislative process. Each of these hampers our elected officials from operating as a high-performance team, or even just a regular performance team behaving like sane people.

Where have all the mensches gone?

Perhaps that should be a headline in one of today's national newspapers.

Mensch is a Yiddish word, by the way, referring to someone of integrity and honor, a human being we can admire and emulate because of one's noble character.

There's another Yiddish phrase that applies here, too: Oy vey!

Members of Congress don't create this atmosphere entirely on their own. Congressional staff make Congress function. I cannot overstate the crucial role that these people play in the success or failure of a member of Congress. While they work behind the scenes and are rarely interviewed or profiled for the public, they form the daily heartbeat of Congress.

Some outstanding professionals worked for me throughout my career, and much of what I accomplished is due in large part to their unwavering commitment to me and my agenda. They are terribly underpaid, I should add, because congressional staffers make a financial sacrifice by choosing public service over the private sector.

In addition to not becoming millionaires, as are quite a few holding office, my staff had to put up with many habits of mine that did not make it into the original job description. For example, any staffer driving me to an event had better be versed in Broadway musicals because much of the trip involved belting out show tunes, the Battle Hymn of the Republic, and the occasional Beatles hit, although we never knew all the lyrics to any one Beatles song.

All joking aside, or at least some joking aside, Myrne Roe, my chief of staff for most of my congressional career, was absolutely critical to my congressional success. She was smart, professional, and always ready to tell me if I was full of shit. But who's counting?

Thanks in part to my staff's outstanding work, I eventually achieved seniority and stature within the Agriculture Committee, leading to my subcommittee chair. All of this helped elevate my role within the Democratic caucus, and as a Democrat representing a conservative district, my party leadership felt I was a good example of the broad appeal of our party to voters. As time went on, I felt I could take on a greater variety of issues, some of which did not sit well with many of my colleagues. But these were decisions I felt I had to make to preserve my independence as a lawmaker. I also felt they were the right thing to do. At the end of the day, that is often enough.

For example, about six months before George H. W. Bush formed a coalition to expel Iraq from Kuwait, I was feeling more and more disturbed by Saddam Hussein's dismal human rights record. Few Americans knew that Iraq and Hussein were receiving export financing subsidies from the US Department of Agriculture to purchase American grain. In essence, US taxpayers were being asked to open their wallets on behalf of a vicious crook without any scruples.

I introduced an amendment to the Food, Agriculture, Conservation, and Trade Act of 1990 (also known as the 1990 farm bill) to stop the USDA from extending export financing subsidies to Hussein and his henchmen in Iraq. Although my amendment attracted considerable support from members of Congress focused on foreign relations issues, the agricultural lobby came out against it in droves. Most of them opposed me because I was shutting down a source of revenue.

We initially passed the amendment in the House, but the vote was reversed in a parliamentary maneuver the next day. Farm and agriculture lobbying pressure prevailed, which goes to show that if you plan to make stands on what you believe and not just follow what the party dogma dictates, you better be prepared to lose some fights.

In the final analysis, my intuition prevailed. Saddam Hussein invaded Kuwait in 1991, in part encouraged by American agriculture assistance, which I had tried to stop. When Congress overturned its earlier decision to continue farm aid to Saddam, I felt a strong signal had been sent to him and his cohorts that domestic politics would prevent the United States from confronting him, and encourage aggressive behavior toward Kuwait and other neighbors; I still believe to this day I was right. The vote to keep farm assistance going to Iraq was not a good signal, either.

I also became more and more focused on consumer and environmental protection issues. My work on the Agriculture Committee enhanced my understanding of how agriculture as a product and nutrition as a commitment could not only coexist but enhance one another. During that time, the first supermarket chains incorporated organic products, and food labeling became much more informative and helpful to the consumer. We also started paying real attention to hidden calories in products, such as soft drinks and juices.

Up until then, the Agriculture Committee and its members were not known as champions of consumer protection, and I was often the lone voice of reason on the subject because those issues captivated me. Later, as secretary of agriculture and beyond, food safety issues and the quality of our food, as well as combating food waste, became causes close to my heart.

For example, I was an early supporter of organic agriculture, as well as farmers markets and locally grown foods. This has helped to augment and diversify farm income, especially for smaller-scale farmers, and was welcomed by the consumer. While I was at the USDA, the Organic Standard Act was implemented, helping to facilitate a multi-billion-dollar industry; farmers markets, with help from the USDA, became ubiquitous throughout the country, and they are continuing to grow, especially in urban areas, where they are needed most.

While serving on the Agriculture Committee, I came to define conservation within an agriculture and farming context, reaching the conclusion that America's farmers had a hugely beneficial role to play in protecting our planet's natural resources. My goal was to help my district and my farming constituents, but I did so while also placing a burden on them to conserve our natural resources. Farm conservation plans became my vehicle for marrying farming policy with environmental protection safeguards.

My commitment to environmental protection would soon be tested when the Agriculture Committee considered what eventually became the Tongass Timber Reform Act. The US Forest Service was actually the largest part of the USDA in terms of employees, with nearly forty thousand of the agency's one hundred thousand workers. By then, I had become an ally of conservation groups, and we worked hard together to pass this legislation, which regulated and curtailed timber cutting in Alaska's Tongass National Park.

The law's purpose was to cancel annual subsidies for the timber harvest, greatly expand off-limits areas to loggers, and incorporate an environmental review into all future logging permits. Although I was not the lead sponsor on the bill, I worked on it incredibly hard as a cosponsor. Kansas barely has any trees, so I find it ironic how much time I spent thinking about them in Congress and as secretary of agriculture.

Most people outside of government may not know that the US Forest Service had the most employees of any part of USDA. Even as a Kansas congressman, coming from a state not known for its abundance of trees, this was a fact I was barely familiar with, but when it came to creating consensus, it was good to know.

Once again, I found few allies on the committee level. However, the bill passed the House with broad support. Unfortunately, it died once it reached the Senate, at the hands of both Republican senators from Alaska: Ted Stevens and Frank Murkowski.

In the process of working on this legislation, I made two powerful enemies. As I would discover a few years later, when the Senate considered my nomination to be the secretary of agriculture, these two had long memories. Fast-forward a few years when former member of Congress, Dan Glickman, is before the Senate to be confirmed as the next secretary of agriculture. In the history of the republic, only the Senate Agriculture Committee had then held confirmation hearings for this post. However, Senator Frank Murkowski, chair of the Energy and Natural Resources Committee, worked with his colleague, Ted Stevens, insisting that I be questioned by his committee as well, making me the only nominee to that cabinet position who had to pass muster with two separate committees.

"Revenge is a dish best served cold" may have been the wishful motto of Stevens and Murkowski, but I ended up being unanimously confirmed, including their two votes.

I have to admit that when I first came to Congress, the Agriculture Committee didn't sound like a ticket to fame and fortune. In fact, I've never seen any of its members on the cover of *People* magazine's Sexiest Man of the Year covers. Just the thought of that makes me laugh.

As it turned out, my experience on that committee was the high point of my years as a legislator and laid the foundation for my future positions as US secretary of agriculture and CEO of the Motion Picture Association of America. Serving on the Agriculture Committee also empowered me to deliver for my congressional district and my constituents like no other committee assignment could have ever done.

Every successful career, especially in politics, builds on the foundation of previous career steps, and mine was no exception. The trick is to maintain your credibility and professionalism in each of those steps and not burn bridges in the process—all while maintaining your own moral code of ethics.

My personal life was also shaped tremendously as a result of this experience. Some of my best friends, like Tom Foley and Pat Roberts, were members I served with on the committee. Many of my most significant bipartisan accomplishments were made possible because we were united in our fight on behalf of America's farmers.

The most important understanding I gained from my work on agriculture issues was the importance of building coalitions of voters if one wants to pass substantial bills through partisan blockades. The key Agriculture Committee coalition was the connection between rural and urban interests. One community needs the other in agriculture policy, and this principle has guided all of my work during and after Congress. The coalition between farming program interests and nutrition interests (for example, feeding programs and food stamps) is still alive, though frayed by the expansion of extreme partisan views in both groups. So far, this rural/urban coalition has kept these programs going, and we can only pray it continues.

This coexistence has also kept our domestic feeding programs alive, most prominently the Supplemental Nutrition Assistance Program (SNAP), which most people think of as food stamps. SNAP, often implemented specifically for poor kids by providing them breakfast and lunch at schools, has been relentlessly attacked by some conservatives as yet another government handout, originally affiliated with inner-city kids rather than rural populations. It seems to be under attack again by many conservative Republicans in Congress. Currently, more rural areas utilize the program, as poverty in those parts of our country has grown. It is not just the urban regions where nutrition programs are essential—not at all. Up until now, our rural/urban coalition of committed members of Congress has ensured that essential programs like SNAP continue to be offered to those in need. Once again, we can only hope and pray that these legislators will persevere and do the right thing.

In today's world of high and rapidly increasing unemployment, SNAP provides an effective safety net for millions of American families who would be in breadlines without it. The program has turned out to be one of the most important social programs in American history. Notwithstanding the good work of the country's food banks, the overwhelming majority of Americans who need food assistance, particularly during times of high unemployment, receive that assistance through SNAP, which enables them to go into grocery stores and use an electronic benefit card to buy food, thereby retaining the dignity of purchasing those necessities, with some restrictions, in a similar fashion to more affluent Americans.

On a larger level, this kind of bipartisan work represents precisely the type of American leadership that is lacking in contemporary politics. Forming coalitions with varied interests and pushing through significant legislation as a unified group seems to be a forgotten art. This kind of thing doesn't happen through dumb luck; it is hard work, which is seemingly beyond or not interesting enough to many of today's lawmakers.

It took years of arduous work by my fellow members of Congress, such as Bob Dole and George McGovern in the Senate, and folks like Tom Foley, Pat Roberts, and myself in the House, to build and defend this rural/urban coalition, and I am proud of the work we did.

When farms thrive, folks in the cities can thrive as well.

When urban interests support agricultural issues, our farmers are empowered. Like everything in life, we are made stronger by working together, and the members of the House Committee on Agriculture lived and breathed that truth every day.

Although my work on agriculture certainly was the driving force behind most of my legislative work, life as a current member of Congress is shaped by much more than a sole committee assignment. I was incredibly fortunate to work with many terrific members from both sides of the aisle, on a myriad of issues that were important to my district, my state, and the country. All of my accomplishments resulted directly from building close working relationships with my colleagues, an aspect of the job unfortunately lost on many current members today.

Perhaps if they looked up the word mensch, things might be better.

Chapter 9

Building Bridges, Breaking Barriers, and Finding Laughs in the House of Reps

Serving in the US House of Representatives is a completely misunderstood vocation. Most Americans and many of the folks who actually serve in Congress don't know how it really works. Hard to believe? If you look closer, I don't think so. Let me explain.

You have 434 colleagues. Each one is assigned specific issues on which to become subject matter experts, apropos to the committee on which they serve. Each member of Congress is also responsible for overseeing a team of professional office staff. Voters give their elected officials periodic job reviews, with the result of positive reviews known as reelection. One moves up within the organization based on things like talent, likability, seniority, skill sets, and knowledge of pertinent issues.

If you haven't realized it by now, as one of these members of Congress, you have a unique opportunity to steer our country in a productive direction. However, you can only do so by working *collaboratively* with as many of the other 434 members as possible as well as with members of the US Senate. Individual members, with few exceptions, aren't particularly powerful on their own. It is only through collective action that Congress can make real change. But when acting together, this chamber is the most powerful part of the American government. What is currently misunderstood is that being successful in Congress requires building relationships and getting along with people, including those with whom you disagree. I should probably repeat that, but in an effort to save paper, let's hope I made that clear the first time.

It's pretty simple, really. Destructive lone wolves rarely succeed in any line of work, but never in a legislative body. From former senator Joe McCarthy to *former* congressman Steve King, we learn again and again that collaboration and mutual respect are key to success. The best people, (according to me) like Ted Kennedy or Bob Dole, had great legislative success by collaborating with the other side.

Unfortunately, we don't have 435 Mister Rogers in Washington, DC, right now, but maybe my example can be enlightening. My strategy was to connect with people by making jokes and always being in good humor. I am a serious person and have a profound interest in substantive policy issues. But I don't have to be boring. I like to make a joke, and over the course of my life, I have found that being myself was not only the right thing to do but a great strategy for getting things done.

There are not many funny people in politics today, at least not intentionally. I even yearn for a few smiles every once in a while. By and large, the tone is caustic. Natural humor, while it still may exist, is too often drowned out by the fear that saying something funny may be politically incorrect and get you into trouble.

In Congress, I was famous, or rather infamous by some people's standards, for my uncontrollable urge to sing. I was no Frank Sinatra but singing not only put me in a good mood it also gave those around me a reason to smile (or, better yet, sing along). It also broke the ice when necessary. During one midyear Democratic Party policy retreat at the Rayburn House Office Building on Capitol Hill, it somehow leaked that I was going to do a small performance of my greatest hits after that day's strategy session. Unbeknownst to me, my colleague Barney Frank organized a walkout. As soon as I hit my first note, the entire Democratic caucus got up and exited the meeting hall. That didn't stop me, though. I kept on singing to an audience of one at the end of an exhausting day of policy discussion; everyone had a good laugh.

I don't think all politicians need to be Rodney Dangerfield or any other prototype of a stand-up comedian. But it does take a pretty secure person to not be afraid to use humor, especially the self-deprecating type, when it comes to discussing policy issues and talking to the public. But the folks there could undoubtedly lighten up. I used humor as a means of puncturing pomposity, defusing tense situations, attracting allies, and even getting people to focus on serious policy issues. Humor, especially when self-deprecating, is another essential key to disarming colleagues and getting your work done.

This worked just as well for me in Congress as it did later as a cabinet member. As secretary of agriculture, I started many meetings or speeches with the simple observation that Bill Clinton certainly had a sense of irony, appointing a Jew to be America's chief spokesperson for the pork industry. There was no worry of him fueling anti-Semitism because a good joke is a great icebreaker, especially a self-deprecating joke.

I guess if you followed me around from speech to speech you would find that joke a bit tiresome, but starting conversations with a little humor always sets a good tone. Besides, most stand-up comedians use the same opener for many shows to make sure they lock in right away with their audiences. Why should a politician be any different?

Besides trying to be funny, I spent a lot of time in Congress thinking about how I could forge coalitions on behalf of what I felt was important legislation. Every single one of us, in the House or Senate, is empowered to drive ideas forward. But to do so, we must build coalitions of support, work with committees and leadership, whip the vote, and essentially convince, cajole, and compromise to get what we want. It's a long and arduous process, often resulting in failure. But this is how the system was designed, and it's the only way it works.

What our founding fathers envisioned has broken down because opportunities for lawmakers to try to build policy expertise and coalitions for legislation have been severely constrained. When I was in Congress, we could insert amendments into bills that funded specific government agencies, requiring them to steer that funding toward issues or projects important to the member or the member's district. This usually happened at the committee level, and nearly all the big committees worked on major legislation at least once during each two-year Congress (and often much more frequently). Committee chairs had enormous influence within Congress to set the legislative calendar for the year. This practice, often known as "earmarking," is now prohibited by House and Senate rules. We got bad publicity for several high-profile earmarks, like the "bridge to nowhere" in Alaska. In many cases, earmarks were a useful way of ensuring bipartisan support for major legislation by encouraging individual members to support bills by bargaining and compromising.

Lookout! There's that bad word again—compromise!

Since the 1990s, when the Speaker's office absorbed so much of the conventional power to set the legislative calendar, members have had little incentive or sufficient experience to hammer out legislation that can pass both chambers by engaging in the committee process.

Imagine you're a committee chairman who spends countless hours working with staff, holding hearings and markups, from subcommittee to full committee, before presenting a piece of legislation that *one* individual party official decides he or she doesn't like. One person! Nope. I have the power and I say no. What's the point of sticking your neck out and compromising with the loyal opposition in order to get a bill through your committee, only to hit a dead end?

At one point, you could rely on the Appropriations Committee to move bills even if things got bogged down in the authorizing committees. But that process has now been weakened, so members of Congress aren't writing authorizing bills and they aren't taking a hard look at how and why the government spends money. As a result, Congress doesn't usually pass budgets on time and they don't use normal processes.

When it comes to congressional oversight of the executive branch on domestic and global issues, this is a fundamental responsibility of those 435 individuals and a key pillar of our constitutional system of three branches of government and through the separation of powers between the executive, congressional, and judicial branches.

When Republicans refused to oversee or review questionable behavior by the Trump administration, they were forgoing their responsibilities to voters and the republic. In fact, it's the exact opposite of patriotism. The battles between Trump and Congress are an example of a historical trend toward centralizing executive power, which means what's needed now is more congressional oversight, not less.

It didn't use to be this way, and it doesn't have to be now. When members of Congress are given a chance to develop subject matter expertise, and committees have an option to move legislation through to the floor for a full vote, every single member of Congress is empowered to do their actual job. Fortunately, our new president, Joe Biden, has decades of experience in Congress, and also understands the legislative process and the need to compromise.

My legislative portfolio was an eclectic mix of issues, such as the Tongass Timber Reform Act and SNAP, and the US Institute of Peace, which I discuss later in this chapter. They first caught my attention because I knew that I could offer bills or amendments that had a chance to be reviewed, debated, and eventually voted on. The system that prevailed for most of my career in Congress is known as "regular order." Doesn't that sound reassuring? It gave individual members and, in particular, committee chairs significant incentive and power to write serious bills and work them hard. Today's system, where leadership determines almost every bill or amendment "allowed" to be considered, has reduced rank-and-file members to simply being a yes or no vote. What you end up with is a lot of legislation that represents the dogmatic political views of a particular party or a subsection of a party. The opposition opposes it; the bill passes on a strictly party-line vote, and frequently, the Senate never even brings it up for debate. Everyone gets to say they were for or against the perfect (or perfectly awful) bill, use it to raise money, and keep their voters animated by negative partisanship.

But nothing serious gets done. If people behaved like this in the business world, they would be fired or demoted to an inconsequential position. How can we create a similar process in Congress that doesn't depend on an election every two years?

It's frustrating to watch a place that worked quite well when I was there now going totally off the rails. Many members of Congress have no experience with how the system is supposed to work. Media coverage portrays "regular order" as if it's a unicorn or a dinosaur. Their portrayal makes it mythical, implying that theoretically, it existed "once upon a time," but it's mostly the stuff of legend, and very few members of Congress remain who have any memory of that ancient process. No matter which side of the aisle you're on, this is shameful.

Our world today is populated by leaders who, for several reasons, think too small. They may be too fearful of the messy legislative process and the challenge of explaining complex policy choices to constituents and donors. They have no patience for incremental progress, which is often the way democracy acts. Don't they realize that we can never set a real agenda for anything, or lead boldly, if we don't recognize the power of big ideas?

Here's what it boils down to: many of our political leaders are afraid of losing (what else is new?), but they also believe that taking any bold action to address major problems will result in just that, losing. They would rather hold onto their seats and do nothing more than swing for the fences and risk staying home.

But as the saying goes, "No Guts, No Glory!"

The safest thing to do in politics is often nothing. In that way, you offend no one. But choosing that means democracy makes little progress in solving America's problems—and we have plenty. The problems we face today—social, political, and economic—are enormous, and the consequences of a failure to act are too large. Could we have defeated fascism, cured deadly diseases, given minorities access to the American dream, or brought down the Berlin Wall with small ideas and an aversion to risk?

Congress was envisioned by the Founding Fathers to be a melting pot of ideas, a way that the concerns we faced as a nation could be debated by our representatives, who came from different areas of the country with contrasting experiences and a variety of challenges. Our legislative process was based on the notion that each representative and senator could bring big ideas to the table but that no single person had all the answers.

Compromise!

The Constitution states that Congress is the Article 1 institution. The executive is next in Article 2. I still believe that the Founding Fathers felt that the national legislature, that is, Congress, should be the most important branch of government. But in recent years, Congress has abdicated power to the executive in many troubling ways. Especially in foreign policy, deference to presidential decisions has created an antidemocratic system. Of course, no member of Congress wants to take votes on risky political decisions in foreign affairs, one of the more difficult and less rewarding issue areas. But placing so much power in the hands of one person is dangerous. For example, Congress has not voted to update the authorization of the use of military force in nearly two decades.

In my almost two decades of service as a representative, I had the opportunity to work on many different issues, pursue a myriad of good—and sometimes bad—ideas, deliver for my Kansan constituents, and push forward big solutions to big problems. I had an extremely satisfying congressional experience and absolutely felt empowered to go down the occasional rabbit hole when something struck a chord with me.

For example, the US Institute of Peace (USIP) grew out of constituent interest from the Mennonite community in my congressional district. Their pro-peace advocacy struck me as a much-needed balance to our outstanding and important military academies. Why shouldn't we have an entity devoted entirely to pursuing peaceful conflict resolution? For years I backed the creation of a US peace academy. This idea, coupled with input from my Mennonite constituents, morphed into an institute created to provide intellectual and academic leadership for global nonviolent crisis solutions.

Getting the USIP off the ground took several years. I worked with several representatives and senators: Dante Fascell of Florida, Sam Nunn of Georgia, Jennings Randolph of West Virginia, Mark Hatfield of Oregon, and Spark Matsunaga of Hawaii. We thought big, worked hard, found the votes, and appropriated the money with the help of Senator Ted Stevens. In Congress, there was mild interest in getting this passed. It took the effort of our group, especially Senator Nunn, during a late-night conference negotiation, to get the USIP inserted into the Defense Authorization Bill of 1987. Thanks to my insistence, as well as our coalition allies in the Senate, we were able to get it done. How ironic was it that an institute dedicated to the study of peace ended up in a military spending and defense bill?

USIP, and similar institutions, train and otherwise facilitate diplomats, business, and academic people, along with the nongovernment world, the skills they need to facilitate nonviolent resolutions to bilateral and global conflicts. For example, USIP was helpful in transitioning South Africa away from an apartheid world in the post-Mandela era.

Today, it works by helping leaders resolve conflicts in the Middle East, Afghanistan, and many other hot spots. I always thought how amazing it was that there was an institution in the United States specifically devoted to peace building and that I had a seminal role in creating it.

The USIP has its headquarters on Constitution Avenue along the National Mall and provides analysis and leadership to find peaceful solutions to conflicts around the globe. It serves as a permanent monument to this country's commitment that peaceful solutions are our first and foremost answer to violence around the world. Every time I drive by that building, I feel tremendous satisfaction and hope.

My congressional service also included being a member and then chair of the House Permanent Select Committee on Intelligence, where I worked to increase public access to US intelligence information. One prominent instance of intelligence issues getting national attention during my chairmanship was the Aldrich Ames spy scandal. We probed Ames's role in leaking classified information to the Soviets and looked at the failures of the Central Intelligence Agency and intelligence community to address and prevent these threats.

I was also considered one of the leading congressional experts on general aviation policy, a proficiency I acquired via the large presence of the aviation industry in my district. I was an early leader in efforts to develop alternative fuels as a member of the House Science and Technology Committee, and in a total non sequitur, I was appointed by President George H. W. Bush to serve as part of the election monitoring team for the Panamanian election that ended up ousting General Noriega.

Congress gave me the opportunity to work on a wide range of issues that were important to me for three reasons: (1) my district and the corporations that employed my constituents, (2) work I had done before coming to Congress, and (3) issues that sparked my curiosity and interest.

I became known as "One-A-Day-Glickman," because, on average, I introduced an amendment once a day. If I had not introduced something by the end of the day, my colleagues would ask, "Dan, are you okay?" The danger of making fun of myself and prolifically introducing amendments was that my colleagues, as well as voters, might not take me seriously or might think of me as a jokester who was legislatively all over the place. I addressed that misconception by working hard, being as knowledgeable as possible on the issues I was addressing, being a tough questioner during hearings—particularly when a witness was clearly stonewalling us—and chairing my committees and subcommittees in a thoughtful and inclusive manner. My colleagues knew they could always get along with me, and they also knew I was an analytical and perceptive politician seeking solutions to problems big and small.

Sounds so reasonable, right?

With agriculture as one of my main legislative pillars, aviation became the other. The aviation industry was one of the largest employers in my district, with companies such as Cessna, Beech, and Learjet building private, corporate, and military aircraft in the Wichita area. McConnell Air Force Base was also in my district. Because of this, Boeing's Wichita division was largely military focused and at one point employed as many as fifty thousand of my constituents. Major parts of all Boeing commercial airplanes, including the Boeing 737 and Air Force One, were assembled by the Boeing plants and its workers in Wichita. The KC-135 tanker modification program was led by Boeing Wichita, and we had a major Air Force base located adjacent to the large Boeing facility.

Aviation was a big deal to my constituents, and as their representative I needed to thoroughly understand their issues. I became actively involved in working on these programs, brought key members of the House of Representatives to Wichita to visit the plant as well as McConnell Air Force Base, and secured continued federal appropriations for the base and the commercial/private aviation sector.

When a tornado tore through the base, it almost destroyed several B-1 bombers, and the damage amounted to tens of millions of dollars. Relationships I had built with my fellow members of Congress—from both sides of the aisle—along with my contacts on the authorizing and appropriations committees, were vital in securing funds to fix and improve the base. They were receptive to my plea for help, allowing Wichita to get the appropriations in a timely manner. Plus, they knew I would be there to help them in the future.

Relationships matter!

In August of 1978, an explosion rocked McConnell Air Force Base. Propellants of a Titan II missile, the most dangerous and toxic part of the system, were spilled due to a ruptured fuel line, and the resulting accident claimed the life of a maintenance worker and injured many others. Several hundred of my constituents were evacuated for fear that dangerous, maybe even radioactive materials were released into the air, and toxic fumes were making their way to the civilian population. Several hours after the accident, the air quality was deemed safe, and civilians returned to their homes. Regardless, I was concerned about whether there was an inherent safety risk located in the heart of my district so I asked to meet with the base commander as I was waiting for my flight back to Washington.

He was eager to answer my questions about the safety of the base and my constituents. To put my mind at ease, he drew a map of the base on a cocktail napkin, marking the exact location of the missiles and warheads on the napkin, which illustrated how far from residential housing the missiles were located. Satisfied with his explanation, I got on my plane. By the time I landed in DC, my office staff had been bombarded by panicked phone calls from the base

"Did Congressman Glickman take the napkin? Where is the napkin? Please tell us the Congressman has the napkin!"

I did not have the napkin, but I never heard another word about it or that any of our Titan II missiles had been stolen by Russians or terrorists. I'm guessing either someone came up with the napkin in question, or the waitress simply threw it away. That was not one of my best moments, but thankfully it worked out. I hope the commander kept his job but learned his lesson.

Use napkins to wipe your mouth, not for state secrets.

Ultimately, my work and expertise on all things related to aviation led to my appointment as chair of the Science Subcommittee on Transportation, Aviation, and Materials. Though most of our work was focused on research and development, as well as NASA and materials we needed to advance our space program, chairing the subcommittee gave me a permanent legislative link back to Wichita and the aviation industry.

My work on the Science Committee also coincided with the meltdown of a nuclear reactor in Pennsylvania—the Three Mile Island accident on March 28, 1979. It began with failures in the nonnuclear secondary system and started a chain of terrible events, each of which could have been prevented with proper safety inspections and procedures, oversight, and regulation. It was a disaster that simply called out for federal intervention to prevent similar incidents in the future.

I became determined that Congress should begin examining how the nuclear industry operates to protect the public while continuing to rely on nuclear technology. In partnership with Congressman Norm Dicks of Washington state, we promulgated new legislation, including the need for full-time inspectors at nuclear power plants and better congressional oversight. We also sought to increase consumer confidence that someone was watching over our nuclear-powered weapons and power-generating facilities.

It was always essential to have fellow members of Congress onboard when pushing through important legislation, working on amendments, or securing funding for an impactful project. Without agreeable colleagues willing to think big and who were not afraid to put their ideas above their party, success would have been impossible.

Working on the Three Mile Island accident with Norm Dicks is one of countless examples of collaboration in Congress. Jim Leach from Iowa and I partnering on campaign finance reform legislation is another. My successful work on behalf of Kansan farmers would have been impossible without Pat Roberts. Bob Dole, former senator Birch Bayh, and I led the charge for the National Alcohol Fuels Commission, which is not a throwback to my fraternity days at Michigan but rather a committee charged with studying the use of alcohol as an alternative fuel source.

I worked with colleagues from both sides of the aisle, mostly members with whom I was first sworn in, back in January of 1977, as well as Agriculture Committee members and the Kansas delegation. Part of the collegiality we enjoyed came from laughing at ourselves, being team players, and being unafraid of failure. Even today, some of my best friends are members from both parties with whom I served more than twenty years ago.

I vividly remember working with Barney Frank as part of the Judiciary Subcommittee on Administrative Law. By the way, I forgave him for staging the Democratic walkout during my beautiful singing.

We held hearings on reparations for Americans of Japanese descent who had been interned during World War II. I actually facilitated and chaired the initial hearings and listened to very moving personal hearings of fellow members Norm Mineta and Bob Matsui, who testified about their personal experiences as children in those internment camps. It was an emotional experience, especially knowing that although approximately sixty thousand Americans who had been locked up were still alive, their numbers were decreasing quickly.

Senator Alan Simpson of Wyoming was particularly supportive of our efforts, and we pushed through legislation to compensate, in a small way, the families our government had hurt so badly. Opposition to the bill was raised by some members because of a fear that we were setting a precedent for African Americans and other groups to point to the legislation as leverage to demand reparations for slavery, but it ultimately passed in a bipartisan manner and was signed into law in the following congressional term under the leadership of Congressman Barney Frank. The legislation provided $20,000 per person for about sixty thousand survivors of the experience.

The legislation was an enormous moral achievement and an acknowledgment that our great country could indeed acknowledge this terrible mistake. It also showed how Congress can be a moral voice on behalf of the American people.

Looking back, I have wondered whether our country's treatment of other minorities deserved a similar response, something I indirectly faced while secretary of agriculture in dealing with discrimination complaints brought by Black farmers.

Had you asked my children in the mid-1980s what their father's most important legislative achievement was, they would have answered "the Pizza Hut Bill." Hopefully, their answer has now changed. Back then, I led the effort to change a USDA rule, which effectively prevented fresh pizza, especially with meat toppings, from being served in the national school lunch program. Under the law at the time, pepperoni and hamburger pizza had to be inspected by a USDA inspector at each school where it was served to make sure it met government regulations. This ridiculous rule had two negative effects: students who wanted fresh pizza left school grounds to drive down to the local pizza joint or Pizza Hut; and frozen pizza replaced fresh pizza since the USDA inspection at the frozen food plant was considered sufficient. In fact, frozen pizzas purchased at a grocery store were exempt from this requirement. In many cases, students leaving school to get pizza did not return to class after lunch, so offering fresh pizza in the school lunch program was actually helping keep kids in school all day.

It might be helpful to point out that Pizza Hut was headquartered in my district at the time. Yours truly got the rule changed to permit fresh pizza from the local Pizza Hut to be brought into school cafeterias *without* USDA inspection at every school serving it.

Once in a while, common sense prevails. This is a perfect example of how members of Congress can make big impacts with seemingly small changes to a law. This little twist translated into hundreds of millions of dollars of additional revenue for a local company and kept high school kids from leaving school during lunch. Most important, for the first time in my congressional history, a legislative accomplishment demonstrated to my children how important their father was, though I am not sure I won any prizes from those working on the obesity front.

I have always felt that you don't have to spend taxpayer money to do something in Congress and I am sure many of my Republican colleagues agreed. I often looked for ways to reduce federal spending on things I believed were wasteful. That mindset did not endear me to everyone. For example, Congressman David Obey, a senior member from Wisconsin and one of the great legislators during my congressional service, once called me a "chicken shit" for introducing an amendment to eliminate elevator operators in automatic elevators in the House of Representatives. At least he used an agricultural reference. These operators were fine people, and my goal was to find better employment for each of them within the building, but I could not wrap my mind around the notion that American taxpayers should foot the bill for someone to push a button in an elevator that I could easily push myself.

This is the kind of common-sense approach to problem solving that makes for good moderate politicians. You have to pair a desire to get bills passed with an understanding that you are there to serve people who are struggling to pay bills, stay in their homes, and build wealth for their family's future.

One day, Scott Fleming, a member of my staff, stumbled across a $50,000 annual earmark for the Franklin Delano Roosevelt (FDR) Memorial Commission. Officially, the earmark was meant to study the feasibility, design, and location of a memorial to President Roosevelt. In practice, however, the entire $50,000 went to pay the salary of one woman, presumably for her to study the feasibility, design, and location of said memorial. She had a wonderful, taxpayer-subsidized office on Capitol Hill, and after God knows how long she had been drawing a salary, she had yet to present any findings that would answer the feasibility/design/location conundrum. It made no sense. I figured this was an easy win for America's taxpayers and inserted language into the Interior Appropriations bill to strike the FDR Memorial Commission earmark. We even had the support of Congressman Doug Walgren to eliminate the Commission, and Walgren's chief of staff was Jon Delano—the same Delano family as in Franklin Delano Roosevelt.

While a vote on my amendment was underway in the House Chamber and televised on C-Span, the electronic voting system failed, which almost never happens. Now the amendment required a teller vote, and suddenly what would have been a little-noticed procedural vote, with members leisurely stopping by the chamber and pushing a button, became a big show of representative democracy at work. Each member was called by name and asked whether they were in favor or opposed to shutting down the FDR Memorial Commission. I happened to be in my office as this was unfolding on television. I often took calls from constituents, and I ended up getting an earful from a lady back home.

"Congressman, you need to vote no and stop this horrible amendment! What sort of fool doesn't want a memorial for one of our greatest presidents?"

Clearly, she didn't know that her own congressman was the fool in question.

"Yes, Ma'am, you are absolutely correct, and I'm so glad you called me!"

Thankfully the amendment lost and FDR eventually received one of the biggest memorials in Washington. I guess he must have intervened from his perch in the heavens.

I continued my crusade to winnow down expensive and wasteful government spending. It was good politics, and protecting taxpayers from feeling like they are being exploited is always the right thing to do. Sometimes, I was a nuisance. David Obey made sure everyone knew that, and I was crushed by his comment at the time. That night, I told Rhoda that my career was ruined. But my constituents loved what I was doing and Obey and I became close friends.

When I worked to eliminate elevator operators in automatic elevators, which dated back several decades, I took that on with a successful amendment on the House floor. Similar amendments eliminated daily printing of the menus in the congressional dining room, even though the menu never changes, and eliminating annual bound volumes of the congressional record being distributed to every member of Congress. Several more senior members took umbrage at this young Turk's escapades, but at home I was viewed as a hero who was saving taxpayers money and exposing the folly of bloated congressional spending.

Besides our staff, our families are integral to any success we might have as elected officials. Being a public servant is a family undertaking, and the spouse is as engaged as the elected member of Congress. As I was developing relationships with my fellow members on Capitol Hill, Rhoda played her own leading role.

The Congressional Arts Caucus was founded by Fred Richmond of New York, the same Brooklyn representative who served with me on the Agriculture Committee. He wanted to educate members on the importance of art in our country, particularly because arts programs in many schools often struggle for funding. Soon after the caucus was created, there was enough interest and (just barely) enough funding to hire an executive director and Rhoda found her calling.

Under her fourteen-year leadership, the caucus became one of the biggest, if not the biggest, caucus on Capitol Hill, with a bipartisan group of more than one hundred members participating in its activities. Ultimately, a majority of Congress members participated. If you have ever had the chance to visit the Capitol, you surely will have noticed hundreds of original pieces of art proudly displayed in the tunnel connecting one of the House office buildings with the Capitol Building. Those works of art are winners of high school art competitions held in every congressional district, thanks to the initiative of the Arts Caucus.

In addition, members have the opportunity to travel and view taxpayer funded arts projects across the country, whether they be special exhibits or museums kept open, thanks to federal grants. One of the best ways to get to know other members of Congress is when you travel with them. One year, the Arts Caucus brought a group of members to Nashville to learn more about country music and its importance to that region of the country. I was part of that congressional delegation, and Tammy Wynette hosted a dinner at her home. Upon seeing a piano, the other members, who knew me all too well, goaded me into singing "Oh Lord, It's Hard to Be Humble," and of course I complied with gusto.

A rather shocked Tammy Wynette listened to my performance, and, after I sang the last, sweet note, she advised me to keep my day job. The next day we all went to the Grand Ole Opry recording studio where the congressional delegation recorded a version of "Rocky Top." As we listened to the recording, the only voice that could be heard was mine, loud and clear. I can't be blamed that the others didn't take their singing seriously.

In addition to giving me multiple opportunities to showcase my inherent singing talents, Rhoda's leadership of the Congressional Arts Caucus was extremely relevant to my success and stature in Congress, as well as an early link to the entertainment world. Rhoda and members of the caucus went to Los Angeles, New York, Nashville, and other entertainment capitals. Not only did she become popular but her work with Oscar and Grammy Award winners helped me too. I was able to introduce my colleagues and have access to significant entertainment figures.

One time, our phone rang at home.

"This is Charlton Heston," a voice said. "Is Rhoda there?"

I put my hand over the phone.

"Rhoda! Moses is on the phone!"

Aside from singing, much of what I did in Congress was centered on serving my constituents, by helping Pizza Hut or aviation companies or steering federal emergency funds toward Kansas after a tornado to help those who lost a home or their crops. Assisting folks with federal agencies, including Veterans Affairs, Social Security, Medicare, farm agencies, or immigration services, was a critical part of my job. For every member of Congress, this is what you need to be thinking of every day: connecting with your constituents— whether they voted for you or not, and as you hear about currently unfulfilled needs, you deliver solutions for your district or state.

My approach to constituent service was to always do it for the benefit of the people of the Fourth Congressional District of Kansas. I came back home to Wichita almost every weekend, and I was always accessible, either in my office, at public events, or going door-to-door during election campaigns, which for better or worse, almost never seem to end.

Being able to use the power of being a congressman to resolve an issue makes you feel like it's all worth it. Inevitably, resolving issues provided the most rewarding and memorable days on the job. For example, during the first Gulf War, I helped bring home an engineer from Kansas who had been detained in Kuwait by the Iraqis. He was reunited with his wife and children in my district office, and I'll never forget the tremendous feeling of joy that I felt that day.

I helped constituents get Medicare benefits for home glucose monitors, which helped with diabetes treatment. I secured funding for funding for Department of Defense contracts, which helped Wichita's defense industry. I also worked hard to get Wichita better commercial air service. We helped people obtain Medicare, Social Security, and disability benefits. Truthfully most members of Congress do a good job in these areas and I like to think I was no exception.

I often brought Congress back to my constituents in Kansas. Today, we risk a real danger in making our citizens feel so disconnected from Washington that they will abandon the process altogether. Voter apathy is the biggest threat to democracy, and I am terrified of how many Americans feel abandoned and deserted by those who represent them. As a member of Congress, I felt it was of paramount importance that my constituents knew how the system worked, as well as what I was actually doing each day on their behalf. On numerous occasions, I organized congressional hearings back home, which brought other members of a specific committee to Wichita and gave local stakeholders an opportunity to testify on related issues. We usually worked with the Agriculture Committee, but we also held hearings on health care or on base realignment and closure because of McConnell Air Force Base.

By the early 1990s, my congressional career had spanned over a dozen years and had resulted in several chairmanships of subcommittees. It had also given me a leading role on the issues most important to my district—agriculture and aviation—and established me as a collegial and bipartisan member who was eager to work hard while also having an enjoyable time.

I did not realize that this part of my professional life was slowly beginning to wrap up. Had my constituents allowed me, I probably would have been happy serving as a member of Congress for many additional terms.

I believe that three simple truths defined my days in Congress: (1) take the process seriously; (2) have humility, humor, and empathy; and (3) don't be afraid to think big. In my long career, nothing quite compares to the work one gets to do as a representative in Congress, fulfilling a role of being a fiduciary or trustee for the American people.

While today's Congress does not permit the same kind of individual opportunities to change the world as I enjoyed, it is still a place where you can push for things you care about, and that will help your constituents and the country. In spite of the skepticism among voters today, I always remind them that it's the best place I can think of to make positive changes in the world. Glamorous or not, it was an honor to affect real change in people's lives.

Chapter 10

Rubbergate, Partisan Wars, and My Last Term in Congress

On January 3, 1993, I raised my right hand for the ninth time and was sworn in again as the representative from Kansas's Fourth Congressional District. Even after winning another hard-fought race, I never dreamed it would be the last time I would enjoy the privilege of serving my hometown constituents and my country.

The first order of business for each new congressional term is to elect and swear in the Speaker of the House. For the 103rd Congress, our Speaker was once again Tom Foley, one of the most capable and decent public servants our nation has ever produced. After the dean of the House (the member with the longest continuous service) swears in the Speaker, the dean turns to the assembled group of representatives and administers the oath of office.

This is a pledge to support and defend the Constitution against all enemies, foreign and domestic. It affirms that as a member of Congress you will conduct your responsibilities within the framework of that most sacred document.

We do not swear an allegiance to our state or constituents, and most definitely do not to a political ideology or party. Political parties aren't even mentioned in the Constitution, and blind loyalty to a party deeply concerned the Founding Fathers.

"Political parties are likely to become potent engines," George Washington warned, "by which cunning, ambitious, and unprincipled men will be enabled to subvert the power of the people, and to usurp for themselves the reins of government, destroying afterwards the engines which have lifted them to unjust dominion."

Partisan loyalty has certainly become a key driver of dysfunction, inaction, and ugliness in politics—particularly in Congress. However, even if we tried to abolish political parties, new divisions would come to the surface, and something like political parties would inevitably come back. This human nature, steeped in tribalism, is inescapable.

By this stage of my congressional career, political parties were hardening around partisanship, and we saw this ramping up in the Congress, sometimes to a fever pitch. Party identity has now become more important to most people than almost any other marker, including citizenship. This level of blind loyalty and a view of the opposition as the "enemy" are the seeds of undoing our great national experiment in self-government.

My former congressional colleague and associate at the Aspen Institute, Mickey Edwards, once said, "It's time to turn Republicans and Democrats into Americans."

I couldn't agree more. Edwards was correct, no matter how much I wished he were wrong. As I began what would become my final term in Congress, I noticed a growing partisanship among my colleagues and the unseen forces supporting them from the shadows.

Since my first successful run back in 1976, my reelection campaign in 1992 was the toughest and closest race I'd ever experienced. My district had always been conservative. It may not have been solidly red when I represented it but it was decidedly a dark shade of purple. This made it tough for me every two years, and my campaigning became more complicated because redistricting had moved some of my more dependable Democratic counties to another district, replacing them with more reliably Republican pockets. As a result, going into the 1992 election, I knew I was in for a rough campaign. However, the national political landscape gave me some hope because Bill Clinton from nearby Arkansas was energizing the Democratic base and bringing voters to the polls who may not have otherwise shown up for me.

Two major events defined that election for me, and either one of them could have taken me down. The first was Multimedia Cablevision's decision to take me out, and the other was the much publicized and infamous House banking scandal. These incidents took the largest toll on me in my congressional career, both personally and professionally. Even though I overcame both obstacles and ended up beating my Republican opponent by a solid ten-point margin, it was still quite a bumpy ride to reelection and my closest race since I was first elected in 1976.

Multimedia Cablevision, a medium-sized national cable TV company headquartered in my district, decided to go after me because I voted for the Cable Television Consumer Protection and Competition Act of 1992. I did so in part because I believed it offered consumers protection from giant cable companies forming a monopoly, which would have forced rate increases and paid content down consumers' throats. Not only was Multimedia Cablevision incredibly powerful as a lobbying organization and a player in congressional politics, it also had hundreds of thousands of customers in Kansas and beyond.

The organization's main objection to that bill was a new requirement that it carry local broadcasting and pay local stations for the content they provided. Suddenly, in addition to running against my Republican opponent, state senator Eric Yost, I was also being forced to run against the largest cable television network in the state—not exactly an even fight.

At that point, before social media and the democratization of media engagement, television advertising was the king of political marketing strategies. As a candidate, if you weren't on TV with the right ads at the right time, you didn't have a great shot at winning a congressional level race.

Having pissed off the company that owned the advertising space through my position in Congress, no matter which channel my constituents tuned into I knew they'd be bombarded with anti-Glickman ads. The cable company wrongfully and self-servingly charged that I was raising their cable rates, but I was on the side of the consumer and supported by most consumer groups.

This was my first real lesson in the political weaponization of media. You can see a much more malignant stage of this phenomenon in cable news across the country today, where bias and spin are the fundamental principles of multiple cable news channels. My battle with Multimedia Cablevision and their reaction were totally unanticipated.

I suppose we could say it's the Fox (as in the network) guarding the hen house.

Up until that race, I had never experienced anything that even came close to such false and negative ads as the ones I saw on TV every single day of that campaign season. They were relentless. The ads were not only about the cable legislation but they came after my overdrafts at the House Bank, which looked to me like the company was in collusion with my opponent. I was less pissed at my opponent than the audacity of the company. I guess they thought that Rubbergate had me weakened and that maybe this could be the straw that would break the camel's back.

As if television spots against me weren't enough, I soon discovered that the cable company was also inserting similarly negative flyers in the monthly cable bills mailed to tens of thousands of voters in Kansas. I just hoped the consumers would be in such a bad mood from getting an arbitrarily high bill from a monopolistic cable company that they wouldn't be persuaded by the flyer. Thankfully, the rule of law and a sense of electoral fairness provided me recourse. My first line of defense was filing complaints with both the Federal Election Commission (FEC) and the Federal Communications Commission (FCC). It was easy to demonstrate that the attacks against me were self-serving and that Multimedia Cablevision was essentially providing my opponent with free campaign ads and in-kind support. Once we sued the company at the FCC and FEC, both agencies required Multimedia Cablevision to air hundreds of my own spots as well, and for free, instead of running their ads against me day and night, essentially unchallenged. This got huge media attention at home and nationwide.

When you take tough votes to defend consumers against predatory behavior by large corporations, you need those regular folks to show up for you. Getting turnout is made doubly hard by the fact that many consumers aren't keenly following daily congressional activity and may not realize that legislation designed to help them was passed, thanks to the support of their own elected officials.

This was another example of speaking truth to a powerful constituency, which was made easier by being on the side of the little guy. That's always been my preference. But in order to pull that off, you have to let them know your position and be comfortable tooting your own horn as you do it.

I organized a massive rally with thousands of my supporters in front of the company's Wichita headquarters, and we received positive news coverage from across the nation. The next day, front-page headlines were everywhere, with photos of voters carrying their posters.

GLICKMAN IS PROTECTING THE CONSUMER

It wasn't the sexiest phrase, I admit, but in the end, what could have absolutely killed my campaign became one of my greatest assets. The publicity turned out to be an electoral blessing as it became a classic case of David versus Goliath.

In almost every situation, if you vote for what you think is right, you can find allies who agree with you, especially if you're on the side of the "little guy." That's an extremely important lesson for aspiring and current politicians. Voters intuitively understand right from wrong. If you do the right thing, perhaps you have to get creative or do some organizing, but people will rally to your cause. That's been true ever since I can remember and it still is today.

That said, the proliferation of money in politics has made it more difficult to champion the causes of the little guy. Certainly the 2008 financial crisis and the Great Recession also made it harder for people to feel that their government was on their side. Years later we are still fighting battles in Congress that began with that economic disaster. On top of that, COVID-19 changed so much, which I get into in the last chapter.

Dealing with the House banking scandal, however, was a different challenge altogether.

The scandal, also known as "Rubbergate," centered around "bounced" checks. The media just can't resist the urge to label things in sound bites, reducing it to sound like a crime before the facts are even in. Basically, the House of Representatives allowed members to overdraw their accounts without a penalty, just like many banks do if you have enough in your account. That unfair practice and its discovery sank more than one member of Congress during that election cycle. I learned one of the most valuable and important lessons in life while navigating this experience. It taught me that in politics, perception trumps reality.

Like all my colleagues in the House of Representatives, I had access to the House Bank, which was not a bank in the classic sense. It was more like an unregulated cooperative, a clearinghouse run by the House Sergeant at Arms, a remnant, if you will, of an almost feudal system that had been established decades earlier. It was closed after the scandal, and most members now use a local credit union or standard consumer bank. We did receive primitive monthly account statements from the House Bank, but they never indicated insufficient funds or bounced or returned checks.

In my case, to my knowledge at the time, there weren't any. The simple statements we received noted checks that came in and checks that went out. They were nothing like the detailed bank statements that include balances, dates of each transaction, and alerts when funds are insufficient to cover a payment.

All my checks, at least to my knowledge, were paid. At the end of the month, if there was not enough money in the account, the checks were held until your salary was deposited on the first of the month. Nothing seemed out of the ordinary at all. This was an easy, uncomplicated way to conduct my Washington, DC, banking. There was a tiny bank branch inside the Capitol Building where we could stop to cast a vote and make a quick deposit or pick up new checks. Even though I conducted my main banking back home in Kansas, the House Bank was convenient as it provided automatic deposit, which back then was not the norm. My paycheck automatically went into my account and needed no additional steps from me.

Because the House Bank had a limited number of customers, it did not need to operate as efficiently or be as regulated as a traditional consumer bank. It's hard to believe today, but back then most transactions were conducted via pencil and ledger, without using any computers. Because we never received a detailed monthly statement, many of us grew sloppy about staying on top of the actual balance in our accounts, particularly when it came time to write checks. The account was a personal checking account, not a campaign account. It held no campaign funds. I simply used it to write checks for normal household expenses.

The folks running the bank knew that there could be a lag between when a deposit was made and when the funds became available. They honored checks written against insufficient funds because ninety-nine out of one hundred times the money was in the account within a day or two and the dollar amounts on honored checks written against insufficient funds were available from other congressional accounts that did have funds at the time.

This entire process became the root of the infamous scandal involving most members of Congress, including yours truly.

A majority of the 435 members of the House of Representatives had accounts with the House Bank. We were certainly to blame for writing checks that would have bounced with any other financial institution. Like almost every other member caught up in the scandal, I wrote checks fully unaware that I did not have enough money in my account to cover them until my next paycheck was deposited. None of my checks were ever returned to the payee for any reason, but in some cases, like those of a great many other members—and unbeknownst to me—they were held until money came in from the monthly salary deposit.

I should have been more careful, no doubt about it, and done a monthly review of how much money I had available versus how many bills I was paying. But that didn't happen. Just goes to show how easy it is to take things for granted. Just goes to show that I was like many of my constituents, too, just an ordinary man representing ordinary people.

In early 1992, I started hearing whispers in the halls of Congress that the Republican faction, led by Newt Gingrich, was going to start investigating how Congress conducted its business. Gingrich and his crew had a take-no-prisoners approach to interacting with their colleagues—Republicans and Democrats—and they were lusting after any opening they could find to twist into a negative message against someone they wanted to oust. All of us were fair game for Gingrich and his minions.

Sound familiar? It should, because what started back then in Congress is now standard operating procedure. Gingrich and his scheming crew understood and exploited the growing partisan rancor in the country. This climate helped Gingrich become a powerful and historically important member of our body. It gave him the Speaker's gavel and elevated him to become a nationally known figure. But it also opened a new and terrible kind of politics in this country, that anything and anybody is fair game.

Much like a Biblical folk tale, however, that level of partisan infighting ultimately cost Gingrich his seat. He resigned in 1999, due to ethics charges, electoral losses, and some personal matters, after being forced to do so by what had once been his Republican caucus. He was succeeded in the Speakership by Dennis Hastert. At that time, though, I'm sure stumbling across the loosely regulated House Bank must have felt to him like hitting a grand slam during the seventh game of the World Series.

All this fit nicely into a narrative the Gingrich-led Republicans were shaping. They claimed that as an institution led by Democrats for decades, Congress had become corrupt, self-serving, and an old-boys network of cronyism.

In addition to the House banking scandal, there were instances of House members violating campaign finance laws, pocketing tax-payer dollars allocated for running congressional offices, and even one or two salacious sex scandals. Gingrich's claim that Democrats had turned Congress into a cesspool was playing well with some voters who demanded action.

The House felt compelled to address the banking scandal by turning the entire matter over to a special counsel, a former judge, named Malcolm Willkie, who worked with the FBI to analyze every account. Most members, including me, were investigated by the special counsel and the FBI and were cleared of any wrongdoing. By receiving this clean bill of financial health, the public was reassured that members had not broken any laws.

The Ethics Committee chastised some members for leaving their accounts overdrawn too long but I was not among them. By receiving a clean bill of financial health from the FBI, I believed the problem was solved, and I could return to the business of legislating and campaigning. After all, the experts in government looked at the facts, determined I had done nothing wrong, and exonerated me. I assumed wrong.

The *Wichita Eagle* and other local news outlets centered much of their coverage of my 1992 reelection campaign on the banking scan-dal. Local and national newscasts kept the spotlight squarely on the number of checks written by each member of Congress. The media coverage provided an important service in keeping elected officials honest and accountable, but it sure did sting seeing my name next to how many checks I had bounced, even though my checks were simply held until the end of the month. This made it extra difficult to capture the voters' positive attention and run a campaign.

I was embarrassed, as this was not the kind of congressman I really was. The anxiety kept me up at night, and I even sought pro-fessional counseling to help me deal with this overwhelming sense of dread and embarrassment, which formed the lowest moment of my professional career.

All in all, the Rubbergate issue in 1992 was a time of high anxiety time for me. It wasn't so much the Jewish issue but the fear of being "exposed" as dishonest, having my reputation tarnished, which was so critical to my very sense of being. But the fact that hundreds of other members of Congress were similarly "exposed" helped soften those fears. Plus, I was fully exonerated.

HI DAN, HOW MANY CHECKS DID YOU BOUNCE TODAY?

That was one of several signs displayed at a parade I attended in Wichita. After one too many times feeling the disappointment of my constituents, I huddled with Rhoda and my parents, who were my closest advisors. We agreed that what my voters needed to hear from me was not a statement explaining the House banking process but an acknowledgement that I had let them down and that my judgment had been lacking. I had to apologize and eat some crow. Some members blamed their spouses. I must admit I thought about doing that, too, but knowing the error was mine, I finally took personal responsibility. I also did my best to convince my constituents that no checks actually "bounced," that they all cleared and were paid, but I must admit it was a tough sell.

This is another area where today's politicians need to step up and issue apologies when they are warranted. Even though I hated doing it, my voters needed to hear from me, and I needed to re-earn their trust. I held a press conference and answered every media question with honesty, sincerity, and humility, blaming no one but myself. I reiterated that no one was harmed by my actions and that voters could still depend on my integrity and credibility. My mea culpa was an important step toward reestablishing the trust I had earned over many years in public service.

Ending the emotional roller coaster of this difficult chapter in my life required one more thing: the 1992 Wichita Gridiron Dinner.

This annual fundraiser, hosted by the Kansas Pro Chapter of the Society of Professional Journalists, donates all proceeds to scholarships for Kansas university students pursuing degrees in journalism. Hundreds of people attend. The evening consists of skits and songs by local media, roasting the newsmakers of the past year. I was invited to make a cameo appearance, knowing full well that my role in the House banking scandal was going to be a major theme of the program. I'm sure the planners of the event didn't expect that I would accept the invitation, but I surprised them and jumped at the opportunity.

Rhoda reworked the song "Hey Big Spender," made popular by Helen Gallagher, Thelma Oliver, and the Sweet Charity Ensemble in 1966, by changing the lyrics to suit my misdeed. Once again, my less than professional singing proved a Godsend for me when I needed it.

"Hey, big spenders—you can always *bank* on me. Just give me one more look, send me back, I'll give them flack; *I'm not a crook.*"

I ended with a big Nixon smile, complete with flashing the symbol V for Victory! My performance brought down the house.

To my delight and truthfully, to my surprise, the press ran many stories, pictures, and lyrics of my grand performance for several days after the dinner. I was happy to note that they commented on how funny I was and how brave and humble the performance had been. While I'll never receive a Grammy, it undoubtedly tops my personal list of greatest hits. It also showed that I had some humility *and* perspective.

With my public apology and that simple song, I put the House banking scandal behind me and won the 1992 campaign, although the race was much closer than my previous races. I had one more big victory ahead of me before my time in the House was over: the General Aviation Revitalization Act of 1994, my most significant personal achievement in legislation.

A majority of small aircraft that carry fewer than twenty passengers were manufactured in my old congressional district of Kansas. I made it a priority to support that industry and the many constituents who were employed by manufacturers such as Cessna, Beech, and Learjet. One huge challenge to any manufacturer's ability to invest in labor and products is paying insurance carriers massive amounts of money for liability protection. Another is tort law, which generally favors the plaintiff in these kinds of cases and inevitably invites the creation of class-action lawsuits aimed at big payout settlements in case of tragedy. These factors and the changing economics of the airplane business threatened the biggest employer in my district. I knew I had to do something, but the politics of this battle were tricky. These companies were paying huge settlements and judgments in court on product liability decisions.

Fighting for my constituents and the businesses that employed them meant taking on a powerful lobby—trial attorneys—who had been growing their influence on Capitol Hill for years. They traditionally supported Democrats over Republicans, so not only was I taking on a powerful lobby but I was going against my own party's funders.

My proposed bill, the General Aviation Revitalization Act (GARA), was intended to shield small aircraft manufacturers from prolonged liability by limiting the duration they can be held responsible to eighteen years after manufacture except when gross negligence or willful misconduct could be alleged. In other words, if a small aircraft older than eighteen years crashed, the accident could not be blamed on the aircraft or its parts unless a plaintiff proved a clear violation of Federal Aviation Administration rules and standards. This pro-business measure, aimed at creating and protecting jobs, established a much higher bar for liability. By limiting the amount of litigation faced by employers, it would save them huge amounts of money and help them stay in business.

This limitation, which I felt then and still do today, was reasonable. Companies should generally have to face the prospect of massive civil liability, especially for gross neglect, but they shouldn't have to be concerned about legal action decades after their product was first sold.

There was vast support for this measure among my constituents, including the rare instance of labor unions coming together with corporate management to help me push the measure through. I also had the support of most pilots' associations, which have a powerful voice in Washington.

Politically, though, GARA was tricky. A similar measure, sponsored by Bob Dole and Nancy Kassebaum, was proceeding much faster in the Senate. I was a bit worried that they would reap all the political benefits of my work by beating me to the punch. As Republicans, they didn't have a problem taking on trial lawyers or Democratic supporters. I was taking all the risks and potentially getting none of the benefits. I was under the gun to get my bill passed. To me, there was no risk. It meant jobs for my district, and it was one of a few areas of industry where the airplane companies and their unions were on my side.

Beyond the external challenge of pissing off a key set of Democratic funders, I had to face down the powerful chair of the House Judiciary Committee, Jack Brooks of Texas, who held up the bill because of all the flak he was receiving at the hands of the trial lawyers' lobbyists. They are a powerful lobbying group that doles out millions of dollars to their supporters, typically Democrats.

The only way to get the bill directly to the floor for a vote was by filing a discharge petition, which moves legislation from a committee to the floor of the House without the approval of leadership or committee chairs. By doing this, you bypass the usual process through which a bill becomes law. You inform anyone paying attention that you do not believe your bill can get a fair hearing at the hands of the committee chair and that the chair needs to be circumvented. This is not exactly the best way to win friends among the most powerful lawmakers in Congress. It's such a drastic measure that it's rarely employed and can only happen if an absolute majority of the members, at least 218, sign your petition. It's almost unheard of to employ this procedural mechanism against a committee chair from your own party. I have always felt that I had to buck my party dogma sometimes, but the discharge petition was an extremely aggressive move, even for me.

It's usually the opposition's last resort to maneuver around the majority party, but in my case, I was not only going against my chair; I was going against my party.

I don't have to imagine how fondly the Honorable Jack Brooks of Texas thought of me as I was knocking on the doors of more than two hundred of his colleagues, looking for signatures. He let me know how he felt in no uncertain terms.

"Glickman, you just ruined your chances of ever moving up in the House."

While neither endorsing the move nor signing my petition, Speaker Tom Foley was sympathetic to my legislation and did not actively fight my efforts. This was my key. By not taking on this fight, he gave his subtle permission for other Democrats to join my side without fear of retribution. This is real leadership, not what we see so often today. Speaker Foley let the process work and didn't feel he had to intervene to prove that he was a confident leader in control of everything. It's just that simple.

Once you have 218 signatures for a discharge petition, you are virtually assured that your bill will pass, unless someone changes their vote. Having secured more than three hundred cosponsors of the bill, I felt confident of success, and I took my signatures back to Chairman Brooks.

"Mr. Chairman," I said, "I have the signatures to successfully file the discharge petition, but I don't want to go down that road because I don't want to publicly embarrass you."

This was an incredibly difficult conversation, especially face-to-face, but I wanted to spare him unnecessary embarrassment. It didn't make sense to burn political bridges. I needed this bill for my district, but I didn't need to make enemies in the process, not if I could help it, especially at Beech and Cessna, and potentially with their suppliers and subcontractors.

Chairman Brooks, realizing how untenable his position was, eventually took up the bill and moved the legislation through the process. But it wasn't until President Clinton signed the bill into law on August 17, 1994, that I could breathe a huge sigh of relief. In addition to providing an excellent service to my district, the bill would make me invincible with my constituents and assure my ree-lection—or so I thought. After all, it would save thousands of jobs in my district and state. It's rare when a congressman can claim that he or she is responsible for legislation that does that, affecting so many families positively in the process.

Back then, the general aviation industry employed nearly twenty thousand people in the greater Wichita area. This was an-other example of fighting for your constituency, even though a powerful lobby stands in the way. Through political perseverance, I had delivered for the people of my district. Hopefully those efforts would inoculate me against any trouble I might face in the midterm election, because it's traditionally a tough challenge for members of the party that holds the White House.

This was a pivotal moment in American politics, though I didn't realize it at the time.

Chapter 11

Naïve Dan

Buoyed by my recent success with the General Aviation Revitalization Act (GARA), I entered the 1994 congressional campaign feeling pretty good about myself and my chances of winning another November race—number ten!

I felt I was in good shape because I could point proudly to the tremendous impact that the aircraft manufacturing bill would have for constituents in my district. Within weeks of the bill being signed into law, Cessna announced more than one thousand new manufacturing jobs when they restarted the assembly line to produce small single-engine aircraft in Kansas. It is hard to engineer tangible results on this scale. You can help people with paperwork and how to deal with government agencies, but playing a direct and consequential role in creating jobs in your community is a rare feat.

My opponent didn't exactly herald my success on the campaign trail. Instead, he gave speech after speech in our district about the North American Free Trade Agreement (NAFTA) and my vote in favor of that bill. Whereas I viewed free trade with other nations as the best way to bring economic stability and growth to our country as a whole, NAFTA opponents saw it as a job exportation program, or as Ross Perot so memorably put it, "the giant sucking sound of US manufacturing jobs going south."

When we passed the NAFTA legislation in the House, it was a bipartisan group of representatives that pushed it over the edge: 132 Republicans and 102 Democrats. I thought the shared support would give me cover to vote for what I felt was the right economic and trade policy for everyone. I soon found out, however, that my previous conceptions of voter preferences no longer held. I believed

I was in good company, but by voting for NAFTA, I likely eliminated any goodwill I had earned with GARA.

The legislation had strong support from President Clinton and
the business community, but it was opposed strongly by organized
labor, especially the Machinist Union, which had many members in
Wichita working at the airplane factories.

Ironically, NAFTA proved helpful to America's farmers, one of
my core group of constituents in Kansas, and I viewed my vote in its
favor as an extension of the work I had been doing all along in support of agriculture and farming. Yet many farmers did not see it that
way, and I made enemies out of some former friends in the Kansas
labor movement even though many of the job losses were more a
result of new technologies than trade. But in the minds of workers,
trade was a much more imminent threat.

The same issues dominate our politics today. In every election,
trade continues to be one of the significant touchstones for members
of Congress, senators, and the American people. Trump campaigned
relentlessly on this issue, and job losses in the manufacturing sector
over the past few decades contributed greatly to our current political situation and to general political instability in the country.

My recent votes aside, it was becoming more and more difficult
to survive as a Democrat in the state of Kansas. And I should know,
since I was the only Democrat who had won an election in that district since before World War II.

A large part of the difficulty was the decision by a prominent
Wichita family to get into politics—in a *big* way. As I described earlier, Wichita is home to Koch Industries and the Koch family. As
everyone knows, they have injected millions of dollars into our political process to put conservatives with partisan views into office.

I was one of their first targets—for two reasons. I don't think
they could stomach a Democrat representing their hometown of
Wichita, and I was a proponent of an energy tax that would have
affected fossil fuels, the major source of profit for Koch Industries.
Koch employees and their PAC poured a great deal of money into
the race to unseat me.

My Republican opponent, a one-term state senator named Todd
Tiahrt, ran a highly energetic campaign, focused on issues that played
well for a conservative community like Wichita. He highlighted my

pro-choice views and my vote in support of the 1994 Crime Bill, which included a ban on semi-automatic weapons.

Guns and abortion rights have become the key issues driving enormous efforts from conservative Americans to go after Democrats. Tiahrt understood this new strategy and employed it with great success. What made matters worse for me was that Wichita became the national epicenter in the fight against abortion.

A local physician named Dr. George Tiller built a national reputation for performing abortions, so the anti-abortion movement zeroed in on Wichita. There wasn't a day that went by without protests, marches, and blockades of his clinic. In interview after interview, I was asked about my pro-choice position. No matter how hard I tried, I could never get the media or the voters to talk about how I created aircraft manufacturing jobs or my history of achievements helping Kansas farmers. The abortion issue trumped everything back then and may still today.

I had an equally tough time explaining my views on the Second Amendment. While I absolutely supported it, I was opposed to any unchecked, unregulated right to bear arms. In my mind, the Second Amendment does not extend to semi-automatic weapons, nor do tighter regulations necessarily infringe upon its intended domain. This is especially true when it comes to regulations for issuing gun licenses to convicted felons and the mentally unstable. I also believed that a reasonable waiting period should be instituted to allow law enforcement to conduct thorough background checks.

To me, all of these measures were common sense. My opponent, on the other hand, was a vocal supporter of a vastly expanded interpretation of the Second Amendment and had the support of the Koch brothers as well as the National Rifle Association. The NRA used this vast grassroots network to alert their thousands of Kansas members as to my position on firearms. And I soon learned that there was no room for compromise on the issue. Many of their supporters were working-class union members who otherwise supported me, but not on gun issues. Still, I thought I had an opening by focusing on Tiahrt's push in the Kansas state legislature to allow the concealed carrying of registered firearms in our state.

This turned out to be a strategic mistake, one I would make again because I found the policy appalling and didn't mind saying so. I ran ads against the concealed carry bill and Tiahrt's support of the measure. As it turned out, although my position made perfect sense to me, I probably lost one thousand votes every time I ran that ad on local television.

Frankly, I completely underestimated the intensity of the gun rights issue and did not appreciate that for the Second Amendment question, where I saw so much room for compromise, most of my constituents saw only one side or the other. The country was being pulled more and more to extreme positions, with little to no room for the spirit of compromise.

Intensity is such a vital factor in politics, and in 1994, issues with NAFTA, abortion, and guns created a huge amount of animosity against me and others when Democrats lost the House. It is only in recent years that the intensity over guns seems to be moving the other way. But during that 1994 campaign, notwithstanding my work on the aviation jobs bill, there were far greater feelings against than for me. It was also the midterm after Clinton's narrow win, a traditional election that often has a swing in the other direction.

During my first race in 1976, the electoral process allowed candidates an opportunity to clearly articulate their positions. But by 1994, tribal politics, which is now the norm, was shrinking any room for dialogue. Both sides of the political spectrum are guilty of this.

For example, when it came to the abortion issue, I could say in 1976 that abortions should be safe, legal, and rare. My constituents would hear my view and understand that I wasn't a huge abortion supporter, that I was just being reasonable about the reality of the issue. But in the 1994 race, and in all races since, you simply can't show any leeway. In many respects, being a "reasonable" person in today's politics is not consistent with the stubborn partisanship of our times. Nothing has changed on this matter in nearly thirty years.

Even though I had earned a reputation as an independent thinker who often went against Democratic Party ideology, my message was drowned out by a well-funded campaign that focused on division and culture war issues while oversimplifying hot-button topics.

I'm not sure if it was the Koch brothers' interests that made me lose through the sheer force of their money, but their support of Tiahrt unquestionably helped him immensely. The Kochs were more interested in my vote for Clinton's energy policy and health care reform than they were in guns and abortion, but every bit of support for Tiahrt, from wherever it came, added up to a powerful adversarial force for my reelection. Guns, abortion, NAFTA, *and* the Koch brothers' support for Tiahrt sealed my fate.

It is disheartening to see that more than twenty-five years later, even with nearly two generations of new voters participating in our electoral system, these same issues—abortion and gun rights—still dominate our political landscape and divide us as a country. They are incredibly powerful forces that have denied Democrats much headway in rural America. That is why there are so few, if any, Democrats in the House or the Senate from predominantly rural districts or states.

Imagine a barbershop quartet with all four voices singing the same melody line. Or even worse, two people supposedly performing a harmonious duet, except they're singing as loud as they can in two different keys.

I recall one moment from the 1994 campaign that illustrates the power of these issues and the discord they provoke. I was on the trail in a Wichita suburb, going door-to-door, introducing myself to constituents and asking for their support when I noticed a gentleman sitting on his front porch. I walked over to him and struck up a conversation.

"I'm an aircraft machinist," he said, "and I want to thank you, Congressman Glickman, for saving my job. Thanks to you, I am able to take care of my family."

I thanked him for his support, assuming he was a sure Glickman vote. But as we shook hands, I could tell he was uneasy.

"I really do like you an awful lot," he said, almost in a whisper, "but Congressman, there's no way I could ever vote for you!"

I was shocked by his admission.

"Why not?" I said, incredulous.

"Congressman, you're against the Second Amendment and taking away my guns is definitely un-American."

There was no explaining to him that I was not anti-Second Amendment or that I had any design on his firearms. He just had it in his head that I was opposed to his right to bear arms, and no action or explanation of mine was going to earn me his vote. So the propaganda worked.

That same story, whether it focused on guns or abortion,

repeated itself throughout my campaign. I was genuinely liked by many of my constituents, but they would not vote for me, no matter how well I delivered for them on a slew of other matters—because I was not 100 percent in line with them on guns or abortion or both.

The intensity of these issues has only grown since I first encountered it, and today's media encourage the base to be vocal and demanding on these and other culture war issues. As a result, many outstanding public servants have been run out of office because they refuse to embrace an extreme position. I worry that we are dissuading the next Lincoln, Roosevelt, Eisenhower, or Kennedy from ever running for office. Even worse, more and more voters are staying home, although the recent 2020 national elections bucked the trend of flat and sometimes declining electoral participation, demonstrated by the fact that a record of more than 155 million people voted. Political scientists will have a field day analyzing why voter turnout was so high, but I suspect the "Trump" effect, both pro and con, was dramatically responsible. Voters either loved him or despised him.

I wish we wouldn't allow issues like guns or abortion to become all-or-nothing litmus tests for our elected officials. These are important conflicts, but they are part of a much broader set of concerns that most Americans have, including health care, immigration, economics, and pocketbook issues, and on and on. Both parties remain locked in a winner-take-all mentality on culture war issues, too, and that creeps into all these other matters where there is much more space for compromise. I understand that culture war issues animate many voters and that people care intensely because of the sense of morality they attach to them.

But in the end, politics is really about dividing up scarce resources in an equitable way. If the culture wars would become less important, you could find that most Americans would embrace the chance to push lawmakers to actually solve a slew of the economic problems we face instead of holding on for dear life to positions that will never be purely winnable.

With all of this doubt and confusion coloring the campaign of 1994, I headed into election night on November 8 with great trepidation.

As I sat with my wife and parents in a hotel room in Wichita and watched the final returns spell out a nearly five-point defeat, I had to come to grips with the fact that I was going to lose. Rhoda and my parents tried to comfort me, but there was nothing they could say that would make me feel better. All I could do was muster up every bit of my strength and thank my supporters for all that they had done on my behalf, and then get back to DC as fast as possible.

However, I did extract a little pound of flesh after conceding defeat. I waited until the beginning of the ten o'clock news to give my concession speech, which ran for about fifteen minutes. The stations carried me live, which meant my opponent couldn't get his live time until later in the news when lots of people had already gone to sleep.

Many people approached me over the next few days, telling me that they really didn't want me to lose, that I had been a good congressman, and that they just wanted to send me a message. Interesting. All I could think of was the famous line from former congressman Mo Udall, who ran for president in 1976; when he lost, he mused that "the people have spoken, the bastards."

I thought of my old friend and colleague, Tom Foley, and how we two moderates had worked so well together across the aisle. Ironically, it was moderate Democratic members of Congress like me who suffered in the Gingrich landslide of 1994, as most liberal representatives survived. I think this was the beginning of a trend of moderates becoming more and more extinct in congressional politics.

I hate to face the music. Politicians eventually lose in real democracies. That's part of what makes these systems healthy. But what's making our political process so unhealthy now is the way many campaigns encourage such deep and negative polarization. During the past two decades, political operatives from both sides of the aisle have eroded safeguards against gerrymandering or undue financial influence. Media of all minds, social and antisocial, keep fanning the flames of hyper-partisanship, which triggers voter fear and anger, leaving today's candidates to only respond to the strong views of a minority of the public.

The moderate consensus builder, the type of politician preferred in poll after poll and vitally necessary to the functioning of the Congress, often cannot find fundraising success or adequate media attention. They are greatly disadvantaged in an electoral system that crowns the winner in primaries instead of general elections.

This is even truer today than it was when I lost this last campaign.

We have essentially removed nearly all competition from our political process by identifying and labeling candidates based solely on their party affiliation and a small subset of extremely contentious and severely narrow issues. There is little room within either tribe for a moderate voter who is conservative on some issues and liberal on the others.

It's as if Hollywood has turned its back on an everyman character like Jimmy Stewart and instead opted for violent action heroes and bloated criminals.

I loved being a member of Congress. That loss on an otherwise lovely autumn evening in Wichita forced me to deal with the reality of no longer being allowed to practice the craft I so enjoyed and respected. I believe I was a good representative for the Fourth Congressional District of Kansas. When I reflect on the many votes I cast over the eighteen years I served in Congress, I am proud to say that I usually did what I thought was right. Once in a while, political necessity would triumph because a congressman will rarely vote against the economics of the congressional district.

This reminds me of a Groucho Marx quote.

"These are my principles, and if you don't like them . . . I have others." That's so perfect!

I didn't know what might come next back in 1994. Just when I was beginning to get over the pain of my loss, I got a call that would change my life. It came from Leon Panetta, the White House chief of staff, who got right to the point.

"Dan," he said, "Now that you're unemployed, how about joining President Clinton's cabinet as his new secretary of agriculture?"

Chapter 12

"Hey Big Spender" Becomes Mr. Secretary of Food

I loved being a congressman for eighteen years. Losing that last race was a bitter pill to swallow, but becoming secretary of agriculture was certainly an excellent follow-up and certainly no consolation prize.

As my son, Jon, once said, my career had a way of "failing upward."

Only a secure child could talk like that, especially if his father agrees.

In my new cabinet position, I was spending my days making public policy on traditional agriculture, food, nutrition, and even the environment. It didn't take long to feel a public spotlight shining on me more significantly than during my entire time in Congress.

For example, the *Pigford v. Glickman* case, which I will explain here in detail, became the most significant issue I faced during my time at the USDA, an accomplishment that still has great impact today.

Fame, even "DC fame," isn't all it's cracked up to be. Take it from me, the most assaulted cabinet member in history. Is that an official moniker? *Guinness Book of World Records* material? I had all sorts of things tossed at me in my position as secretary of agriculture—organic seeds by naked men and women in Rome, bison guts in Montana, and tofu pies in DC. It turns out people *really* care about their food.

In 1996, I led the American delegation to the United Nations Food Summit in Rome. As delegates gathered for a panel discussion and I prepared to speak, about two dozen men and women in the front row stood up and took off their clothes. Right in front of me, a rather portly gentleman turned around to face me, naked as the day he was born, and launched into a tirade against bioengineering as a way to produce more crops. He and his fellow protesters were adorned with body paint, baring the slogans "No Gene Editing" and "The Naked Truth."

With seconds to spare before Italian police could tackle him, the man looked directly at me and others in our delegation and announced that he was going to spread "organically produced seeds." Having gone nearly bald by this time, I was hoping that he might produce the hair I had been missing.

Actually, I stood there quite frozen in terrified anticipation at what was about to come flying in my direction, and boy, was I relieved when the only thing he spread were actual seeds, though I'm still not sure if they were organic.

My parents watched the entire episode broadcast live on CNN, and though my mother vigorously voiced her concern that my new job was too dangerous, my father seemed much more interested in the nudity. Once my mother stopped her scolding and worrying, my father got a word in edgewise.

"So, what did everybody look like?"

My dad was more interested in what the women looked like.

I soon realized that I had gotten off relatively easy that day in Rome. Back home in America, the assaults continued.

A couple of months later, I was at a meeting in Yellowstone National Park, along with Montana's two senators and Governor Marc Racicot. The event was focused on the plight of bison when they stray from their zoned areas on federal land. Whenever that happens, they leave feces, which end up being consumed by grazing cattle, which causes disease that can often be fatal to livestock and dangerous to humans.

As the governor made his remarks, a woman approached the podium with a bucket of rotting bison guts and hurled its contents toward us! Although Governor Racicot took the brunt of the projectile, all of us were splashed with the putrid intestines. CNN was right there once again, providing coverage that reached Wichita, and my mother wasted no time letting me know how worried she was about what her son had gotten himself into.

Airborne bison guts were nowhere to be found in my job

description, but I soon learned that bison guts were a real issue to some folks in the region.

During a subsequent hearing of the House Agriculture Committee, I was right in the middle of my testimony when a man stood up and announced that he was going to kill himself. As we discovered later, he was upset about a shipment of contaminated soda to Eastern Europe, He smashed two bottles during his tirade, showering me and the room with glass and carbonated soda. Just after he swung the bottles against the table, he gave me a menacing look, with the broken bottles still in his hands. I thought he was about to lunge at me when Congressman Earl Pomeroy, who was a standout rugby player at the University of North Dakota, put all his training to effective use and came flying across the witness table. He performed a lifesaving tackle that would have made Vince Lombardi proud.

This entire scene was covered extensively in the media, and my mother's phone calls, demanding that I find a new job, were growing harder to laugh about. Maybe she had a point.

Sometimes in politics you can get caught up in issues for which you were not at all responsible, though to this day I have no idea how I was to blame for any of these personal attacks on me. It could have been I was in the wrong place at the wrong time. Or maybe that many people feel so strongly about food and agriculture issues that they demonstrate their rage more aggressively than any reasonable person would have expected.

Just a couple of weeks after escaping the exploding soda incident, I was the keynote speaker at the National Nutrition Summit in Washington, DC. I had just begun to speak when a protester jumped onto the stage and hurled a pie at me.

"Shame on you, Dan Glickman! You're a meathead! Shame on you for being a pimp for the meat industry!"

The pie in question was made of tofu, with whipped cream, of course. Having learned my lesson by then, that people—naked or clothed—enjoy throwing eccentric objects at the secretary of agriculture, I was fast to duck, and the pie sailed by me, leaving just a touch of whipped cream on my jacket. Most of it landed on Secretary of Health and Human Services Donna Shalala. Bob Dole was on the platform with me, too.

"Bob, I don't think we're in Kansas anymore."

As the protester was detained by police, I addressed the crowd.

"This was not a very balanced meal," I said, referring to the pie she had thrown at me, before pivoting back to my prepared remarks on nutrition.

Humor always lets you move on and I was happy to do that as fast as possible. I did have a security detail with me, but obviously it was not enough. Who would have thought the secretary of agriculture would be so vulnerable? Maybe someone in the State or Defense Department, but the USDA, who could have imagined? From that time on, security details for future secretaries were "beefed" up. And I found out that people really do have intense feelings about food.

Notwithstanding these hilarious, dangerous, and odd assaults, including those on the phone from my mother, being secretary of agriculture was one of the best times of my life.

I learned a couple lessons during my tenure: bison guts smell bad, secretaries of agriculture make their security detail work almost as hard as the president's, and it is amazing and alarming to see how worked up folks actually get about food and agriculture.

During many speeches I've given since then, I've included stories of those assaults, which shows that you can make lemonade (not tofu pies) out of lemons. They certainly provided surprising and funny material, which always seems to loosen up my audiences.

Despite all the stuff thrown at me—literally and otherwise—I'm grateful that I had the opportunity to serve in the cabinet as secretary of agriculture. After losing my seat in Congress, I had been down on my luck and feeling a little sorry for myself. I will always remember the moment Leon Panetta, then the White House chief of staff, reached out to me to talk about joining the Clinton administration—that the president wanted to hear my vision for the Department of Agriculture and was hoping to speak with me as soon as possible.

In that moment, I was still worn out from a long campaign and nearly two decades in Congress, so I spent a bit of time wondering if that would be the right move. Ultimately, and thankfully, I decided it was too good of an opportunity to pass up. The truth is, even if I had been offered the job after being reelected, I would have grabbed the opportunity. But since it came after a loss, my emotions were stirred up.

When Panetta called, I had just landed in Los Angeles, having flown out there ten days after losing the election, looking for a job. I was alarmed by a voice over a loudspeaker in the airport calling my name as I headed to pick up my luggage.

"Paging Dan Glickman, go to the white courtesy phone, please."

Rhoda was on the line.

"Leon called, and they are interested in you for secretary of agriculture."

I was on my way to the Walt Disney Company to interview for a government relations job with Sanford Litvack, the senior executive vice president of Disney at the time and a former senior Justice Department official. I had a massive anxiety attack right there in the airport and started sweating bullets. I don't know why. Maybe it hit me then that I was entering a period of massive change in my life.

I went to Disney shortly after the call. Litvack wisely advised me that if given the opportunity to become a cabinet secretary, I should jump at the opportunity, that it would give me a chance to really change the world. He was spot on with this sage advice. I collected myself and jumped at the opportunity, which prompted a set of very positive changes. Ironically, years later, when I became CEO of the Motion Picture Association of America, long after Litvack had left Disney, I used to meet with senior Disney officials in that same office.

I went to the White House in late November 1994, excited to discuss my vision for the USDA with the president. I waited three hours while our meeting was repeatedly pushed back, until finally, the White House cancelled because the president's schedule had been usurped by more pressing business.

The next day I returned, worried slightly that President Clinton might be wavering on my appointment. My worry proved to be unfounded, as I was ushered into the third-floor presidential living quarters and had a long and productive conversation with Leon Panetta. When he had first floated my name as a possible nominee with leaders such as Al Gore and Bob Dole, he had received unanimous positive feedback. Panetta must have also briefed the president extensively on my policy work when Panetta and I served together on the Agriculture Committee in the House. Making and keeping friends across the aisle was vital in securing the attention and approval of President Clinton. This is a good lesson for everyone in politics.

Making friends at the White House level and with folks around the country—especially in Kansas—doing favors for colleagues, and building and not burning bridges, were instrumental for me in generating support. I did not have a lot of enemies. Of course having the support of Bob Dole, the Senate majority leader; Al Gore, the vice president; and Leon Panetta, White House chief of staff, were also critical.

When Bill Clinton finally entered the room, we spent little time talking about agriculture issues. The president told me he knew my record as a member of Congress and was comfortable with my experience. Instead, most of our conversation concerned the recent election, my own loss, and the path forward for Democrats. The main topic centered on our agreement to make economic development in small towns and rural communities a priority, a commitment he maintained throughout my career at the USDA.

The president wasted no time making a decision and offered me the post right then and there. Panetta, Gore, and I had entered Congress together in 1976 and we remained good friends. This helped to establish me as a viable candidate in Clinton's mind. Bob Dole's endorsement didn't hurt, either. I believe the president saw a chance to score an easy political victory after the brutal midterm election he had just endured. The Republicans had taken over the House and the Senate, and President Clinton needed a nominee who could get confirmed by both parties, someone with the same policy views as most Democrats but independent and moderate enough for Republicans to accept. I fit the bill and accepted the invitation.

In December of 1994, only six weeks after losing my reelection bid, without delay, advance public notice, or press speculation, I was announced as the president's nominee at a ceremony in the majestic Rose Garden at the White House, where the president of the United States announced my nomination to be the next US secretary of agriculture.

Rhoda and our children were with me, as well as plenty of national and Kansas press. As I took in the scene, an image entered my mind: my grandfather, near penniless, entering the country through Ellis Island after having left Belarus. Here I stood, two generations later, about to go to work for the leader of the free world. That is why America remains the land of opportunity and why countless men and women still make the same journey as my grandparents.

What a country!

The response to my nomination was generally positive, especially in Congress, where I had a solid track record of working well with members from both parties. Policy makers in the agriculture community, especially folks from the Midwest agriculture, wheat, corn, soybean, and cattle counties, also voiced their support. I had lots of allies in both the House and Senate. Al Gore, Leon Panetta, Bob Dole, Pat Roberts, and Dick Lugar were invaluable in pushing through my nomination. It also helped that in almost twenty years on Capitol Hill I had made few enemies and had burned as few bridges as humanly possible in this tough business.

In Washington, however, nothing can escape politics, certainly not a presidential nomination to a cabinet post. I knew that although I had a clear path to confirmation, the vetting and hearing process would inevitably come with surprises. My biggest concern was that Republicans had taken a majority in the Congress, and I didn't know if there would be partisan objections. After all, my eighteen years in Congress had no doubt produced a few controversial votes.

The first bump in the road came in the form of the two senators from Alaska: Ted Stevens and Frank Murkowski. While the nominee for secretary of agriculture must always appear before the Senate Agriculture Committee, the brand new Republican chairman of the Senate Energy and Natural Resources Committee, Mr. Murkowski, insisted I answer before his committee as well. The two senators had not yet forgiven me for my position on timber cutting in Alaska, which I often voted to restrict, and my opposition to deforestation in national forests.

In the Alaska delegation's view, my hope to protect trees was a direct assault on their timber industry, and the two senators were obviously eager to continue that debate. I became the first nominee in the history of the USDA who had to answer the questions of not one but two committees in the US Senate.

Bob Dole gave me a heads-up that Murkowski and Stevens were still upset with me, and he suggested that a personal meeting before a public hearing might diffuse the situation. We arranged for a get-together in Murkowski's office, and things got a bit testy.

"How would you like for us to support efforts that would ruin the Kansas wheat industry?" Murkowski said.

I chose to hold my tongue and we parted on cordial terms. I thought I had handled the situation well, but they insisted on having a hearing and used the occasion to extract from me a public commitment to, as they said, be "fair and balanced" when it came to policy on national forests, over which the USDA has jurisdiction.

Both senators eventually voted for me, and I suspect Bob Dole worked his magic behind the scenes to appease them. Can you imagine a Republican senator these days going to bat against his own caucus for a Democratic cabinet nominee? I doubt it very much. People don't want to build these kinds of relationships anymore and they can't claim that they don't have the opportunity because they do. They are choosing to stay in their caves.

My hearing in front of the Senate Agriculture Committee went smoothly, thanks in large part to Senator Pat Roberts introducing me with his stinging but funny sense of humor, which was undoubtedly a terrific way to disarm the panel. Senator Lugar was kind and generous and ran a fair hearing process, and most of the senators asked questions about substantive agriculture issues affecting their states. Pat Leahy of Vermont was particularly interested that I keep him in mind on dairy policy, which I agreed to do.

The FBI vetting process was a different story altogether, and quickly became a public review of every single decision and vote I had ever taken, with a heavy focus on anything that could be construed as negative. It ranged from bad jokes I had made in regard to the House banking scandal, with unpaid parking tickets and credit card use thrown in for good measure.

The vetting process was intensive. Giving the FBI five years of cancelled checks and bank records, extensive credit card statements, and numerous interviews was exhausting. I guess it goes with the territory, but I saw many newspaper articles with quotes, which I assumed contained FBI leaks. One article talked about spending campaign dollars for my daughter's travel, which was not true. This produced a lot of anxiety and cost me thousands of dollars in legal fees. At times, I thought about withdrawing, but White House counsel and others said I didn't have any serious problems, and I was confirmed within ninety days, which was fairly quick for this type of thing.

Part of the issue was distrust by some in the FBI toward President Clinton. I got caught up in that by virtue of my connection to him. One of the ironies is that I took the USDA job after Secretary Mike Espy, the first African American secretary of agriculture, resigned due to ethics charges for which he was later exonerated. Though Espy began to address some of the problems within the USDA, he only held the position for two years. I felt a special obligation and saw it as part of my legacy to work toward a comprehensive solution to the problems that festered over decades. In today's world, Espy's alleged wrongdoing would pale in comparison to most of the allegations against several of Trump's appointees.

When the whole House banking fiasco came up during my vetting, I briefly thought of withdrawing my nomination. In addition to Rhoda and our kids standing by me, White House counsel Jack Quinn stood by me, providing particularly great support.

It's fair and necessary for cabinet nominees to be vetted, but the process is invasive and uncomfortable. It was an incredibly difficult three-month period, and I grew agitated that my name and reputation were being so publicly judged. Elected officials are used to being in the spotlight and having to live their lives under a microscope, but nothing compares to an FBI investigation into your whole life.

During one or two dark moments I was tempted to pull my nomination and walk away from the entire process. Rhoda and the kids were my rocks and kept me sane, but others were asking out loud why the Glickman vetting was taking so long.

The lesson I learned most was that our government has powers that reach beyond anyone's imagination. Via agencies, such as the FBI or the Internal Revenue Service, they can come after a citizen with a vehemence and impact that is simply overwhelming. Unchecked governmental authority is an incredibly dangerous thing, and I for one will always be the most vocal defender of our civil liberties. I hope this belief is still shared by all Americans and their elected representatives.

In the end, the FBI investigation concluded without any major issues, and the Senate Agriculture Committee unanimously recommended to the Senate that I be confirmed. On March 30, 1995, the

Senate voted 94–0 that I become the next secretary of agriculture. I'll never know what happened to those other six senators.

I was on the Hill during the vote for my confirmation: Bob Dole had invited Rhoda and me to stay in his majority leader office in the Capitol while the vote was held, which showed yet again what a class act he is. After the vote, we went down Independence Avenue to the headquarters of the USDA, where the acting USDA secretary, Richard Rominger, a California tomato farmer and former California state secretary of agriculture, administered the oath of office. The ceremony was repeated the next day in the Old Executive Office Building so that friends and family could witness Al Gore swearing me in.

What a thrill.

The first person I went to visit once I began the job at USDA was our inspector general, who was our lead anti-corruption and antifraud employee, and had previously held a high-level position at the FBI. Needless to say, he became an important friend and ally while I was at the department, and we worked together closely for the next six years.

When I took over the USDA, the department was huge, with more than one hundred thousand employees and an annual budget topping $60 billion. I quickly learned that even though I was knowledgeable about farm policy and feeding programs, I had little experience in timber and forestry issues, food inspection, and other USDA activities. I had a lot of learning to do, and I was helped immensely by a talented career staff and my brilliant chief of staff, Greg Frazier.

The issues under our jurisdiction included food, farm, and rural development, the environment, international trade, national forests, nutrition policy, food safety, animal and plant health, and agricultural marketing, to name the major ones. While the work of the USDA touches on the lives of nearly every American, few citizens really understand—or even want to understand—agriculture policy. This may not necessarily be a terrible thing because it leaves some complex issues in the hands of experts well-versed in policy who are cognizant of the impact of the decisions made by Congress and the administration. The USDA could facilitate issue experts, representatives and senators from farming communities, or farm groups representing specific industry sectors to work together on developing sensible policies about complicated issues.

I continually found it ironic that while most folks do not understand agriculture policy, they feel strongly about the safety, quantity, and quality of the food supply. Considering the fact that every American citizen eats food on a daily basis (or so we hope), these issues formed a gigantic tapestry of challenges and concerns.

For me, this meant expanding my managerial skills from running a congressional office of about a dozen full-time staff members to supervising one of the largest agencies of the federal government, tasked with overseeing issues that literally touched every person in the country, if not in the world. My experience in Congress gave me a great comfort level with most of the USDA's jurisdiction, but some issues, such as overseeing national forests, were new to me.

I had some learning to do, that's for sure. Thank God I was a curious person by nature and welcomed new challenges. I suppose I can credit my adventurous parents for that.

Fortunately, I had an excellent staff, especially the senior team, including Rich Rominger and the dedicated career employees of the USDA. The entire department has always been full of devoted and talented civil servants who make government function. I made it a habit to always be available to USDA staff, especially career employees. This was a great management practice that kept the team involved and engaged and helped me facilitate high-performance teams. I frequently had lunch at our cafeteria and often sat with groups of employees I had never met. Once they got over the shock of the secretary sitting down with them, I think they were pleased. They often shared their thoughts about particular policies or problems within the department, which was helpful to hear and good for department morale.

Civil service is a foundational building block of good government. No matter what the pundits and looneys out there may say, our federal government is a pretty good and reasonably well-run organization. It agitates me when candidates running for office—usually on the Republican side—make denigrating statements about the federal workforce and the need for changes as part of their campaign pitch to voters. Naturally, in any situation involving so many people and challenges, you can find a few slackers here and there, but they do not represent the majority of government workers. If these candidates think that the government is so infested with inferior people, why would they want to join them?

Most of the dedicated professionals who implement our domestic and international policies are outstanding public servants, well educated and trained, who come to work each day for the purpose of moving the nation forward. Most of them could probably make more money in the private sector. They work hours equal to or longer than most of America's workforce. Most of them turn out a superior work product that has kept our nation in a leading position globally when it comes to economic output, innovation, or military might.

But full disclosure, in case you had any doubt. It's true. Our government is not perfect.

We strive, as always, to be better with each passing year. In fact, one of the first issues I had to deal with upon arriving at the USDA was a class-action lawsuit brought against the department by Black farmers from across the nation.

Pigford v. Glickman addressed racial discrimination going back as far as the 1930s and continuing through the 1980s. Many of the issues alleged in the lawsuit had been going on for generations, caused by some USDA employees and political appointees making decisions without much oversight, which reflected the civil rights conditions of the era. It became especially significant for me because of my central role as head of the USDA and certainly as a result of my name becoming inextricably linked with the entire case as the named defendant.

The first day I set foot inside the USDA office after being confirmed, a group of Black farmers were gathered in front of the building on Independence Avenue, picketing the department and seeking justice. Although they were courteous to me, this became the first of many times I had meetings and confrontations with this group, and some but not all were pleasant, in part because in all my eighteen years in Congress, and to the best I can recall during my confirmation hearings as secretary, this particular issue of racial injustice had unbelievably never been raised.

I have long thought about why I wasn't aware of it. Was it my own ignorance? Was it that no one in my home district had ever raised the issues with me? Was it the fact that the Congressional

Agriculture Committees during those times had few if any minority members and there hadn't been serious hearings on the subject? Was it because the national civil rights groups did not prioritize their historic plight?

I am not sure, as we dealt with so many issues, including farm and commodity programs, food safety, hunger, conservation and natural resources, farm exports, etc., but the intensity of this issue surprised me, and it turned out that racial discrimination became one the most significant issues I dealt with during my six years as USDA secretary and in all my public life.

We held a series of national hearings at the USDA about discrimination against minority farmers, and to a lesser extent, minority employees around the country, where we heard gripping stories, many of them years, even decades old, about farm loans being improperly denied and poor treatment given to cases filed at USDA offices. Those hearings were instrumental in developing the necessary record for later settlements of many of the cases. US district judge Paul Friedman was particularly helpful in getting the cases organized and presided over for several of the settlements. Those hearings proved useful in building public support as well as support in the civil rights community.

The *Pigford* case represented a long history of racial discrimination and malpractice, which began long before my time, and a final settlement was reached at last during the Obama administration, when Tom Vilsack was secretary of agriculture.

Even after serving on the House Agriculture Committee for eighteen years, the *Pigford* case was complete news to me. Amazingly, we had never held a hearing on racial discrimination issues as it applied to our country's Black farmers. This just shows what a major problem this issue truly was—that it had not been the focus of the legislature or the department. During the entire Pigford litigation and discussion, and during all my years in the House, there was barely any minority representation on the House Agriculture Committee. It was hardly diverse during this period, and I am glad to see that the committee is changing its racial representation. It's another demonstration of the vital importance of diversity in our government.

Once I arrived on the scene at the USDA, I knew I had to deal directly with this crisis. The lawsuit alleged that Black farmers, particularly in the South, had been discriminated against for decades when local USDA officials decided on farm loans and other assistance programs. While rules within the department and laws governing our support of farmers were written to be applied without bias, many of those executing the law on behalf of the USDA let racism guide their decisions. Even though the law was colorblind, many of the implementers were unfortunately not. There was virtually no minority representation in the local committees where the bias occurred, and a disproportionate number of Black farmers were denied credits and benefits, whereas a much larger number of white farmers had no problems at all. If a loan application was time-sensitive because the money was needed to rescue a crop or rebuild following a natural disaster, some local USDA officials dragged their feet and only approved loans after a farm had already gone under.

Unconscionable but true.

When Lincoln first created the USDA, it was known as the "People's Department" because most Americans at the time lived in rural settings and were directly impacted by the newly created entity. The USDA later became known as the "Congressional Department" because compared to other federal agencies, it had the most active give-and-take with Congress and committees of jurisdiction. I learned that for more than a generation, Black farmers had called the USDA "The Last Plantation." When this became clear to me as secretary of agriculture, my goal was to eliminate that nickname and the reasons it was created in the first place.

The discrimination claims against the USDA, most but not all legitimate, often could not be processed because they were old, and the statute of limitations had run out, barring the claims from any further consideration. The claims were largely applications for farm loans by Black farmers who had been rejected or not acted upon over the years. Many were deeply rooted in the historic culture of parts of the USDA and the legacy of discrimination in geographical areas of the country, largely but not limited to the South. Locally elected farm committees composed almost entirely of white farmers made many of the decisions denying the claims. The system was the product of the Depression and the government's desire to give more authority to local officials to actually administer farm programs.

Under my supervision, we did not contest efforts to create the class action litigation that was filed to address the claims, notwithstanding the statute of limitations, and we worked to allow the cases to proceed in class action form. However, to accomplish this, we needed to get Congress to pass short-term legislation to waive the statute to allow people who believed they had a legitimate case to file as part of the class on older cases.

It took the leadership of Maxine Waters, a liberal Democrat from California, and Henry Hyde, a very conservative Republican from Illinois, who were not members of the Agriculture Committee but still had major influence in Congress. At the time, most members of Congress were not interested in any of this, and even civil rights groups had not prioritized these issues. Although they represented extremely different ideological philosophies, Waters and Hyde, along with a few others, somehow managed to work together in a bipartisan way to lead the effort to pass legislation extending the statute of limitations, giving aggrieved farmers a time extension to file their claims against the government. This did not mean they were automatically approved, but they could be considered by a court.

My relationship with Waters and Hyde, plus the advocacy of the organization of Black farmers, helped to facilitate the approval of the class and the partial settlement that resulted in payment in excess of $1 billion to claimants. The case also led to other litigation involving allied cases for certain USDA employees and other minority farmers and employees, including Hispanic workers.

Some technical legal problems still existed with the case, and the USDA could probably have mounted a strong defense based on those technicalities, statutes of limitations, and procedural issues. However, with the complete support of President Clinton, I decided that the accusation was so grave that the only way to move forward was to settle the case and implement a system to compensate those who had been wronged. Furthermore, we would take a much closer look in the future at how the USDA was conducting its business in these areas and beyond. It was an enormously challenging problem and certainly not one I had ever anticipated when I took the job as secretary of agriculture.

I knew that we could not appeal the judge's decision to grant class status. The department might have prevailed on either or both counts had it fought harder, but a legal victory like that would have been a civil rights disaster. These two actions, or lack of action, were decisions that indicated our commitment to proceed to the underlying discrimination claims, allowing us to address the larger civil rights problems at the USDA.

The decades of neglect in investigating and enforcing discrimination against minority farmers, as well as allegations of discrimination against some USDA employees, to some degree mirrors the current discussion of racism in America. Black and other minority farmers suffered from years of active and pervasive discrimination in farm lending, resulting in significant numbers of foreclosures. I took a great interest in trying to remedy these problems, and I credit Secretary of Agriculture Tom Vilsack for furthering many of the solutions we initiated.

The case and my decision to settle it unveiled historic discrimination within the agency. We eventually set up a process to compensate any injured farmers who had suffered from discrimination. Many people claimed that the settlement was insufficient, and several critics complained that payments were made in error. My guess is few Black farmers benefited from it because they had already lost their farms and the settlements were not sufficient to re-establish themselves, as by then, growing trends of concentration in agriculture had swamped them. In one respect the settlements were a form of reparations, payments for damages done. The USDA made some changes, though. A new assistant secretary for civil rights was hired, and even if it was fleeting, there was some priority on elevating Black officials within the agency.

The process of correcting racial discrimination in farm lending and related farm program administration as well as racial representation in certain USDA farm programs, was certainly imperfect, but it was significant in America. It was an important achievement in the ongoing battle for civil rights. Frankly, it was probably my biggest achievement in public life, certainly at the USDA. Not only did we focus on how to bring compensation to the farmers but we also made monumental changes within the USDA and created a department-wide civil rights action team. All of this resulted in farm loans to minorities dramatically increasing, and the USDA workforce becoming more diverse than ever.

Sadly, though, mainstream agriculture never invested in resolving these problems, and though the broader civil rights movement chimed in from time to time, it never embraced the case as fully as it might have. The long-term results are mixed. But some of the lessons of this case are appropriate today: cultural and structural change is hard; it doesn't move in a straight line, and it has to have the entire culture invested in its success. No matter how this episode is viewed, it was the right thing to do.

I fundamentally believe that this was one of the most important, if not the most important, matter I worked on in all my years of public service. While I did not get the issues fully solved and resolved, I moved the ball forward significantly. My name will forever be the listed defendant on a case (in my representational capacity as secretary) on one of the most important anti-discrimination cases of this generation.

At local levels, USDA oversight over the administration and implementation of programs increased substantially during my tenure, an improvement continued by subsequent secretaries, especially Tom Vilsack. I am proud to this day that the case bears my name because I did not want racial injustice to stain my legacy or that of President Clinton.

We faced another pressing issue as the bridge between the White House and Congress on negotiating the 1996 Farm Bill. Every five years or so, Congress reviews the nation's agricultural and food programs, setting the policy direction for the USDA as well as its budget. During my hearing, I sparred with senators on cuts to USDA spending, particularly when it came to workforce reduction and curtailing initiatives, such as eligibility for food stamps.

Pete Domenici of New Mexico envisioned a draconian cut of up to $50 billion over five years, while the Clinton administration was holding on to a $1.5 billion cut over the same period. During my hearings, I made the point that any cut beyond that amount would have a markedly negative effect on land prices and farm program stability and should be avoided, lest we want to risk the solidity of our entire farming community.

Even though the Congress had changed hands and become much more partisan by the early 1990s, Pat Roberts became the chairman of the Senate Agriculture Committee. He had previously been the chair of the House Agriculture Committee and was the only member of Congress to have occupied both posts. I knew him well and could work with him. That relationship was important because the most serious negotiations were held just with him and his staff, so I didn't have to work with folks who were out to screw over President Clinton and the Democrats just to score partisan points.

The political atmosphere became more toxic in the mid-1990s, in part due to extreme partisanship precipitated by Newt Gingrich and Republican control of the Congress. But Clinton was very pro-farmer and had good relationships with farm state members; certainly my relationships with Dole and Roberts, the latter of whom was chair of the House Agriculture Committee at the time, helped soften the partisanship. We had three Kansans running farm policy in America.

Even though change was underway in Congress, people still wanted to work things out through legislative negotiations. In the end, President Clinton had some reservations about the bill, but I convinced him it had good provisions and was worth signing.

The 1996 Farm Bill we negotiated, which provided a seven-year framework for the USDA to administer agriculture and food programs, was eventually signed into law in April and encompassed the bulk of my legislative activities during my tenure as secretary of agriculture. One of the reasons Bill Clinton had chosen me as his secretary of agriculture was my obvious network of contacts and working relationships from both parties on the Hill. As a matter of fact, the Clinton White House held off engaging Congress on the subject until I was in place as the new secretary of agriculture, and my team and I became quite involved in every step of the negotiations.

The primary focus of the USDA is to help farmers. We could deal with natural disasters, such as droughts or tornadoes, or respond quickly to falling crop prices. My relationship with Congress was critically important throughout my years at the USDA, particularly because low farm prices were the norm for much of the time I was there. Because I had earned a reputation as a moderate who could work well with colleagues from both sides of the aisle, I was an effective secretary of agriculture, and the 1996 Farm Bill became the blueprint for moving forward.

My position also gave me a platform to create and advocate visions for a better America regarding how we fed the nation and the world, and how to leave a better planet for the next generation. Conservation, the environment, eating healthy and safe foods, eliminating food waste, and helping those in need via programs such as SNAP were subjects that had grown incredibly important to me during my time in Congress. Through my work at the USDA, I could actually do something directly about them.

We held a well-attended forum on popular diets, including two created by prominent physicians, Dean Ornish and Robert Atkins. There was an enormous amount of press interest, as it was the first time that the USDA had focused on diets, as opposed to individual foods or food groups. Ornish was an advocate of a diet low in fats and protein and Atkins was famous for his low-carb diets. In my judgment, each believed that the other was preaching death and evil. The tension between the two was high, and I thought it might lead to a physical altercation. Talk about a food fight! Nonetheless, the enormous national attention they received helped establish a national debate on nutrition and food consumption, which continues to this day.

We significantly boosted US food assistance to famine and drought-stricken areas around the world. At home, food stamps were restored to thousands of legal immigrants, and we launched a new food stamp education outreach effort. We organized conferences on childhood obesity and published new dietary guidelines that included, for the first time, recommendations on exercise and food safety. This work involved developing farmer's markets nationwide, including opening the USDA farmers market outside our Washington, DC, headquarters. At the time, there were only a handful of farmer's markets, and now there are approximately ten thousand nationwide. They were a big part of my desire to expand farm income and bring consumers and farmers closer together. They presented an opportunity for people to buy fresh produce directly from their local growers.

I am thrilled with how farmer's markets have grown significantly nationwide, and to this day, I absolutely love going to farmer's markets.

We also took one of the first close looks at organic food and genetically modified organisms (GMOs), meaning foods produced via genetic engineering instead of being grown through traditional farming and harvesting.

The Organic Food and Production Act was implemented under my watch. The regulatory process generated an incredible amount of consumer comments, in part because the first attempt at regulation did not explicitly rule out GMOs in the definition of organic. The feedback we received from the public was intense.

"How can you lump organic and GMOs together?"

That was a tame comment. Organic agriculture not using GMOs and conventional agriculture using GMOs gave consumers a real choice of what they wanted to eat.

Although GMOs were considered safe by an overwhelming majority of experts, consumer pressure prevailed, and we struck the GMO reference, which opened the door to today's organic food movement bearing the blessing and imprint of the USDA organic seal. Today, the organic food movement is one of the most profitable parts of the agricultural sector.

It is important to note that the organic food movement and the science behind GMOs were relatively new when I became secretary of agriculture. We created regulations and precedents as we learned on the fly about this new way of farming. As with any learning process, there were some hiccups along the way, but I strongly believe that the work we did set the tone for today's understanding of what defines organic food and how GMOs can be an important part of the agriculture industry.

Under the USDA seal, organic-labeled products completely avoid modified ingredients. This means that an organic farmer cannot plant GMO seeds or an organic cow cannot be fed GMO feedstock. While organic food is totally divorced from GMOs, one should not ignore the potential benefits they can bring.

Proponents of GMOs will tell you that the process can feed the hungry, assist farmers by making certain crops more resistant to insects or harsh weather conditions, and can improve many foods. For example, they can pull seeds out of the grapes we all buy at local supermarkets. The again, maybe we could do that ourselves without risking any unnecessary genetic modifiers.

Many opponents of GMOs are worried about putting food on the table that is not found in nature or that is scientifically altered in any way. They feel that we do not yet know enough to declare GMOs completely safe.

The organic food versus GMOs debate was an extremely interesting intellectual challenge when I became secretary of agriculture, and it just shows how farming, even though the practice goes back millennia, continues to evolve.

Under the USDA umbrella, we employed more than forty thousand public servants as part of the US Forest Service. We shifted their policy focus away from merely timbering and toward a multiuse philosophy. As part of this plan, I protected nearly sixty million acres of pristine national forest land from additional road building, and President Clinton created a national monument to protect the world's only remaining giant sequoia trees. Ironically, one of Trump's last acts as president was to restore logging in pristine areas of the Tongass National Forest in Alaska, which partly reversed one of the Clinton-Gore administration's most significant environmental achievements.

At the USDA, with the head of the US Forest Service reporting to me, I was placed smack in the middle of a war between the timber industry and environmentalists, and I must admit that I leaned heavily in favor of the spotted owl who made its home in these majestic trees. It most certainly helped to have Al Gore as an ally, who to this day remains the leading voice and good conscience of the environmental protection movement.

Virtually every timber sale offered or not offered became a battle with the industry and Republican members of Congress, most notably Senators Murkowski and Stevens of Alaska, my old sparring buddies. They believed they had heard a promise from me during my nomination hearings to let them chop down trees at will. Really? That's what they actually heard me say? Interesting. My commitment to them had been to be fair when considering deforestation proposals without any mention of chopping down trees.

While I thought I was being fair, our differences of opinion came to a head one year when Murkowski, Stevens, and Senator Larry Craig of Idaho defunded the USDA undersecretary in charge of forestry matters. I ended up taking the highly unusual step of crafting a handwritten note to every single senator, placed on each of their desks when the bill was considered. Ultimately, the money was restored. I didn't go to the media to get the job done while risking embarrassment to my colleagues. Instead, I took my case directly to the lawmakers and won that battle.

In addition to serving the farmers' interest on Capitol Hill and implementing nationwide agricultural policy, the secretary of agriculture is the industry's world ambassador. I had the opportunity to represent our nation's interests at conferences and negotiations across the globe. Trade agreements with other countries often contain a robust agricultural component, and the secretary's leadership is crucial in protecting the interests of America's farmers.

I had the honor of representing the president during negotiations in Japan, South America, Europe, and China—often during contentious sessions focusing on thorny issues, such as genetically modified foods, livestock hormones, and export subsidies.

I specifically recall many meetings with European counterparts regarding GMOs and hormones. European standards are much stricter, and a trade war based on hormones would have prevented US beef from reaching European Union markets. Clearly, this would have been disastrous to the US economy, especially our farmers, and it took rounds upon rounds of negotiations to find a mutually agreeable solution.

Public attitudes, even my own, on issues like appropriate utilization of pesticides and hormones, as well as related food and agriculture products, have evolved over the years. Today there is a much stronger consumer force in agriculture and food production techniques than we saw twenty-five years ago. Consumers are much more interested now in what is in their food, how it's produced, and where it's grown or raised.

Those trips around the world were incredibly rewarding, but one incident almost cost me my marriage.

A group of senior USDA employees and I were traveling to Africa in the summer of 1999 to see how our food assistance program was working. We visited a Maasai village in southern Kenya, not too far from Nairobi, where we received royal treatment from the villagers, who presented us with flowers and could not have been more gracious and hospitable. As the food trucks were driving by on their way to deliver the food aid, I kept hearing the screams of a nearby woman.

"Chicago, Chicago!"

That was the only word she was saying in English, which I thought was rather unusual. I asked our translator what the woman was saying and why she kept repeating "Chicago."

"Secretary Glickman, the woman is saying that she has a cousin in Chicago and wants to know if you'll marry her so she can come to Chicago to see him."

Of course I was flattered but asked my translator to let her know that I was already happily married, and that in the United States, that type of thing is frowned upon, especially by a woman I know who goes by the name of Rhoda Glickman. I explained that, as opposed to Kenyan tradition, it was against American law to have more than one wife, so I could not oblige her request.

I could see from the grimace on her face that she was disappointed. I felt kind of bad, but the rest of our crew thought the entire incident was quite amusing. Rhoda and I have not spoken of my potential Kenyan wife since then, but I did make a promise that the next time I went to Kenya I would take her with me.

Once a diplomat . . .

On the same trip to Africa in 1999 I met Nelson Mandela.

With the help of President Clinton and State Department staff, my USDA team and I visited former president Mandela in August. What was supposed to be a thirty-minute courtesy visit turned into several hours of discussion about South African history, agriculture, politics, and American investment in South Africa. We spent a lot of time discussing reconciliation and peace in his country, especially how he could forgive his previous enemies. I was particularly interested in the amount of Jewish memorabilia in his house, and he spoke movingly about the number of Jewish supporters in the anti-apartheid movement, as well as the Jewish lawyers who gave him job opportunities earlier in his life when few others in the white community would.

I had a copy of his autobiography, *Long Walk to Freedom*, which he autographed.

"To Glickman: Best Wishes to a Wonderful and Generous Philanthropist. Mandela. August 6, 2000."

I will treasure this forever.

Serving as Bill Clinton's secretary of agriculture was the honor of a lifetime and the pinnacle of my career in public service—putting aside the occasional bison intestine flying in my direction. In addition to shaping and implementing the nation's agricultural policy, I had a front-row seat to the significant issues that influenced the last decade of the twentieth century.

President Clinton's leadership style was one of inclusion. In other words, his analytical process needed the input and opinions of those he trusted. There was never any doubt that he was the final decision-maker and would go against the majority opinion if he felt it prudent. He could raise his voice in anger, no doubt about it, but he never personalized his irritation or belittled someone who worked for him. He understood that politics requires pragmatism and that relationships matter. That was something we had in common.

He was also a classic "good old boy" from Hope, Arkansas, whose understanding and appreciation of rural Americans and farmers was in his DNA.

Bill Clinton and I got along extremely well. We had quite a few things in common, the two most prominent being our sense of humor and our love for golf. The first opportunity to play with him almost never happened. I was in Wichita when the call came from the White House that the president would like to play golf with me at Andrews Air Force Base the next day. I had many meetings planned in Kansas and had not seen my parents in a while so I was going to pass, but my father insisted I go back to DC.

"Danny, drop what you're doing and play golf with the president, but for God's sake, don't beat him!"

I didn't take my dad's advice too seriously. After all, Bill Clinton was the president of the United States. He didn't need to be flattered by beating his cabinet secretary at golf.

I flew back to Washington. The next day, I joined Bill Clinton and Vernon Jordan, a classic Washington insider and close friend of the president. Despite disagreeing with my dad, I absolutely tried to play my worst just in case he was right. On the first hole, I scored a par. On the second shot on the second hole, I scored an eagle on a par four when I hit it blind from over 150 yards to the pin. It was dumb luck.

By now, the commander-in-chief appeared upset. I was wondering whether some sort of Russian invasion had happened without me hearing about it, but I should have listened more closely to my father's advice.

"Let's just make sure that ball is actually yours," Clinton said, commenting on my near-pro level drive.

On the third hole, I birdied. That's when I realized my dad was right and I was in trouble. Mustering all my focus, I concentrated on playing the worst golf of my life on the remaining holes, which probably saved my relationship with the president as well as my future in government. In fact, I might have saved the future of farming altogether.

In typical Bill Clinton fashion, which has endeared him to many cabinet members, he sent me a picture of the two of us with a handwritten inscription.

"Anytime you can play golf, have an eagle and say, *"Screw the President,"* you're having a good day."

Twenty years later when he met my son at an event in Los Angeles, Bill Clinton told him that golf story and cracked himself up in the process.

We bonded over humor and golf so much, in fact, that during my vacation in St. Croix in the US Virgin Islands, someone tracked me down on the golf course one day.

"A Mr. POTUS is on the phone for you, Sir."

I knew that Clinton would forgive me for finishing my round before calling him back, especially since I was playing really well. As soon as I finished, I rushed to the club's pro shop to return his call. True to form, the first thing President Clinton said to me was about the golf course and not the policy issue, the latter of which was his real reason for calling.

"I think I played that course in St. Croix."

What came next made that call one of the more surreal experiences of my life as a cabinet member. Bill Clinton had just received a call from Jimmy Carter about the price of pork. Apparently, during a Bible study at the former president's church in Georgia, one of the farmers there had lamented the decline in hog prices. President Clinton wanted to update the former president and needed immediate information from me—vacation or not—about hog prices. This led to me briefing him on the current value of America's pigs while standing in my golf duds in a St. Croix pro shop, surrounded by dozens of amused golfers.

Somehow, too much of my life was revolving around pork.

This also prompted greater attention on food safety, which was a high priority to prevent food-borne pathogens like salmonella and ecoli, both possible killers. That said, during this time, we didn't focus enough on the health and safety of employees, especially in meat and poultry plants. Part of this was due to the regulatory anomaly that the health and safety of employees was not in the

USDA statutory authority, as it resided under OSHA and the Labor Department. Today, with the COVID-19 crisis, it is abundantly clear that a serious review of these separate regulatory authorities is needed because the health, safety, and reliability of the food supply is intrinsically related to the safety of the employees handling the supply. Many in the food industry oppose tightening this regulatory review, but the viability of our modern and complicated food supply system demands it.

Back to the White House. Bill Clinton the man is no different from the President Clinton we have seen on television for decades. He's absolutely one of the smartest people I have ever met. He is highly analytical; he is compassionate to a fault; he retains names, faces, and information in that computer-like brain of his, and he can recall it all at a moment's notice. He can focus on you and make you feel like the most important person in his life at that moment. In my opinion, he was one of our greatest presidents, with a list of achievements and sound policy that clearly demonstrates the tremendously positive impact he has had on our country. He was also one of the best policy minds on American agriculture with whom I have ever worked.

However, his presidency will, of course, forever be remembered for his extramarital relationship and the resulting impeachment. When the Monica Lewinsky story no longer could be ignored and had to be addressed by the White House, President Clinton convened the cabinet and gave us his side of the story, which at that time, still included a complete denial that there had been a sexual relationship. He had just completed his deposition and was sharing with us the position he had taken with the independent counselor's office. He more or less dictated to us a series of talking points that we should take to the press and use to defend him.

It was, without a doubt, the expectation he put on his cabinet members: step in front of the microphones and plead my innocence to the American people.

As cabinet members filed out of the room and left the White House, the Washington press corps was lined up with cameras, waiting for statements. Bill Daley, Madeleine Albright, and others chose to participate and defend the president in front of the cameras.

I trusted my gut feeling when a story does not ring true. The one I had received that day in the White House's cabinet room did not sound accurate to me at all. You have to be a good loyal soldier in politics, but if your instincts drive you in a different direction, you're left with a difficult decision. I trusted my instincts. I was lucky to exit out the side door and avoid commenting to the press about the president's remarks.

Fast-forward to the infamous blue dress with the president's DNA as evidence.

The cabinet and senior White House staff were called to the White House, this time to the Yellow Oval Room, which is in the president's residential quarters. White House staff had arranged our chairs in a semi-circle around the president's chair, and one by one, the president asked us to share our thoughts on the situation. In a way, this was the world's most high-level group therapy session, with many cabinet members reassuring the president that he still had their support. Then the president turned to one of the female cabinet members, making her the first woman to address the group.

She gave him holy hell about how he had betrayed women with his behavior.

"You ought to be ashamed of yourself," she said, and that was it.

You could hear a pin drop.

I remember everything she said, almost word for word, but I can't remember anything that came out of my own mouth. I could not wait to get out of that room and be anywhere else. That group therapy session, however, may have saved Bill Clinton's presidency, because it gave all of us a chance to voice our emotions and then cool down. Not a single cabinet member resigned, which provided Clinton and the country a sense of stability during a time of crisis. Clinton had a huge amount of good will with his cabinet. Firing an able and extremely competent cabinet member would not have been in his character, unlike what we saw with former president Trump.

Knowing how well-connected I was on Capitol Hill, President Clinton asked me to make some calls to Republican members of Congress to take their pulse on the scandal. He was wondering whether there was a genuine appetite for impeachment. I could have told him the answer without talking to a single one of them. It was more than obvious that the Republicans, led by Speaker Newt Gingrich, were out for blood and could not wait to go nuclear on the Lewinsky affair. Newt was such a hypocrite!

Bill Clinton, though certainly flawed, had enough support on Capitol Hill and within his party that he could survive the impeachment trial once it reached the Senate. He was so likable that few from his own party were going to go against him (in the end, there were only five Democrats in the House who voted in favor of at least one of the four articles of impeachment). There were even quite a few Republicans who liked him as a person and voted against impeachment, even though their leadership was trying to force them to hold the party line.

I have often been asked how I would have voted on impeachment if I had been a member of the House. I would have voted against impeachment. His conduct was seriously improper, but not impeachable. Clinton never put the country at risk. And all things being equal, on most things he was truly an excellent president. The last balanced budgets we had were in his term. America was respected around the world.

This is another lesson that likability is one of the long-term keys to success in politics, no matter how trying the circumstances may be.

We can juxtapose that climate with the Senate voting pattern during the impeachment and conviction of Trump, where except for Mitt Romney, the vote was totally partisan. Same in the House. Clinton's impeachment had the ring of some partisanship but much less than what we see today—on just about everything. Even Nixon's impeachment in the House was bipartisan. The later (second) impeachment of Trump was slightly more bipartisan.

A wounded Bill Clinton served out his term and handed the Democratic mantle to my friend Al Gore, who would have made an outstanding president. However, the Clinton administration, despite the many tremendous accomplishments we brought to the country, most notably a strong economy and balanced budget, had become a tarnished brand, and that was one big reason that cost Gore the Oval Office, although just barely.

In the tightest election in the nation's history, the presidency was decided by a handful of votes in Florida and eventually required the Supreme Court to determine the winner. I might have considered continuing my public service in a Gore White House, but clearly, that was not an option under President George W. Bush. On January 20, 2001, my time as secretary of agriculture came to an end, as did my career as a public servant. Bush wanted his own team, which he was entitled to. He did keep one Clinton cabinet member, Norm Mineta, as secretary of transportation.

When my final run for Congress ended in election defeat, I thought my world had come to an end. Weeks later, I was nominated in a Rose Garden ceremony to become a member of the president's cabinet. Fast-forward another few months, and I took the oath of office to be our nation's secretary of agriculture, embarking on the six most remarkable and impactful years of my professional life. Being committed to building relationships with my colleagues from both parties and getting things done was the key to my success then, as much as it is now.

A partisan operative hell-bent on pushing through an agenda that appeals to only one party would not have been successful in this job. It is because of my moderate approach to politics that I was able to do a lot of good for the American people. That philosophy continued to provide me with so many interesting opportunities that likely would not have happened if I had been viewed as an extremist or as a partisan troublemaker.

Plus, folks always remembered my jokes and singing.

Even after leaving the USDA, I have continued to work on domestic and global hunger and related nutrition issues, especially through partnering with my friend and former secretary of agriculture, Ann Veneman. I had previously focused on strengthening the food stamp program and other feeding programs while in Congress and at the USDA, and it remains one of my key passions today. I also have become a strong advocate for a well-funded federal food and agriculture research program, so critical for preserving a safe and adequate food supply to feed a hungry world. Congress in 2014 created the Foundation for Food and Agriculture Research, to find innovative ways to fund food and agricultural issues, and I was pleased to be its founding chair.

I am proud that the United States continues to lead the world in fighting hunger and malnutrition at home and abroad.

We still have at least fifty million people on SNAP, millions still access the nation's food banks, and as unemployment has skyrocketed in the past year, this demonstrates the constant problem of food insecurity in the United States, not to mention the significant problem of food waste and loss across the food supply system, where it is estimated that more than one-third of all food produced and sold is thrown away. Still, by and large, a bipartisan coalition in Congress has worked to keep our feeding programs to the poor as a high priority. This is one of the great bipartisan achievements of the past forty years.

That said, we must do better.

Chapter 13

From DC to Harvard to Hollywood and Back: Life After Public Service

After leaving government for the last time after George W. Bush was elected president, I became a lawyer lobbyist for a short while at the law firm of Akin, Gump, Strauss, Hauer, and Feld. While I did no actual lobbying that required registration under federal lobbying laws, I did work on food and agricultural issues. But I must admit that although the law firm was helpful and generous, it was not a natural fit for me. I loved public service. A year or so later, I accepted a position at the Harvard University Kennedy School of Government as the director of the Institute of Politics. I quickly came to love the daily interaction with bright young minds as I tried to impart some wisdom from my long career in public service. What an excellent job, helping students advance their interest in politics while working with a fascinating collection of people—authors, politicians, and other leaders from here at home and around the world.

Ironically, the most famous student at the time was Mark Zuckerberg. I can't actually remember if I met him but I do know that I did not invent Facebook. Sadly, I was not smart enough to invest in it, either. Former presidential candidate (and former mayor of South Bend, Indiana) Pete Buttigieg was also a student on campus while I was there. He was one of the smartest kids I met while at Harvard, and we have remained good friends.

One Monday, I was sitting at my desk in Cambridge, Massachusetts, answering my typical daily load of emails. I had a full day ahead of me to review our lecturers' syllabuses, meet with students, return phone calls, and meet with my staff of fifteen. We ran one of the largest lecture series in the world and interfaced with some of the brightest young minds in America, including students like Buttigieg.

As I settled in with my second cup of coffee, my phone rang and I noticed a number with a Washington, DC, area code. Leslie Hortum was a headhunter working with the DC office of the international firm, Spencer Stuart, and I had met Hortum during my years in Washington. She had a reputation for placing top political and business leaders in high-profile jobs around the country.

"Hi, Dan, it's Leslie, and I'm calling to let you know that Jack Valenti is leaving the Motion Picture Association, and I figured you would want to know."

Jack Valenti was a legend in DC and Hollywood. He was originally a public relations consultant from Houston who had done some work for President Lyndon Johnson (LBJ) until he was hired full time after the Kennedy assassination; he was on the plane that carried Kennedy's body back to DC. After a few years with LBJ, he was hired to head up the Motion Picture Association of America (MPAA) in Washington, DC, where he led the group for over thirty years and became Hollywood's representative in DC. He was suave and handsome, and members of Congress loved him.

"Dan, how would you feel about throwing your hat in the ring as his successor?"

"What a question," I said.

I was so intrigued.

Leading the MPAA was my private-sector dream job, an opportunity to combine my love of movies with my love of politics. But many thoughts flashed through my mind in that moment, like what would it be like heading up a trade association representing the glamour of Hollywood? How would a Midwestern politician with little knowledge of the film industry survive in this environment? Harvard's Institute of Politics was a comfortable, interesting, intellectually stimulating job (and the only way I got into Harvard).

I have always loved motion pictures. I can still smell the aroma of fresh popcorn when my parents took us to the movies, which was almost every week. Sometimes my dad sent me and my brother and sister to the Crest Theater in Wichita to buy popcorn, even when we weren't seeing a movie. He said theater popcorn was better than my mom's, and we didn't disagree. The Crest held twelve hundred people, making it one of Wichita's largest. When it opened in 1950,

I was a happy six-year-old, sitting in awe, watching some of that year's top releases: *Cinderella, Treasure Island, Abbott and Costello in the Foreign Legion, Kim,* and *The Jackie Robinson Story.*

Once we had our own children, Rhoda and I made family movie night a tradition, a staple that no Glickman ever wanted to miss. I thought of the rich tradition that movies had played in my life, as a child and a parent, and if I would become Jack Valenti's successor at the MPAA I could combine my political experience with my passion for the silver screen. The love of movies was so ingrained in our family that my son Jonathan, a Hollywood film producer, had already been involved by then in the production of over a dozen films—before I was ever considered for the job.

Valenti made it clear to the headhunter that "of the various people the headhunter is talking to," I was the preferred candidate, and a fair amount of leaking to the media took place soon after my initial consideration by the headhunter and Valenti. Valenti supported me in large part because I was a former cabinet member, which gave me stature, and I had worked with the MPAA on many issues, such as film piracy and intellectual property issues over the years, both when I was a member of the House Judiciary Committee. Plus, he knew me and my family. Valenti knew Rhoda especially well because she had been director of the Congressional Arts Caucus for a dozen years, bringing members of the House and Senate to Hollywood and Hollywood to Congress, where they worked on issues of mutual interest. Sometimes I think Rhoda would have been a better head of the MPAA as she knew the issues and the people so well.

Succeeding a legend like Jack Valenti would be a challenge. I knew there would be many other highly qualified people vying for his job, both in Washington and Hollywood. Valenti's shoes would most certainly be tough to fill. Like with many important decisions, I took time to think it through carefully and ultimately realized that I had to jump at the opportunity and pursue the job. I had nothing to lose, except a bruised ego, and plenty to gain, personally and professionally.

I felt good about my chances for the job. I had been a member of the House Judiciary Committee in Congress, where I'd been active in many of the issues that concern the movie industry, especially intellectual property rights and trade issues. I knew that stuff and I knew the people in government who made it happen.

Who was I to disagree?

After deciding to accept the offer, I had to get out of my agreement with the Kennedy School, where I had fulfilled two years of a three-year commitment. I was managing their speaker series and their fellows program. I didn't want to be someone who goes back on their word, but the opportunity at MPAA was once in a lifetime, and the salary was significantly higher than what I was making at Harvard. Since my staff there was already doing an excellent job of managing projects without my daily supervision, I hoped to leave with a relatively clear conscience and my reputation intact.

Leaving the Kennedy School as quickly as I did to join the MPAA created some ill will with a few members of the Kennedy family, but another problem arose once I was announced for the MPAA job, which reflected the new, partisan reality that continues to metastasize like a cancer in our government.

I became a target of something called the K Street Project. This was a Republican strategy created in 1995 by Grover Norquist (the man behind binding all Republicans to a completely unrealistic no-new-taxes pledge) and Gingrich-led House Republicans to persuade and pressure Washington lobbying firms to hire "Republicans only" to fill their top jobs.

After the Gingrich gang took over the House in 1994, they informed corporate America that only Republican lobbyists would get anyone's attention on Capitol Hill. Because most of their offices are located along K Street in downtown DC, the entire undertaking became known as the K Street Project. Many law firms, lobbying shops, and corporate government affairs offices staffed up on the Republican side to build and maintain the relationships that are the lifeblood of their businesses.

When you think about how to be the most effective lobby shop, you want to have folks with relationships on both sides of the aisle. This happens naturally, but what Norquist and Gingrich were doing was pressuring lobbying groups based purely on partisan affiliation. This was a vivid example of negative partisanship, the kind that is still dominating our political landscape. I'm not arguing that top jobs in lobby shops on K Street should be held exclusively by Democrats; a diversity of networks is necessary when pursuing business goals. But to make the letter between the parentheses next to a person's name—Glickman (D)—the benchmark for everything else is as foolish as it is divisive.

House Majority Leader Tom Delay was a key player in the Norquist/Gingrich movement. Because he was putting pressure on major trade associations and corporations to fill their plum jobs with no one but Republicans, I knew he would vehemently oppose me for the position at the MPAA and take serious umbrage at such a prize job going to a Democrat.

God forbid!

Thanks to years of building bridges with my colleagues, I had a few Republicans chime in on my behalf with K Street Project leaders and MPAA board members. I even put Bob Dole down as one of my character references. My friends in the Kansas congressional delegation weighed in for me, as did former president Clinton, my friend and former secretary of commerce, Mickey Kantor, and several others. After the internal vetting process concluded without any red flags, the MPAA board, with Jack Valenti's endorsement, voted to offer me the position.

As expected, the K Street Project folks weren't happy and Norquist said as much in an article he wrote in *The Hill.*

"Hiring Glickman is a studied insult by the film industry."

Ouch!

He went on to say that hiring Democrats was "stupid."

Well, that was just plain silly.

Valenti stood by me through their criticism, and even though I had public pushback from the K Street Project, I enjoyed great bipartisan support from Capitol Hill. The negative partisanship that is so effective today in shutting down the process didn't stop me from getting such a great job. At times it was daunting, but I went from office to office in the House and Senate, trying to build bridges with Republican lawmakers.

Folks in Washington thought this MPAA job was the most glamorous one in DC, in part because of Valenti's long tenure, his history with LBJ, and the fact that he knew everyone in Washington, Hollywood, and around the globe. As a result, I received enormous press coverage when I was announced as his successor. The *New York Times*, the *Washington Post*, the *Wall Street Journal*, and all the Hollywood trade publications ran big stories announcing it. I was a little intimidated by my lack of recognition by the entertainment media and community, but Valenti acted as my agent, mentor, and rabbi to secure my reputation and image as well suited.

When Valenti planned the succession and announced my appointment in July 2004 at the Hay Adams Hotel in Washington, DC, (next to the MPAA building) he did it the old-fashioned Hollywood way. I stood behind a curtain in the ballroom, and just as he announced me to at least one hundred members of the media, I walked out from behind the curtain, almost as if I was the Wizard of Oz finally revealing himself. The irony to the Kansas connection was not lost on me.

As I spoke, it became immediately clear to me that a lot of the entertainment reporters had no idea who I was other than a former congressman from Kansas and the former secretary of agriculture. Even though I had actually been hired by the heads of the seven major studios, who knew my background well, others in Washington and Hollywood were suspicious that a person from the world of agriculture could be the leading figure in the film industry—notwithstanding my long-time work in Congress on trade and intellectual property and anti-piracy issues.

Quite interestingly, two of America's leading exports are agricultural products and movies and entertainment. This connection made a lot of sense to me.

In spite of what I considered my classic Midwestern Jewish good looks, I was not exactly Mr. Glamour, at least not in the Hollywood sense. Former attorney general Eric Holder told me at the time, "You've got the greatest job," and he may have been right, but I spent a lot of time early on working overtime to introduce myself to the world of film and television.

"I used to grow popcorn, and now I sell it," became one of my favorite and frequently told jokes. Yet most of the work was not glamorous. We didn't consort with movie stars frequently. Instead, we were policy nerds on issues such as piracy, censorship, taxes, and trade.

I spent the first few weeks listening to my employees, learning about time-sensitive issues, and getting to know the studio heads who had given me this incredible opportunity. By that time, in November 2004, the Bush/Cheney ticket had just won reelection against John Kerry and John Edwards.

Republicans had picked up some seats in the House while defending the Senate. As a Democrat with farm issue experience, I had to lean on my reputation as being independent and bipartisan, as well as my record as a moderate Democrat who found common ground with congressional Republicans.

The MPAA had several crucial issues that I focused on right away. Copyright and piracy concerns were paramount at the time, and tensions were high between the movie and tech industries because of these critical issues. Internet piracy was becoming ubiquitous, and movies and TV shows were being ripped off and made available online for free. This hurt the business prospects for Hollywood and TV studios, and something had to be done.

I also faced the challenges of how to increase American box office revenues and open markets abroad for our films. I really enjoyed this because I think few elements of American culture export as well or are as popular as blockbuster Hollywood films. As if those issues weren't enough to fill my days, I needed to address the partisan perception that Hollywood was strictly a liberal industry that was out of touch with conservatives, even though it employed more than two million people from all walks of life, including actors like Charlton Heston, Jon Voight, and John Wayne, who were not exactly die-hard Democrats.

As a diplomat by nature and someone known to possess a moderate and inclusive voice often independent from the Democratic Party, I knew I could be a bridge builder between Hollywood and Washington, even with the Republican lobby machine making so much noise. But, just to be on the safe side, I hired two respected Republican aides and invited Republicans to screen Oscar-nominated films at the MPAA's private screening room. I was hell-bent on eliminating the vitriol between the Bush-bashing by many Hollywood celebs, as well as the backlash against movies that conservatives felt were offensive. This became my mission.

At the end of the day, Americans think Hollywood and movie actors are cool. It doesn't matter if you are conservative or liberal. Revering big-name stars and the industry in general is a part of American culture. That was my belief as I tried to break down the walls between conservative politicians and liberal Hollywood. I initiated and hosted the first two major Hollywood/Washington MPAA symposia, which brought around four hundred industry representatives and elected officials in DC together, as well as movie stars and the media. During the day we held discussions on substantive issues, and in the evening we hosted a large reception and dinner. In my judgment, this was a successful attempt to gather these disparate groups under one roof to talk and wine and dine in a Washington, DC, setting.

During one of these events, which I moderated, Will Smith came and spoke about the power of the movie industry and the significance of film in changing people's attitudes. He told a compelling story about the movie *In the Heat of the Night*, starring Rod Steiger as the white sheriff of a segregated town in the South and Sidney Poitier, who played a Philadelphia-based detective investigating a murder in Steiger's community.

During one scene, Poitier confronts a local businessman about the alleged crime. The businessman insults Poitier with a racial slur and Poitier and the businessman soon slap each other in the face.

Fast-forward years later to when Nelson Mandela was in the Robben Island prison in South Africa. Incredibly, they showed this movie (among others) to the prisoners but only showed Poitier being slapped. But in the context of the movie, Mandela and his colleagues figured out that Poitier must have slapped the other guy because otherwise it didn't make any sense. The upshot was that this scene gave Mandela and his colleagues the belief that others watching this movie must have seen a reciprocal face slap, and this was a huge boost of morale for the prisoners.

I assume Mandela must have told Will Smith this story. In any event, he heard it from a reliable source. You could have heard a pin drop when Will Smith told the story, as it demonstrated the power of movies in delivering a compelling story. Of course *In the Heat of the Night* won the Academy Award for best picture that year.

At another event, Clint Eastwood discussed his role in broadening audiences. Dwayne "the Rock" Johnson spoke at a lunch, and we hosted producer and director John Landis, famous for his movie *Animal House*. I love that movie, which shows exactly how sophisticated I am. In fact, John Landis signed a poster to me with the following inscription:

It was Glickman against the Rules, and the Rules lost.
Dan, Toga, Toga.
John Landis.

I treasure that almost as much as the Mandela autograph, which I keep on display right next to an *Animal House* picture.

Congress is the seat of absolute power, and Washington, DC, is the beating heart of the world's last true superpower. The decisions that the men and women walking the halls of Congress make—or do not make—have real impact on the lives of millions across the country, and those legislators take themselves quite seriously, as most of them should. But watch what happens to them when you announce that a Hollywood celebrity will be in room S-120 of the US Capitol. Many of these buttoned up folks turn into giddy adolescents, hoping for an autograph or a selfie. I am no exception. I loved hanging out with movie stars.

Even though Hollywood is filled with its fair share of lefty liberals, most members of Congress, including conservatives, love the industry. The events I organized didn't lead to much drama over Hollywood activism. Instead, breaking down barriers with good dialogue and a healthy budget for alcohol and pigs-in-blankets proved to be a positive strategy.

The MPAA screening room was a popular place to show movies to members of Congress, and invitations to those screenings were some of the most coveted in DC. This helped with my popularity and access with Congress. Lots of stars came through Washington, including Will Smith, Clint Eastwood, Martin Scorsese, Woody Allen, Matthew Broderick, Sarah Jessica Parker, Jon Voight, and many others. Members of both parties loved meeting these people, and most of the celebrities were thoughtful and sensible about the issues.

Getting Republicans and Democrats together with luminaries from Hollywood gave everyone a chance to learn about the issues that affected them and helped build the long-term relationships that are critical for success in any endeavor.

For example, California's own senator, Diane Feinstein, was highly critical of the industry for putting way too much emphasis on violence. Her comments were actually pretty gutsy at the time, considering she was criticizing Hollywood as a senator from California. Through our symposium, we had a chance for a real back-and-forth discussion on that and several other issues.

At one conference, we presented a special award to Clint Eastwood, and another year we presented the same to Martin Scorsese, both for their catalogues of great directorial work. These events and advocacy paid off in spades. As a result, we reached out to dozens of members of Congress and their staff on piracy and other issues, and successfully helped pass major tax legislation worth hundreds of millions of dollars for the studios. The bridges we built were priceless, and they continue to this day.

I can't say I succeeded in breaking down the barriers between conservative elected officials and Hollywood, but like any true moderate, I tried my best to make a real impact on the divide. I'm proud of the work we did at the MPAA to build and strengthen those relationships. I even donated thousands of dollars personally to Democratic and Republican legislators.

In spite of this perceived progress, some Republicans in Congress, along with several in the administration, continued to demonstrate the kind of partisanship that takes no prisoners. They didn't make legislative matters any easier, but I did my best to keep the MPAA bipartisan and independent.

I always invited roughly an equal number of Republicans and Democrats to our dinners and events, and spent a lot of time visiting members of both parties. I helped members of both parties set up fundraisers in Los Angeles, even though raising campaign money was not one of my favorite tasks.

The television and movie industry is a powerful force for producing jobs in America. My job, and the role of the MPAA, was to talk about the economic and cultural impact of this industry, which faced good and bad regulatory initiatives from Congress. I had to fight the bad ones and help shape the good ones. One of my successes at the MPAA was navigating congressional adoption of a film production tax credit, worth hundreds of millions of dollars to the studios.

Another big accomplishment during my tenure at the MPAA was managing our movie-rating process, where we rated movies and related advertising based on factors such as sexual content, violence and language, and drug use. This was the brilliant creation of Jack Valenti, conceived to avoid the local censorship boards of his predecessor. It worked amazingly well by providing people, especially parents, information about the content of movies through the various letter grades—"G" to "NC-17"—along with descriptors that accompanied the ratings, which we substantially expanded during my term.

We also added "smoking" as a factor affecting ratings and the specificity of the descriptive language, which accompanied the ratings. We democratized the ratings process, allowing more transparency and input into the decisions. This was an enormously important and interesting part of the job, one that gave me and my team significant influence and power over the motion picture production process, especially because a specific rating could impact the revenues for a particular movie.

For example, an "R" rated movie usually drew a smaller audience than a "PG-13" rated movie. Studios and the creative production teams often did their best to work with the ratings staff to get the least restrictive rating possible. This was the area where I primarily interfaced with the great producers and directors of American films, and while I personally did not review many of these movies (there were a few hundred a year), I often became involved in the more controversial decisions.

One incident I particularly remember was the "R" rated movie, *The Hangover*, which I thought was a more recent version of *Animal House*. No one objected to its "R" rating because it met all the criteria. It became one of the most popular "R" rated movies ever, along with its sequels. Nonetheless, in watching the outtakes at the end of the film during the credits, I noticed a particular clip, which appeared to show a graphic moment of oral sex. Although I was convinced this was done in a simulated and humorous way, I was disturbed because this was not to be permitted in an "R" rated movie, and it had somehow slipped through the process.

That is why we had the "NC-17" rating, which had replaced the old "X" rating of previous years. After a thorough review of the process, and recognizing that the clip was not live action but an attempt to be funny during the credits, we got a commitment from everyone involved that this would not happen again.

There's a joke here somewhere, and as you can see I am diplomatically avoiding it.

As my five-year contract neared an end, I received a one-year renewal with recommendations from the MPAA board for things they wanted me to do the next year.

By that point, I had already decided to move on. It wasn't solely my decision, but I came to a mutual agreement with the board that I would not continue as president at the MPAA. While I enjoyed the job tremendously, I felt that I had accomplished everything in my power to move the organization forward.

The truth is, I loved parts of the job, especially working on the movie ratings system, but it was clear that some of the CEOs of the companies wanted a more aggressive leader on issues like fighting piracy. I had been there six years, had a good ride, and all of the CEOs came to my goodbye party and wished me well, even promising to help my son, who was already in the business. Let's be honest, following a legend like Jack Valenti was never going to be easy, as he was glamorous and well coiffed, as if he were cut from some glamorous Hollywood cloth. I was not so slick, to say the least, but was as comfortable being with a group of farmers as I was schmoozing with Hollywood stars. It was never a perfect fit, but I never regretted being part of America's greatest industry. I had met my goals and was feeling restless for a new challenge.

Out of all the jobs I know of in Washington, DC, heading the MPAA is probably the most exhausting and energy zapping. The movie industry is an incredibly fast-paced environment, and the folks you report to tend to have a short attention span, with an even shorter fuse. The three-hour time difference between DC and Hollywood didn't help either. The phone never seemed to stop ringing at all times of the day and night.

I don't know how Jack Valenti lasted for decades because I felt pretty burned-out after a little over six years. By that time, Valenti had passed away, and I'm sure on some subconscious level that also affected my decision to leave. I let the MPAA board know that I would not be staying for the full year, as I would be moving on to the nonprofit world to tackles issues like the debilitating partisanship I had observed in Washington for far too long.

I was happy to learn that my colleague and friend, former senator Chris Dodd, would become my successor. He moved on after six years, too, succeeded by the former US ambassador to France, Charlie Rivkin. Both men are talented and creative, a real plus for the organization.

I have never regretted taking the MPAA job; in fact, I feel quite the opposite. Out of all the positions I held, this afforded me the greatest opportunity to learn a new industry and translate my experience in government into an entirely different setting. There was no way I could lobby on behalf of something that I didn't love, and I most certainly love movies. We all have different taste, and although there were movies I didn't care for, I wasn't offended by them; if the movies were produced by one of the MPAA member companies I worked for, I was careful to be diplomatic.

My son Jon has been a film producer for many years and has formed his own production company. He has given me many reasons to be proud of his movie-making success, inspired in part by his early experiences at the movies with Rhoda and his sister during the many weekends I spent in Kansas during my congressional days. We talked about movies all the time and even relived some of them.

The *Godfather* and *Godfather II* were among our favorites, and we replicated the scene when Michael Corleone kisses his brother Fredo (who participated in an assassination attempt on Michael) on the mouth, with the comment, "I know it was you Fredo." Jon would kiss our beagle, Reuben, on the mouth and repeat the phrase, "I know it was you Fredo." That scene was repeated quite frequently.

I spent a huge amount of time on the road, much of it overseas, serving as an ambassador for American movies. Rhoda and I, and our daughter sometimes, too, enjoyed going to Berlin, Cannes, and Venice, as well as Sundance in Utah, for film festivals, and I cannot lie that we didn't love walking the red carpet at the Academy Awards and the Golden Globes. Who would have thought? A Jewish guy from Kansas, a former secretary of agriculture, whose grandparents came from the old country, walking the red carpet in Hollywood.

Chapter 14

Lessons from a Self-Deprecating Moderate

After my six years with the Motion Picture Association of America (MPAA), and after a brief time at Refugees International, a global policy refugee organization, I joined the Aspen Institute Congressional Program as well as the Bipartisan Policy Center, the latter a Washington, DC, think tank promoting constructive partisanship, founded by four recent Senate majority leaders. Throughout my political career, I have come to believe that we have an excellent system of government, but it can only function well if it has a crucial ingredient: *moderate* politicians who are willing to compromise.

The Founding Fathers essentially institutionalized gridlock by creating a separation of powers, ensuring checks and balances so that no one branch of government can control the others. They wanted one foot on the brake and one foot on the gas pedal, even in the days of horses and buggies. However, a system where power is not centralized requires consensus and compromise to get anything done.

There's that word again—*compromise*.

Our government, as envisioned and drafted by the first Congress in Philadelphia, relies on collaboration and empathy as a template for how one party views the other when it comes to moving the country forward. Unless actors within the system—voters and politicians—seek to build coalitions, especially on challenging issues, then you will be left with benign neglect, or in some cases, harmful inaction.

Today, most of the incentives in our political system do not favor consensus or—God forbid—compromise. Notice how that word keeps coming up, as if it's important or something even essential, like oxygen?

Party loyalty trumps devotion to country, and an excess of money in the system discourages political risk-taking and leadership. Our conflict-driven media encourages Americans to fear and loathe those who hold political views different from their own and to celebrate conflict and division, further exacerbating a lack of risk-taking and leadership.

This is not a prescription for a thriving country, let alone one that functions well for everyone.

My political life has taught me many invaluable lessons, which can all be summarized by one guiding principle:

Life is about building bridges between rivals, not making permanent enemies. This principle must exist if we are ever going to achieve fairness and equality.

To build bridges with genuine intention, several fundamental truths need to be accepted. First and foremost, be guided by integrity so that your peers respect and trust you. Be a man or woman of your word. To build the bridges needed to help you achieve your goals, find ways to connect on a personal level, which for me meant using humor. Don't take yourself too seriously but also be known as a person of substance and intellect. Come to a discussion committed to civility and empathy but ready to defend your views. In a political context, this means you are willing to hear dissenting opinions and recognize that the person across the table is as convinced about their beliefs as you are about yours.

For this formula to ultimately succeed, it relies on one central factor: personal character. The bottom line is, if you don't make people with whom you disagree your enemy, you can find the space to work together. Plenty of politicians today perceive the risk of doing something, anything, beyond what is dogmatically party doctrine, as a political risk that could lead them to lose their seat. They believe they could be defeated in a primary or a general election if they stray too far off the predetermined path set forth by activists within their party coalitions. But members of Congress, keep it firmly in your mind that losing your seat is not the end of the world. It certainly wasn't for me. So please, dear elected officials, live a little and vote what you think is right for your district and the country, not just for your party. Don't be a fool about it, but pick your moments to be a leader and make those moments the ones that really matter.

Shortly after I was sworn into my first term in Congress, I experienced an extraordinary event that has stayed with me ever since. Former vice president Hubert Humphrey, who had returned to the Senate after losing his bid for the White House in 1968, addressed the entire House of Representatives. Humphrey was still a sitting senator but was extremely frail because he was dying of cancer. Most of the current House members, Republicans as well as Democrats, came knowing that this was a historic occasion and probably one of the last times this highly respected public servant was going to speak in public. Few moments in my life have been as moving as listening to this speech. He stood (clearly with heroic effort) in the well of the House, with Daniel Webster's quote "Do Something Worthy to Be Remembered" visible behind him.

His message to us was so simple, yet remarkably crucial:

"Fight every legislative battle with vigor, passion, and the belief that it is the most critical issue of your life. When that fight is over, no matter what the outcome, cross to the other side and shake your opponent's hand, because he or she could easily become your ally in a future fight. There will be future fights, and you will need allies. Never burn that bridge that is so flammable in the heat of battle."

Then he said what I believe every voter, candidate, and elected official needs to hear:

"Respect for your opponent and your opponent's opinion does not weaken your integrity or your position—quite the opposite."

Hubert Humphrey died two months later, on January 13, 1978. I wish every sitting member of Congress today would read his remarks and take them to heart. To be fair and transparent, did Humphrey's voting record prove his point? I'm not too sure about that.

I served as an elected or appointed official during four presidencies: Jimmy Carter, Ronald Reagan, George H. W. Bush, and Bill Clinton. I campaigned as a Democrat during a Republican administration, and while in Congress I opposed a specific policy promulgated by my own party's president. It never occurred to me, nor to many of my fellow members of Congress, that the president was my enemy or that the other party had set out to destroy our nation. All of our presidents in my tenure as elected officials were true patriots, a fact I never doubted as they each presented their vision for America to the voters. I may have strongly disagreed with their views on how to move the country forward, but I never assigned them any motive other than a love of our country. Even those who followed Clinton, especially George W. Bush and Barack Obama, are men of honor and decency. Not so with Donald Trump. I have great hope in our new president, Joe Biden; certainly his years as a senator and vice president have exemplified excellent character.

Nothing is a clearer example of the intrusion of vicious and small-minded partisanship into our government than the presidency of Donald Trump. In my opinion, he changed the country in a raw and vulgar way, feeding off the dysfunction that enabled his rise to power in the first place. He embraced the role of a great divider, understanding the deep-seated tribal nature of our current politics and he played the political system to keep himself and his party in power.

Our biggest challenge in this era is to ensure the continuation of America as a nation based on sound values and good character. We cannot allow the institutionalization of the dark tendencies that Trump's election legitimized. Even those presidents with whom I disagreed, like George W. Bush in his decision to take us into Iraq, deserve my congratulations for the display of transformational leadership in the fight against AIDS, and malaria in Africa.

I refuse to believe that our current division is permanent and that what ails us cannot be overcome. We have surely descended into tribal politics that stifle our success rather than nurture it. But the "better angels of our nature" described by Abraham Lincoln, are still, deep down, part of America's DNA. Where we are today is a reflection of uncertainty, economic inequality, fear, and insecurity. Our nation's psyche is fragile, much like the America we witnessed during the Vietnam era. We have been struggling for America's soul for almost an entire generation, and as our society is changing from a white majority to a minority majority, we need to understand and appreciate that the change is challenging for many Americans. At the same time, we need to remember that one of this country's greatest strengths is our diversity.

That said, even when Trump is gone, hopefully by the time you are reading this, his voters still live among us, so what do we do about them and their belief system?

What can see us through to a more civil era is for voters who believe we are on the wrong path to commit to supporting moderate political candidates. And for those candidates, once elected, to stand firm in the belief that pragmatism and civility must be the guiding principles of governance.

In 2007, I watched a town hall with then GOP presidential candidate, John McCain, where he argued with a voter who made outrageous claims about then senator Obama's citizenship and religious affiliation. McCain was booed by some people in that audience for simply saying, "Barack Obama is a citizen and a family man, but I disagree with him about many things and that is why I want to be president."

Senator McCain's response was a class act by a man who held deeply conservative views but embodied the principles of pragmatism and civility. It was the same commitment to working together for the common good that made John McCain one of the leading Republican voices against the divisive tactics employed by Donald Trump and his minions.

Having now observed candidate after candidate succeeding by using messages of fear, anger, and even outright hatred for their political opponents, I wonder if common manners, decency, and civility are values no longer taken seriously in politics or society itself. Seeing people respond to brash self-promotion, or regarding schoolyard bullying and direct ad hominem attacks as qualities of leadership is deeply disturbing to me, not just as a former politician, but as an American and a citizen of the world.

The bottom line, which deserves repeating, is that political leadership, like any type of leadership relies on character. The foundation of democratic politics requires leaders of deep integrity and good character, who are committed to the ideals of democracy, as well as working within the system to advance the interests of their constituents.

We have arrived at this challenging crossroads for several reasons, which must be addressed and resolved. This should begin with vastly improving how we elect our officials, who we elect, and to what standards we hold them. This means focusing on money in politics, gerrymandering, and divisive hyper-partisanship. Grassroots efforts to address these ills are springing up all over the country. I am involved in several of them through my work with the

Aspen Institute, the Bipartisan Policy Center, and the Former Members of Congress Association.

No issue is more vital than addressing money in politics. Everybody talks about the corrosive role permanent fundraising plays in our representative government, but no one from either party really wants to do anything about it.

Jesse Unruh, former Speaker of the California state legislature, said in 1966 that "money is the mother's milk of politics." By now, it has become the cottage cheese, yogurt, and pretty much the entire meal of politics.

What we used to call "payola" is suffocating our political system.

With rare exception, the ability to raise money has become the primary criteria to judge a candidate's political worthiness. Consider how the political world judges the success of presidential candidates. If they can't meet an extraordinary threshold of fundraising, they are deemed not viable, regardless of their leadership qualities, policy positions, experience, or charm. Proposals to help the country are an afterthought to a candidate's fundraising prowess.

Although politicians of all colors, stripes, and backgrounds claim to hate what is happening to the system, when push comes to shove, few are serious about changing the corrosive influence of money. This is because gaining exclusive access to the sources of funding gives them a competitive edge over would-be political challengers.

This is disgraceful. It is ridiculous to believe that money, especially large sums from individual donors and corporations, comes with no strings attached. As Adolf Rupp, former basketball coach at the University of Kentucky, used to say, "If it doesn't matter whether we win or lose, why do we keep score?" If it doesn't matter where the money comes from, why do people give it, and why do candidates obsess over raising it?

My first run for Congress in 1976 was a door-to-door operation where money was a nonissue. My seat was not gerrymandered for or against me, even though I was from a Republican-dominated state. I unseated an incumbent because I outworked him and connected with voters. My election would not be possible in today's money-driven campaign environments. I would need $3 million to

$5 million simply to be competitive. There would be no time for direct voter contact because fundraising and schmoozing with deep-pocket donors from out of state would occupy most of my calendar. What a screwed up sense of priorities!

Though money was not a factor in winning my first election, I am convinced it was a factor in losing my last campaign. By 1993, Koch Industries, headquartered in my hometown of Wichita, had decided that Democrats who supported an energy tax were jeopardizing their corporate interests. Because campaign finance laws were murky, made even less transparent thanks to the atrocious *Citizens United v. Federal Election Committee* Supreme Court decision, there's no way of telling how much money they funneled into the campaign against me.

I am also convinced that Koch Industries' concern over their corporate bottom line, as well as their own philosophical views, made funding my opponent a sound investment, with an anticipated positive return. This was also known as "let's fund the other guy" and spend whatever is necessary to smear and even ruin his opponent.

Things have only gotten worse. Now a handful of supremely rich families can steer millions toward any campaign or candidate of their choosing, whether that means supporting a senator in their home state or a representative from a district hundreds of miles away. They can do so entirely cloaked in secrecy, thanks to nefarious political operatives steering bundled millions of dollars toward politicians via PACs and super PACs, the mother of all corruption. It's all completely legal, but in my opinion, it's highly unethical.

Political party resources have been outstripped by super PACs since the *Citizens United* ruling opened the floodgate of dark money campaign expenditures. This deregulation effort now resembles the arms race between the United States and the Soviet Union, with each side trying to remove all barriers and rules preventing them from raising unlimited contributions. The political parties promulgated this development to fight fire with fire, but the result just further increases the importance of high-net-worth donors and further marginalizes most of the voters in our political system.

As a result, donations flow directly to candidates rather than to either party, which results in extreme candidates finding success by simply embracing a single issue that wealthy donors care about, like eliminating the estate tax. As long as a candidate supports a pet issue of wealthy constituents, unscrupulous donors will turn a blind eye to the zany, radical, or outright insane policy views that candidate may hold in any number of other issues. It is the height of irresponsibility to invest in candidates to protect or extend things like tax benefits without regard for the rest of the dangerous nonsense that comes along with supporting that candidate.

All of this has had a paralyzing effect on our legislative bodies at state and federal levels. There are only twenty-four hours in a day, and once you subtract time for sleeping, eating, traveling to and from the district, and hours upon hours for fundraising, there is little time left to shape policy, engage in true debate, build relationships with your colleagues, and put in any genuine effort to move the country forward.

This also doesn't take into account the fact that most dollars are given to preserve the status quo. Donors ask that you don't do something legislatively, for example, like create new regulations to address changed energy production such as fracking. Big donors generally do not support big ideas; they usually fight them. They also want to preserve the systemic inequality that exists in our country. One positive development on this front is how social media has empowered many small donors to contribute, offsetting some of the need for candidates to rely exclusively on the rich and powerful.

At the same time, this compounds the disconnect that average voters feel toward their elected officials. I would suggest that many voters on both sides have a legitimate belief that our political system is irrelevant to the lives of everyone except those at the financial top. Candidates offer this or that on income inequality or tax or social policy, but most of the public policy we need for a better America, like infrastructure investment and education reform, is completely stuck.

Voters are unhappy because they are not being served by a government paralyzed by money: political donations bind candidates to the views of a handful of Americans, stoking the flames of partisanship and keeping Congress from doing anything truly transformational. The system feeds itself via ruthless professional fundraisers who care little about the damage they are doing to the nation. They are much more interested in earning their consultancy fee from candidates who are convinced they can only win because they've engaged the best hired gun to essentially buy their way into office.

This dependence on fundraising has had an additional debilitating effect. We are turning away highly qualified candidates for office who simply want nothing to do with a system that requires them to constantly ask strangers for money. It is a privilege to ask someone for their vote. It is embarrassing to ask someone for their money. While candidates can be recruited to do the former, they are now turned off by the latter.

Add to that the personal attacks most candidates endure at the hand of their opponents, there's little motivation left to seek higher office. Citizens see political dysfunction causing policy gridlock, and fewer and fewer potential public servants view Washington, DC, as an opportunity to fulfill Daniel Webster's mandate: to do something worthy to be remembered.

We are not only alienating future senators and representatives—we are also turning off future federal bureaucrats, foreign service officers, and political appointees. Because fundraising is the single most determinative factor for congressional committee assignments and top leadership positions in the House or Senate, new members of Congress are told to not only raise money for their reelection but also for the party and their colleagues. That gives those wanting to rise within a committee little incentive to become issue experts and lots of incentive to cozy up with that committee's corporate interests.

This is a recipe for failure as a democracy.

An all-too-comfortable relationship between members of Congress and the interest groups they regulate also contributes to making an incumbent member almost unbeatable. Back in 1976, when I took on incumbent congressman Garner Shriver, it was already considered a fool's errand to challenge a politician who was seeking reelection and did not have a scandal dragging him down. While there are wave elections that sweep an unexpectedly considerable number of sitting members out of office, most of the time the incumbent enjoys a clear advantage over the challenger and handily wins reelection.

One other thing we can do to make our politics better is to end the extreme politicization in gerrymandering of member districts. One of the reasons our election campaigns are uncompetitive is that congressional districts are drawn by most state legislatures in a partisan manner, with the sole purpose of keeping each seat safely in the hands of whichever party happens to control the redistricting process following a census.

These gerrymandered districts (named after a salamander-shaped Massachusetts district then governor Gerry created in 1812) produce almost no competition on Election Day because the outcome is pretty much predetermined. That leaves the real contest to the favored party's primary, where very few eligible voters determine the eventual representative of that seat. This has also led to more extreme candidates winning primaries, since the 10 percent of eligible voters who do show up for a primary tend to be on the far right or far left.

Gerrymandering is one of the truly bipartisan aspects of our electoral system because given the opportunity, both parties gleefully reshape congressional districts. Only a few states have adopted a nonpartisan or bipartisan redistricting process because whichever party cedes its advantage to a neutral body also gives up its sure grip on the seat.

Part of the discussion about gerrymandering should also analyze whether our nation is served best by holding on to a two-party system. We are a multiparty nation, with differing political points of view within each party that form a coalition under one of two labels: "Republican" or "Democrat." In recent years, we have allowed this within-the-party coalition to yield to the most extreme political persuasions within the party, which effectively diminishes the voices of reason that each party's moderates bring to the table.

Two-party labels no longer allow for a broad definition of "liberal" or "conservative." Politicians are loath to work with each other because there's no political gain from crossing the aisle. Though some politicians actually do work with "them," it is not the norm. In fact, the opposite is true: your party's primary voters will punish you for being too close to members from the other party, but few politicians get punished for being too close to a super PAC moving unregulated dark money.

Our current system produces too many one-issue voters who make a single question (usually a social issue, such as abortion) their litmus test for support and are willing to accept a host of fringe positions on any other topic. Gerrymandering and our primaries process support the continuation of the two-party system to the detriment of our ability to elect the best and the brightest. This system also punishes the moderate candidate who has a much harder time winning a primary than a general election.

Beyond tribal politics, the influence of money, recruiting top-notch candidates, and gerrymandering, the viciousness of our political rhetoric has reached new heights. I cannot recall a president of the United States bullying political opponents daily, either via Twitter, in speeches, or by sending out his press secretary or a nasty statement with no possibility of questions from the press.

As president, Donald Trump had little or no filter on anything he said or did. His use of Twitter did not allow for any depth of discussion and only triggerd friction and confusion because of the way he used it. He remained in constant campaign mode, and his announcements, whether confined to 280 characters or a two-hour speech, were aimed at a single audience: his own voters. Every other president in the history of our nation has approached the job with a willingness to unite, and a recognition that he is responsible to all Americans, not just the ones who voted for him.

What message does this send to young Americans who need to trust their government, engage in the political process, be responsible citizens, and work for change? It turns them off and makes them run for the hills rather than run for office.

We should not forget, however, that Donald Trump was not the source of our tribal politics and hyper-partisan rhetoric, but rather its logical product. He was also a product of our national obsession with TV and celebrity. Those same politicians who want to meet a Hollywood actor were dazzled by Trump because they had seen him on TV for so long.

By abandoning civility, empathy, and a willingness to collaborate, we have enshrined a different type of leader than what our nation used to demand. The goal for all who care about our democracy needs to be that we return to leadership based on integrity, good character, sound morals, and a vision to move the country forward rather than suppress those who think or look or sound different.

We most certainly can regulate campaign finance better. In this age of social media, elections will be fundamentally different in the future, and the traditional model that candidates can simply be outspent by buying TV airtime may eventually become a thing of the

past. In a rational system of government, there is absolutely no reason why members of Congress should spend more time fundraising
than legislating.

At a minimum, it should be prohibited for members of Congress to dial for dollars while Congress is meeting or in session.
That would at least eliminate the immorality of a member simultaneously raising money from a corporate supporter and working or
voting on an issue important to that corporate entity. Fundraising
should simply be banned while Congress is in session to eliminate
even the appearance of a quid pro quo. It would also free members
to do what they were sent to Washington to do—legislate!

Running for office should be based on wanting to change the
country for the good and contributing big ideas. By making the
path toward a candidacy and electoral success much less focused
on fundraising and much more focused on policy, we will encourage
big thinkers to pick up the mantle. Let's support these idealists by allowing them to create solutions rather than exploratory committees.

Let's also embrace the notion of professional politicians who
have made public service their calling. In the age of Trump, where
our own president disparaged Washington, DC, as a swamp filled
with despicable creatures either running the government or working for it, we somehow have become persuaded that political experience is a detriment.

I prefer experienced pilots to fly my plane and experienced sur-
geons at the operating table. Why would I want *in*experienced legislators to formulate our laws or lead our country? This notion that
by having worked in government, a candidate for office is somehow
tainted is completely nonsensical. Let's stop falling for candidates
who run for Congress or the White House by denouncing the institutions to which they want to be elected. We need individuals of
character and integrity, who possess a moral compass as well as a
healthy respect for our representative democracy.

Former Arizona senator Jeff Flake retired from Congress because his moral compass prevented him from blindly siding with the
president from his own party. I respect him for that and completely
agree with him that Congress must pursue strong, independent, and
bipartisan oversight of the actions undertaken by the White House
and all the cabinet departments. Donald Trump seemed disinter-
ested in learning that the White House must deal with Congress, the

courts, and the media, all of which are empowered by the Constitution to provide checks and balances, to keep our democracy from turning into something sinister.

John F. Kennedy (JFK) wrote an outstanding book called *Profiles in Courage*, which highlights the integrity of eight US senators. In each of the stories, their actions went against their perceived self-interests, as they probably would have benefited politically by staying on the sidelines rather than taking a stand and following their moral compass. History showed that voters rewarded them for doing the right thing.

Since much of my current work focuses on bringing Republicans and Democrats together, if I were to write a sequel to JFK's book, my theme would be bipartisanship. Let's recognize those elected officials who cross the political aisle and are willing to approach colleagues with a sense of empathy and a commitment to collaboration.

In the era of Trump, American journalists have risen to the challenge of covering this bizarre and dangerous administration. Unfortunately, in the process of doing their job, they have also given him a bullhorn to promote his bigotry.

But our journalists need to rediscover a degree of professionalism that abhors any implication of bias. It's easy to go on social media and see the political views of almost any journalist. This erodes their credibility and gives space for actual peddlers of fake news to spin lies and propagandize on behalf of their masters. Professional journalists should seek information and the truth, no matter where the story takes them, and must always be conscious of being accused of bias. The First Amendment protects our freedom of speech and a free press, and encourages the fourth estate to look over our leaders' shoulders, which remains as vital to our democracy as our system of checks and balances.

We need to push society to move toward a more unified and civil place. The first step is restoring civic education into America's classrooms. Though largely a state responsibility, we need to eliminate the ignorance of so many Americans, especially the next generation, who need to be taught the skills necessary to make informed decisions when it comes to their vote. They know little of the basic tools of public service: listening to opinions, making your own argument, building trust, and engaging in the art of compromise.

There it is again: compromise.

Remember comedian Jay Leno's shtick called "Jay Walking," where he asked folks on the street simple questions, like how many branches of government there are? The answers usually revealed that average citizens are woefully and ridiculously uninformed.

We need a real push for young Americans to strengthen their communities by performing public service. While I am not advocating conscription or a draft, I believe we all would benefit as a society if young adults were incentivized by thoughtful and realistic options for public service. All Americans between the ages of eighteen and twenty-five should have an opportunity to come together under a service umbrella, including military and civilian programs. This would give our next generation of citizens a way to interact with people of different economic backgrounds, races, cultures, and levels of education.

Much like the greatest generation that fought in the Second World War and returned home to see the country safely through the Cold War, America would benefit enormously from a citizenry working together on the common purpose of moving the country forward. Sadly, this is a missing ingredient in American democracy, especially considering our public school system, where economic class and race are still enormous factors in determining the quality of our children's education.

We know that all power flows from an educated, informed, and engaged citizenry. Grassroots efforts could achieve proper and objective congressional redistricting, based on actual census data rather than partisan politics. A large citizen movement might be able to enact even bigger changes to the system, which could spur politicians to behave better. Citizens as a whole should demand government action on everyday issues, such as a national effort to improve America's infrastructure or our entire education system. Most important, if politicians know that an educated, informed, and engaged citizenry is watching their every public move, they will be committed to constitutional principles, especially First Amendment rights, freedoms of expression, and separation of powers to preserve a check on the executive branch.

I am convinced and optimistic that what has made America great for hundreds of years is still alive and well: our sense of community, our willingness to help and support each other in times of crisis, and the strength we derive from our diversity. We have abundant resources in our people: bright minds that can pursue and receive top-notch educations, can-do attitudes toward problem solving, and an overarching entrepreneurial spirit that has made us the strongest economy on the planet. Our schools, religious institutions, and community groups can all do a better job extolling the values of respect, good character, and compromise. Our complex social and political challenges cannot be fixed with magic bullets, but I remain optimistic because I remember American history.

We have always overcome times of great divisiveness, whether it was the Civil War, McCarthyism, the Vietnam War, or Watergate. Throughout those challenging times, we have demonstrated that we are a resilient country with a destiny unequal in human history.

Adlai Stevenson said, "America is much more than a geographical fact. It is a political and moral fact, the first community in which men set out in principle to institutionalize freedom, responsible government, and human equality."

Bill Clinton shared a notion that "there is nothing wrong in American that can't be fixed with what is right in America."

Both of these great speakers reminded us of our nation's exceptionalism. Now, in this time of division and hyper-partisanship, we need to focus on the great strength of our democracy, which means delivering tangible results for the American people by thinking big—rather than the great weakness of democracy, which is just saying "no." Some of the brightest moments in our country occur when citizens come together from all walks of life to serve, putting aside their differences for the common good. That's the America we all love, and that's the genuinely American DNA that has made us who we are and that continues to make us great.

I often think of Daniel Burnham, an American architect and urban designer, who opined on the difference between having small ideas and pushing hard for big ones, when he said, "Make no little plans; they have no magic to stir men's blood and probably themselves will not be realized. Make big plans; aim high in hope and work."

In politics, shying away from big ideas might keep you in office a bit longer, but it defies the purpose of being there. If we think small, how will we ever manage to rebuild America's infrastructure, explore space, or cure diseases? If we think small, how can we be a worldwide leader in the search for freedom and liberty? If we think small, how will we ever erase our growing national debt?

Economists estimate that we will be in the red to the tune of $30 trillion by the end of the decade. Only twenty years ago, we had four years of balanced budgets. This demonstrates that restoring fiscal responsibility can be done while still engaging in big plans for the future.

The key is leadership, character, and courage.

That means compromise.

Our leaders need courage to make tough choices, like creating a sensible but fairer tax system, restraining the growth of federal spending on entitlement programs, and just good old effective management practices. That means some candidates of character may risk losing an election, if necessary.

We recently saw character and courage in the votes of a select few Republican House and Senate members, most of whom risked their political careers on making unpopular votes on the impeachment and conviction of President Trump. In my judgment, these people put country over party, put deep personal values over obsequious support for a president who had committed unpardonable offenses against the country. They made sacrifices for the larger historic good. Not every elected official, including yours truly, can honestly say that we always voted courageously on every hot divisive political issue. But these folks wrestled carefully, independently, and thoughtfully, and did not compromise their principles. In most cases compromise is needed to make the system work, but in others fear of losing a political race is an enormous sign of weakness. Personal dignity and respect is more important than a committee chairmanship.

Perhaps the example of my life you have read about here has defined what a moderate is and how moderation is a necessary ingredient for our country to move forward. Based on my experiences, in politics and life, it can lead people to deal with issues and conflicts—and each other—in a healthy and productive way. It's simply better than any rigid, ideological political philosophy. That's my opinion, and I'm sticking to it. I don't care how much you think compromise won't work. I'm not budging on my view. It's compromise or bust!

All joking aside, one can hold conservative or liberal political views, but if you are an asshole with a closed mind or have little to no empathy for what your adversary or competitor is feeling, or what struggles one has faced, you are not only a jerk— you will never be a positive force to solve any of our nation's problems.

That is what being an elected office is all about. Don't be a jerk!

If you have the ability to listen, if you can cultivate a general sense of empathy and are respectful in tone and substance, you can still advance any of your liberal or conservative views with a sensible and moderate tone, and you may even find that people will listen to you much more and consider your position in a reasonable way. You may even change some minds, or quite surprisingly, when you listen, too, you may even change your own mind.

Our nation's great leaders have certainly mastered the art of active listening. Will our current crop of politicians ever learn from the wisdom of our past leaders?

Whether you agreed with him or not on specific issues, former senator Everett Dirksen once said quite a wise thing, which most politicians today could do well to emulate.

"I am a man of principle, and my first principle is flexibility."

You see, principles and flexibility are not inconsistent with one another. They are necessary tools for creating a genuinely bipartisan and effective government because, as we know all too well, the alternative is gridlock. Dirksen and LBJ were examples of politicians who used both techniques to work across the aisle to achieve great things for our country, especially when it came to the civil rights laws of the 1960s.

I had the privilege of a long and successful career in public service, shaped by outstanding public servants from both sides of the aisle. We always found much more in common than what divided us politically. We always found ways to work together because we never forgot that we are stronger together than standing alone.

Is America vulnerable? Yes, of course it is. Our democracy is only as strong as our commitment to perfecting it, and right now, our country faces huge challenges on multiple fronts. In spite of that, I am optimistic that the opportunities are even greater than the challenges. We are an extraordinarily resilient nation, founded on common sense principles, and the bedrock of our exceptionalism is the ability of the American people to persist, sometimes by taking two steps forward in response to when we falter and regress. Our Kansas state motto, "ad astra per aspera" or "to the stars through difficulties" is especially relevant now. We must maintain our determination to overcome adversity and find a better way, as this is what separates America from so many other nations. Each of us must turn our hopes into responsible actions, and together "we shall overcome."

Hopefully, your experience will mirror mine in some respects and you will enjoy a productive, happy, and enriching life. Oh yeah and have some fun along the way. Tell a joke, be humble, be yourself. Remember the words of Yakov Smirnov, reflecting on this remarkable place where which we are privileged to live.

"What a country!"

Epilogue

Life in the Age of COVID-19

Citizen activism, including marches for justice and peace, combined with the impact of COVID-19, means we are (or should be) in revolutionary times. I think we are at a turning point in this country, but notwithstanding this, the same skills I talk about that made my career successful are needed now more than ever in facilitating change in America and for getting things done.

Change and progress must begin with leadership, which we are largely missing on a national level. This lack of consistent leadership has impeded the country from coming together as fast and as necessary as is needed. It must begin at the top, meaning from the White House, because no matter how effectively individual governors and mayors respond to any matter, their efforts can only go so far without the support of the federal government.

Sometimes we succeed and sometimes not. Sometimes we as a country and a society succeed in meeting the challenges of our times; more often it is two steps forward and one step back, making slow but steady progress along the way. But that is the nature of a democracy where compromise and collaboration, while critical, often prevent instant solutions to the problems and challenges of our society. Fortunately, I can go to sleep at night, knowing that while I served in government, I did whatever I could to move the needle forward when it came to making America a better country—for everyone.

In addition to the *Pigford* case, which I discussed in chapter 12, the issues of racial discrimination called for cultural changes at the USDA and in Congress. As I mentioned, these issues had never to my knowledge received congressional attention from the

Agriculture Committee during my tenure in Congress, or before or after, until the early 1990s. However, under my tenure we began making substantive and procedural reforms that improved internal operations within the USDA to prevent discrimination against minority farmers and employees, and those reforms have largely continued through the current administration. Congress has become much more attentive to the problems as well.

As our country examines issues of systemic racism, the *Pigford* case and related issues I faced at the USDA present excellent case studies and historical evidence of how racial attitudes impacted the implementation of agricultural policy in a very significant way and are an important part of the history of the civil rights movement. They are also indicative of challenges our country faces in so many other areas beyond the USDA, even as we have made substantial progress in racial fairness and equality in so many other areas of our civic life. Certainly the election of Barack Obama in 2008 and 2012 and of Kamala Harris in 2020 would not have even been possible in years past.

That said, we have a long way to go. The protests of an expanded Black Lives Matter movement, which burst on to the national stage following the murder of George Floyd in May of 2020, exposed America's long history of government failure when it comes to race relations and genuine equality.

Donald Trump was a disaster as president, in my humble opinion. He diminished America's role in the world, directly threatening our global leadership in so many areas. Furthermore, he helped reduce trust in our American institutions at home, which is so critical in our democracy, especially as we deal with a national epidemic with no unanimous public opinion about solutions.

We can, however, make lemonade out of lemons, as I have suggested throughout this book. This approach raises some fundamental questions as we consider our path forward.

Can we reestablish the prominent role of Congress, the Article 1 institution of our government, to its equal status with the president?

Can we continue, as Daniel Webster said, to do things worthy to be remembered?

As an optimist I think we can but only if the people demand it and participate in the solutions. As we have seen the events of 2020 unfold, our political system writ large has responded inconsistently at best. Will our society reward good leadership, or is it impossible in the toxic world of today? If this continues to be the case, the outlook is bleak, at least until we have an opportunity to usher in new leadership through the power and possibility of elections.

COVID-19, this terrible debacle, has demonstrated a need for a more comprehensive national health care system, focusing on prevention and the inclusion of lower and middle- income people, who have often been ignored. This is where my longtime work on food, health, nutrition, and medicine is relevant. Time to move to an intelligent national health care system.

We also need a dramatic increase in public funding for research in public health, medicine, food and agriculture, the environment, and technology. These areas have seen declines in support in real terms over the past two decades. This is unfortunate, because as we know, an ounce of prevention is worth a pound of cure.

Let's remember the words of that great American philosopher, Pogo.

"We have met the enemy, and he is us."

Pogo states the problem well. The citizens of America and its leaders in the public, private, and nonprofit sectors must lead us through this time with viable and valuable solutions.